Tracing Your
Scottish
Family History

Tracing Your Scottish Family History

Anthony Adolph

FIREFLY BOOKS

Published by Firefly Books Ltd. 2009

To our very good friend Dean Laurent de Bubier.

First printing

Publisher Cataloging-in-Publication Data (U.S.)

Adolph, Anthony.
    Tracing your Scottish family history / Anthony Adolph.
[224] p. : photos. (some col.) ; cm.
includes bibliographical references and index.
Summary: A book that demonstrates how the reader may trace his or her Scottish family history using family trees, the internet, contact information and other resources.
ISBN-13: 978-1-55407-457-0 (pbk.)
ISBN-10: 1-55407-457-6 (pbk.)
1. Scotland -- Genealogy -- Handbooks, manuals, etc. 2. Scottish Americans - Genealogy - Handbooks, manuals, etc. I. Title.
929.1/0720411 dc22   CS464.A465 2009

Library and Archives Canada Cataloguing in Publication

Adolph, Anthony
    Tracing your Scottish family history / Anthony Adolph.
Includes bibliographical references and index.
ISBN-13: 978-1-55407-457-0
ISBN-10: 1-55407-457-6
    1. Scotland--Genealogy--Handbooks, manuals, etc. I. Title.
CS463.A36 2009   929'.10720411   C2008-906450-X

Published in the United States by
Firefly Books (U.S.) Inc.
P.O. Box 1338, Ellicott Station
Buffalo, New York 14205

Published in Canada by
Firefly Books Ltd.
66 Leek Crescent
Richmond Hill, Ontario L4B 1H1

Printed in China

The publisher gratefully acknowledges the financial support for our publishing program by the Government of Canada through the Book Publishing Industry Development Program.

Illustration p. 2: "The Red Man," painted by Allan Ramsay (1713–84), shows Norman, the 22nd Chief of the MacLeods of Skye and Harris, in 1747.

Contents

Introduction

This book was written to mark the 250th anniversary in 2009 of the birth of Robert Burns, the Ploughman Poet, whose words captured the spirit of the Scottish nation. His anniversary year has been declared Scotland's Homecoming Year, which aims to encourage Scots all over the world to come back to visit, and to assure them of a warm welcome when they do.

To come home you need to know where you come from. Underpinning Homecoming Year is genealogy, the study of family trees or pedigrees, and its associated discipline of family history, the study of the stories behind the pedigrees. In many countries, computerization of records has rocketed genealogy from a minority interest into an immensely popular

With a population of just over five million, there are many parts of Scotland where the ubiquitous sheep are more easily found than people.

obsession. But in Scotland, knowing your roots is nothing new. Right back in the 16th century, the French joked of any Scotsman they encountered, "that man is the cousin of the king of the Scots," for that was what he would surely claim. A rather more cynical view was penned in the mid-18th century by Charles Churchill (1731–64), in his *Prophecy of Famine*: "Two boys, whose birth beyond all question springs/ From great and glorious, tho' forgotten kings,/ Shepherds of Scottish lineage, born and bred/ On the same bleak and barren mountain's head ..."

Sarcastic, yes, but accurate, for many of the widespread Lowland families and Highland clans were indeed founded by scions of Scotland's ruling dynasties, be they in origin

Pict, Briton, Gael, Viking or Norman. And such knowledge was not lost, especially in the Gaelic-speaking parts, when ancestors' names were remembered through the *sloinneadh*, the patronymic or pedigree, in which two or more — often many — generations of ancestors' names were recited, and which was a natural part of everyone's sense of identity.

Such essential knowledge was threatened, diluted and sometimes lost by migration, whether to other parts of Scotland or over the seas in the white-sailed ships. Nonetheless, it results today in many people all over the world being able to point at a particular spot on the map of Scotland and say, "that is home."

This book is for those who can't but want to, or who can but want to learn more. I know that many aspects of genealogy such as DNA and nonconformity can seem terribly complicated, and that some specific aspects of Scottish genealogy (such as services of heirs, wadsets and precepts of clare constat) seem to have been designed purposely to intimidate the faint-hearted. And, given the great amount of contradictory information flying about, does your Scottish surname actually indicate that you belong to a clan, or may wear a tartan, or doesn't it?

I hope this book will help guide you through these issues, to develop a much fuller understanding of your Scottish family history, and to find your own way back, so to speak, to your Scottish home.

Future meets past: old Ally Alistair MacLeod was a Highland crofter, descended from Viking chieftains. His tiny granddaughter Moira Hooks was born after her mother (whose sister is shown here) had moved away to Glasgow. Now she and her descendants all live in England. This picture captures the only time they ever met (courtesy of the MacLeod Family Collection).

Abbreviations

FHC	Mormon Family History Centers
GROS	General Register Office of Scotland
NAS	National Archives of Scotland
NLS	National Library of Scotland
NRAS	National Register of Archives of Scotland
SGS	Scottish Genealogy Society
SHS	Scottish History Society
SoG	Society of Genealogists (London)
SRS	Scottish Record Society
TNA	The National Archives (Kew, London)

PART 1

Getting started

The very first steps in tracing your Scottish family history are to talk to your relatives and keep a note of what they tell you. This section suggests what to ask and how to record your growing store of information about your family tree. The next step is to identify archives or organizations that are introduced in this section. Before diving any deeper into your research, it is helpful to gain a background understanding of Scotland's geography and naming systems.

Old family photographs provide the perfect backdrop to your research, helping bring the past to life.

CHAPTER 1

How to start your family tree

Ask the family

The first resource for tracing your Scottish family history is your own family. Meet, email or telephone your immediate relatives and ask for their stories and copies of old photographs and papers, especially family bibles, old birth, marriage and death certificates or memorial cards. Even old address books can lead you to relatives worldwide, who will be able to extend your family tree. Disappointingly, old photographs seldom have names written on the back: they may show your ancestors, but they are anonymous. Old ones often show the photographer's name and address, and some firms' records are in local archives. Directories (see p. 88-9) can show when the photographer was active, helping to give the photograph a rough date, and the mere location can be a clue as to which side of your family is being depicted. And, please, write names on the back of your own photos, to save future generations this frustration, or even include a family tree in your own photo albums to show who's who.

When you interview a relative, use a big piece of paper to sketch out a rough family tree as you talk, to keep track of names and dates. Structure your questions by asking the person about themselves, then:

- their siblings (brothers and sisters)
- their parents and *their* siblings
- their grandparents and *their* siblings

... and so on. Then, ask about any known descendants of the siblings in each generation. The key questions to ask about each relative are:

- full names
- date and place of birth
- date and place of marriage (if applicable)
- occupation(s)
- place(s) of residence
- religious denomination, whether Church of Scotland, Free Church, Catholic, Jewish and so on
- any interesting stories and pictures.

Next, ask for addresses of other relatives, contact them and repeat the process. Once you know the name of a village where your ancestors lived, try tracking down branches of the family who remained there since people

This photograph of Catherine and Jane Wilson in 1923 is usefully marked on the back, "Drummond Shields Studio, Edinburgh," thus suggesting the area where these girls may have grown up (courtesy of Jane's daughter-in-law, Helen Taylor).

Sennachies

Before Christianity and literacy came to Britain, a special class of Druid, the *seanachaidh* or sennachie, memorized and recited the royal *sloinneadh* or pedigree. Long after other forms of Druidism had fallen away, sennachies remained, some as villagers who remembered the local family histories, others in the clan chiefs' households. In about 1695, Martin Martin wrote in *A Description of the Western Isles of Scotland* (Birlin, 2002): *"Before they engaged the enemy in battle, the chief druid harangued the army to excite their courage. He was placed on an eminence, from whence he addressed himself to all of them standing about him, putting them in mind of what great things were performed by the valour of their ancestors ..."*

Martin, who used the term 'marischal' for the chief's sennachie, also said he was, *"obliged to be well versed in the pedigree of all the tribes in the isles, and in the Highlands of Scotland; for it was his province to assign every man at table his seat according to his quality; and this was done without one word speaking, only by drawing a score with a white rod which this marischal had in his hand, before the person who was bid by him to sit down; and this was necessary to prevent disorder and contention; and though the marischal might sometimes be mistaken, the master of the family incurred no censure by such an escape."*

It's good to know that, occasionally, we genealogists were allowed to get it wrong.

Dr. Johnson (1709–84), the London essayist and lexicographer who traveled around Scotland with the writer James Boswell in 1773, had trouble finding whether the bard and sennachie were different people, or one and the same, though he acknowledged different customs may have prevailed in different places: touring the Hebrides, he found

Aristocrats, such as John Campbell, fourth Duke of Argyll, shown in this painting by Thomas Gainsborough, have always had the help of sennachies or genealogists to record their family history.

that neither had existed there for some centuries. However, we do remain: Lord Lyon is High Sennachie of Scotland, and all genealogists worth their salt have inherited their share of this ancient Druidic mantle.

who have never left may know a lot about the ancestors you have in common, and might have tales about your ancestors who migrated away.

What you are told will be a mixture of truth, confused truth and the odd white lie. Write it all down and resolve discrepancies using original sources. Watch out for "honorary" relatives. While writing this, I received an email telling me, *"I recall as a boy, being introduced to people named to me as Uncle Ned, Auntie Jo and Cousin Francis. Many years later, I found during my family history searches that none of them were in fact relatives, just very close friends at that time. Yet the oldest relative I was interviewing still described them as Uncle, Auntie and Cousin, even under my challenge, with the result that I spent many weeks searching records for these people as relatives, and I never found any of them — but I eventually did find them as ordinary individuals shown as living in the same neighborhood."*

Photographs of family holidays are particularly valuable when people used the time to retrace their roots. Alexandrina ("Alice") MacLeod left her ancestral home in Badnaban, Sutherland, to become a servant in Glasgow, marrying Walter Hooks there in 1935. They came back on vacation, bringing along Walter's parents: here she is with her parents-in-law and sister Annie at nearby Achmelvish. There is more on tracing the roots of this family on pp. 50–1. (Photo courtesy of MacLeod Family Collection.)

The internet

Genealogy has been revolutionized by computers, bringing data and even images of records to your own home and, more significantly, making them really easy to search. Being able to look at the whole Scottish 1851 census online is useful: being able to search it in seconds for your great-granny is revolutionary. Scotland has led the way in making its national records accessible and searchable online, and the website www.ScotlandsPeople.gov.uk is a unique resource that has changed the face of Scottish genealogy for ever. It is your great good fortune to be tracing your Scottish family history now.

Computers are readily available in libraries or internet cafés (or friends' houses!). If you don't use the internet already, I would strongly recommend learning from a friend or joining a class, as it will make tracing your Scottish roots vastly easier. If you absolutely can't bear the idea, ask an internet-savvy friend or relative to do your searches for you.

There are several excellent websites that put like-minded genealogists in touch with each other, particularly the British-based www.genesreunited.com, though sites such as www.onegreatfamily.com will contain many families of Scottish descent too. You enter names, dates and places for your family, and the sites tell you if anyone else has entered the same details. When new people join and enter the same relatives, they'll easily find you. It's a new method that really works.

LEFT: **A page from www.genesreunited.com showing a list of references to ancestors called Lachlan MacLeod. You can tell which may be relevant by the years and places of birth. By clicking on the name you can send an email to the person who submitted the information.**

RIGHT: **The front page of the ScotlandsPeople website.**

Doctor Who's Dutch cousin

Register of Proclamations & of Marriages.

Joining a contact website such as Genes Reunited is seldom a waste of effort. Kenny Graham, who lives in the Netherlands, had been tracing his mother's MacDonald family tree since about 1990, and a few years ago put it on Genes Reunited. His children never took much interest in it until an email arrived from me. "Suddenly," wrote Kenny, "Daddy's 'boring' hobby became cool."

I was tracing the family tree of David Tennant, the West Lothian-born actor who is the latest incarnation of science fiction hero Doctor Who. David's real name is David MacDonald. His father, Alexander, Moderator of the Church of Scotland, was the great-grandson of John MacDonald, son of Alexander MacDonald, a road laborer at Kilmadock, who married Isabella King at Lecropt, Co. Perth, in 1824.

I wanted to see if David had any relatives out there, so I looked these ancestors up on Genes Reunited, and found their names had been entered by Kenny, whose great-great-grandfather Peter MacDonald was another son of Alexander and Isabella's.

"I couldn't believe it when we got the email," said Kenny, "because it is not every day you find out that David Tennant is your fourth cousin!" His son Ben, nine, was even more excited: "When I told my friends a few believed me but most of them didn't. It seems a bit different watching David on TV now because I try to imagine what he is like in real life." His sister Kirsty, aged seven, said, "I was really surprised when I found out. My friends didn't believe me but when they found out it was true they were amazed. My friends and I made a Doctor Who Club at school where we talk about the last episode." Kenny told me that, "this experience has helped us greatly in keeping the children aware of their 'Scottishness' and also brought to life my hobby to my siblings."

TOP: **The marriage proclamation of David Tennant's great-great-great-grandparents in 1824 reads:**
> *Alexr McDonald and Isabella King, both of this Parish,*
> *Paid 4s/ to the poor's funds.*
> *No Objections offered*
> *Proclaimed 31st Octr 7 Novr*

This entry employs a number of abbreviations for the months and also Alexander's name. It was found on the ScotlandsPeople website, but only after using the Soundex option (see p. 49), as he was indexed as "Alexr," not "Alexander."
LEFT: **David Tennant.**
RIGHT: **The Graham family (courtesy of K. Graham).**

Original records

Original records are usually held in the archives of the organization that created them or in public repositories, local or national. Since it is not always practical to visit an archive, there are other options:

1. The Church of Jesus Christ of Latter-day Saints, also called the Mormon Church, has an ever-growing archive of microfilm copies of original records from all over the world, including Scotland, many of which are indexed on the Mormon website **www.familysearch.org**. Founded in 1830, the Utah-based church has a religious mission to trace all family trees, and they hold ceremonies that allow the deceased to become Mormons, should their souls desire. They have Family History Centers (FHCs) in most major towns, so find your nearest at **www.familysearch.org**. FHCs are open to all, entirely without any compunction to convert, and here you can order any microfilms to be delivered from the Mormon's Family History Library in Utah.

2. Many Scottish records have been published, as indicated where appropriate in this book, especially by the Scottish History Society (SHS) **www.scottishhistorysociety.org** and the

Scottish Record Society (SRS) **www.scottishrecordsociety.org**. Volumes can be bought, examined in genealogical libraries or ordered through interlibrary loan.

3. You can hire a genealogist or record agent. Genealogists like myself charge higher fees and organize and implement all aspects of genealogical research. Record agents charge less and work to their clients' specific instructions, for example: "Please list all Colquhouns in the Old Parochial Registers of Oban between 1730 and 1790." Most archives have a search service, or a list of local researchers. Many advertise in genealogy magazines or at **www.genealogypro.com**, **www.expertgenealogy.com** and **www.cyndislist.org**. Some belong to the Association of Scottish Genealogists and Researchers in Archives, **www.asgra.co.uk**, whose members charge a minimum rate of £20 per hour, though membership does not guarantee quality. The NAS website has links to some genealogists on **www.nas.gov.uk/ doingResearch/remotely.asp**.

Most professionals are trustworthy, and many offer excellent services, though ability varies enormously. Generally, the more prompt and professional the response and neater the results, the more likely they are to be any good. Hiring help is not "cheating" — if you only want one record examined but are not sure it will contain your ancestor, it makes no sense to undertake a long journey when you can pay someone a small fee for checking for you, and a local searcher's expertise may then point you in the right direction anyway.

4. Use the ScotlandsPeople Centre in Edinburgh and its website. In the "Old Days," the only way to trace Scottish family history was to go to New

General Register House, Princes Street, Edinburgh, where the ScotlandsPeople Centre is housed.

Register House, Edinburgh, and search the indexes to births, marriages and deaths (from 1855), and the censuses (currently from 1841 to 1901), and then walk round to the National Archives of Scotland to examine the Old Parochial Registers (that can go back to the 1500s) and testaments (also from the 1500s).

Since 2002, however, these records have become available on **www.ScotlandsPeople. gov.uk**. This is run by the General Register Office for Scotland (GROS), the National Archives of Scotland (NAS), the Court of the Lord Lyon and an internet company, Brightsolid. You purchase a block of credits using a credit or

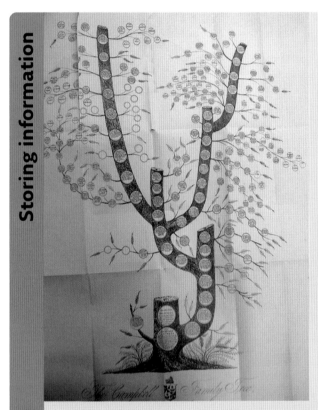

A family tree of the Campbell Clan, drawn as a real tree, complete with trunk and branches, from *The House of Argyll and the Collateral Branches of Clan Campbell* (1871) — courtesy of SoG.

Some people enjoy using family tree computer programs. A comparative table of those available is at **www.My-history.co.uk**. Many are based on the transferable "Gedcom" format, so once you have typed in your data you can move it between programs, including the one used in Genes Reunited.

Others (like me) aren't so keen: most have limitations, or pester you for "vital data" that you don't have, almost

forcing you into making misleading assumptions. Many demand dates of birth, marriage and death. From 1855 onwards in Scotland this is all fine, as these are very well recorded. Before then, however, Old Parochial Registers (and most non-Established church registers) can record baptisms, not births, and proclamations, not marriage; few programs make allowances for such subtleties, resulting in people entering the former as the latter. Just recently I saw a Family Group Sheet giving a death date of July 5, 1617. The evidence was a burial dated July 6, 1617, and my poor client, browbeaten by the computer's demand for a date of death, had simply guessed that the burial was the day after the death — which is in fact rather unlikely.

I prefer hand-writing family trees and keeping more detailed notes in computer documents. The following "narrative" method allows much flexibility.

Alexander Matheson
Write everything you know about Alexander. Then write "his children were" and list them:
1. **Donald Matheson**, *the next member of the direct line, so after his name type "see below"*
2. *Alexander Matheson. Put anything you know about Alexander and his descendants here. If he had children, then write "his children were:"*
   1. *Hamish Matheson*
   2. *James Matheson. If he had offspring, then ...*
      1. *Jean Matheson*
3. *Margaret Matheson. If you have absolutely loads on Margaret and her descendants, you might want to open a separate "chapter" for her and put her at the top of her own narrative document.*

Donald Matheson, *son of Alexander.*
Write what you know about Donald, and so on.

Pedigree conventions

- = indicates a marriage, accompanied by "m-" and the date and place.
- solid lines indicate definite connections: dotted lines indicate probable but unproven ones.
- wiggly lines are for illegitimacy (though straight lines are now acceptable) and "x" for a union out of wedlock.
- loops are used if two unconnected lines need to cross over, just like electricians' wiring diagrams.
- wives usually go on the right of husbands, though only if that doesn't interfere with the chart's overall layout.
- Common abbreviations are:

b.	born
bach.	bachelor
bpt. or c.	baptized or christened (same thing)
bur.	buried
d.	died
d.s.p. or o.s.p.	died without children
d.v.p. or o.v.p.	died before father
inft	infant
m.	married
MI	monumental inscription
m.i.w.	"mentioned in the will of ..." followed by f. for father, gf. for grandfather and so on.
m. proc.	marriage proclamation
spin.	spinster
test.	testament
unm.	unmarried
wid.	widow or widower (as appropriate)
w.wr./pr.	will written/proved

debit card, and spend them making searches and viewing digital images of the records themselves. Searching the index to wills and testaments is free but you pay to view an image of the document. At the time of writing, the site contains the following material:

- Statutory (General Register Office) Registers: Births 1855–2006; Marriages 1855–2006; Deaths 1855–2006.
- Old Parochial Registers: Births and Baptisms 1553–1854; Banns and Marriages 1553–1854.
- Censuses: 1841, 1851, 1861, 1871, 1881, 1891 and 1901.
- Wills and testaments: 1513–1901.

If, by the time you use the site, more material has been added, all well and good!

Births, marriages and deaths are *indexed* up to nearly the present day, but for privacy reasons, digital images are only available up to 100 years ago for births, 75 years ago for marriages and 50 years ago for deaths, though you can order "extracts" of these from GROS, or examine the originals at the ScotlandsPeople Centre.

The website works out to be more expensive than visiting the archives in Edinburgh, but if you don't live nearby then **www.Scotlands People.gov.uk** is a godsend. Besides bringing indexes to your computer, it has indexed the indexes, making the searching process vastly easier than ever before. And, because it's now possible to view images of the original documents online, people across the globe can now trace their Scottish ancestors properly. This has encouraged many new people to start exploring their Scottish roots.

Take a few minutes to explore the site's extra features. There are fairly detailed explanations of the records, and "Research Tools" contains many helpful features, such as tips on reading old handwriting and understanding old money.

The calendar

Up to 1582 Britain and Europe used Julius Caesar's calendar with years starting on Lady Day, March 25; but that year many other European countries started using the calendar of Pope Gregory the Great, with years starting on January 1. King James VI and I ordered the adoption of the Gregorian calendar starting on January 1, 1599/1600 — now that the year started in January, not March, New Year quickly absorbed many surviving pagan Winter Solstice traditions, creating the great Scots New Year festival of Hogmanay. Although James became king of England and Ireland in 1603, the calendar there did not change until 1752.

Dealing with written records

Reading old handwriting is called palaeography. Old ways of writing, or simply bad handwriting, present a real problem for genealogists. You can learn to read the former, but ghastly scrawls can defeat the most seasoned professional. For old hands, see G.G. Simpson's *Scottish Handwriting 1150–1650* (Tuckwell Press, 1973) and A. Rosie's *Scottish Handwriting 1500–1700: A Self-Help Pack* (SRO and SRA, 1994).

The site **www.scottishhandwriting.com** offers online tuition on old handwriting, and there are palaeography classes available at places like the ScotlandsPeople Centre.

Older records in Latin can be intimidating, but you can always pay a translator or experienced genealogist. Good guides to Latin include R.A. Latham's *Revised Medieval Latin Word-list from British and Irish Sources* (OUP, 1965), and there is a useful list of Latin words used in genealogical documents at **www.genuki.org.uk**. Here are some basics that appear in legal documents:

- *Annus* — year
- *Dies* — day
- *Eod. die.* — same day
- *Est* — is
- *Filia* — daughter
- *Filius* — son
- *Inter alia* — amongst others
- *Mater* — mother
- *Matrimonium* — married
- *Mensis* — month
- *Mortuus* — died
- *Natus* — born
- *Nuptium* — married
- *Obit* — died
- *Parochia* — parish
- *Pater* — father
- *Pro indiviso* — undivided
- *Qua* — as
- *Sepultat* — buried
- *Uxor* — wife
- *Vide* — see
- *Vidua* — widow

Knowing what a document is likely to say can help enormously. Examples of old documents, highlighting where to find the genealogically relevant parts, are in P. Gouldesborough's *Formulary of Old Scots Legal Documents* (Edinburgh, 1985).

If you're stuck over a word you cannot read, look for others in the document that you can. By doing so you can work out how the writer formed each letter, and you can use this technique to decipher otherwise illegible words.

This extract from a 19th-century sasine or land grant is relatively easy to read: earlier documents can be harder to follow.

CHAPTER 2

Archives and organizations

Before you start research among records, it's sensible to have a good idea of where to find the ones you will need, whether online or on the ground. Here is an overview.

Edinburgh

Many of Scotland's records are found in Edinburgh. The main port of call there is the new ScotlandsPeople Centre, opened in 2008, and housed in two adjoining, venerable institutions at the end of Princes Street, New Register House (home of the General Register Office or GROS), and General Register House. The Centre has several searchrooms, including disabled access, and offers a free two-hour "taster session" each day for newcomers.

Visitors are allocated a computer terminal for a fixed daily fee (currently £10), or you can pay an

The old Sasine Office of the National Archives of Scotland, now the entrance to the Historical Search Room.

hourly rate for expert help. Via the terminals you can search broadly the same material that is available on www.ScotlandsPeople.gov.uk — General Registration records, censuses, Old Parochial Registers (OPRs), testaments and wills to 1901 and the Public Register of All Arms and Bearings (not yet on the website). The terminals can save up to 200 images, that can be downloaded to a memory stick for a fee, or returned to on a later visit. Check the website for the Centre's opening times and details of how to book a visit.

The original heraldic records are in the Court of the Lord Lyon, on the first floor of New Register House, www.lyon-court.com.

General Register House is one of the two buildings of the National Archives of Scotland (NAS, formerly the Scottish Record Office or SRO), containing many national and local records. Located here are the Legal Search Room and the Historical Search Room; the latter being the one most frequented by genealogists. The NAS's other building, West Register House, home to its maps and court records, is a mile (1.6 km) away in Charlotte Square. The NAS's official guide is *Tracing your Scottish Ancestors* (NAS, fourth edition, 2007) which, despite its title, is mainly concerned with its own holdings. The NAS website includes its catalog (called OPAC, the Online Public Access Catalogue) and guides to the records at www.nas.gov.uk/guides/. You can simply type a place name or family name into the catalog and see what appears — usually a great deal. To hone searches, choose specific time periods or categories of record. To find the kirk session records for a specific parish, for example, you would type in the parish name followed by the reference CH2.

The National Library of Scotland (NLS, **www.nls.uk**) contains many useful journals and books, as does Edinburgh City Library, which also has a good collection of Scottish newspapers. The NLS Map Library is in Salisbury Place, and its collection is now accessible online at **www.nls.uk/maps/index.html**.

Archives across Scotland

Scotland is well supplied with local archives, business and institutional archives. There is an increasing number of small visitor centers catering to local interest in history and genealogy, and to genealogical tourists, such as the Comainn Eachdraidh or Western Isles Historical Societies. For addresses, see the slightly out-of-date *Exploring Scottish History* (M. Cox, ed., Scottish Library Association, 1999), or look at the tourist information website **www.visitscotland.com/** under "visitor attractions."

At present, 52 archives are linked in the Scottish Archive Network (SCAN), whose catalogs can be accessed at **www.scan.org.uk**. It's worth looking at the site's "knowledge base" that has information on all manner of things from old legal terms and old money to a gazetteer of "problem places" (SCAN includes **www.scottishdocuments.com**, whose records, a bit confusingly, are accessible via ScotlandsPeople).

Other websites useful for locating archives and records are:

- **www.archon.nationalarchives.gov.uk** — covering local archives, museums, universities and similar institutions.

Edinburgh addresses

GROS and the ScotlandsPeople Centre
New Register House,
3 West Register Street,
Edinburgh,
EH1 3YT
www.gro-scotland.gov.uk

The National Archives of Scotland (NAS)
HM General Register House
2 Princes Street
Edinburgh
EH1 3YY
www.nas.gov.uk

National Library of Scotland
George IV Bridge
Edinburgh
EH1 1EW
www.nls.uk

Scottish Life Archive
National Museum of Scotland
Chambers Street
Edinburgh
EH1 1JF
www.nms.ac.uk

See also pages 215–17 for more useful addresses.

The websites of the National Archives of Scotland and the General Register Office of Scotland.

- **www.familia.org.uk** — public library holdings of genealogical material.
- **www.archiveshob.ac.uk** — focuses on holdings of academic institutions.

Before visiting any archive, always check its website or telephone for opening times, what identification you may need, fees charged and whether you need to book. Also, make sure that the records you are planning to search are likely to tell you what you are hoping to find out — this guide should help you do that.

The National Register of Archives of Scotland

The NRAS (**www.nas.gov.uk/nras**) catalogs privately- or publicly-held papers of many individuals, families, landed estates, clubs, societies, businesses and law firms. Its online catalog is particularly useful for finding estate papers of families who may have been your ancestors' landlords, or archives of businesses that may have been your family's employers.

Genealogical Societies

The Scottish Genealogy Society (**www.scotsgenealogy.com**) was founded in Edinburgh in 1953 to promote research into Scottish family history and to encourage the collection, exchange and publication of material relating to Scottish genealogy and family history. It has an excellent library, keeps a register of people researching specific

The old kirk at Inchnadamph, Sutherland, now beautifully restored by Historic Assynt (www.historicassynt. co.uk) as a focal point for studying the genealogy and history of Assynt.

surnames, and publishes a quarterly magazine, *The Scottish Genealogist*.

The Society of Genealogists (SoG) in London has a vast collection of printed and manuscript sources covering all the British Isles, including a great deal for Scotland. A summary of its Scottish holdings is at **www.sog.org.uk/prc/ sct.shtml**. Its largest manuscript collection is The MacLeod Collection, comprising the working papers of Rev. Walter MacLeod and his son John, both professional genealogists in Edinburgh from about 1880 to 1940. Its 83 boxes are in rough surname order, though seem to contain mainly notes, not finished reports.

The GOONs or Guild of One Name Studies (Box G, 14 Charterhouse Buildings, Goswell Road, London EC1M 7BA, 0800 011 2182, **www.one-name.org**) includes many members studying Scottish surnames.

Scottish family history societies can be found via Genuki (see p. 33) or the Scottish Association of Family History Societies on **www.safhs. org.uk**. The latter publishes much of local interest and members can be sources of local lore. Many family history societies in Australia, New Zealand, Canada and the U.S., incidentally, have Scottish-interest groups, and there are Scottish Societies, including strong genealogical elements, in many countries. The Netherlands, for example, has a flourishing Caledonian Society (**www.caledonian.nl**) whose members are mainly descendants of Scots sailors, soldiers and merchants who settled in the Dutch ports.

Most Scottish clans now function through clan societies, that are effectively family and social history societies, as described on p. 160.

The site **www.rampantscotland.com** provides copious links to Scottish-interest sites, including travel, cooking, clans and history. The genealogy links page is worth exploring.

The Seallam! Visitor Centre, and its founders, Bill and Chris Lawson, with their fantastic files of island pedigrees.

A fine example of a small local archive is Bill and Chris Lawson's Co Leis Thu? (which means, "what people do you belong to?"), housed at the Seallam! Visitor Centre, An Taobh Tuath (Northton), Isle of Harris, HS3 3JA, 01859 520258, **www.seallam.com**.

Realizing that the fantastic oral history surviving among the Gaelic speakers in the Hebrides was threatened by the spread of English, Bill learned Gaelic and approached as many Gaelic speakers as possible. Few were willing to talk on tape or even in front of a notebook, so he had to remember what he heard, and record it later. He combined the results with close scrutiny of the available written records. Of these, he comments,

"Written records in the Islands are generally poor, and were often kept by incomers with no knowledge of Gaelic, and even less interest. Oral tradition, on the other hand, comes from within a community and is much more likely to be accurate, even though it does tend to be more localized. Neither by itself is a complete record, but if the two are amalgamated, a more complete picture emerges, sometimes with surprising results ..."

None more so than in the wonderful cases of people who could recite their patronymics — their father's name, followed by their grandfather's, great-grandfather's and so on. Some patronymics also appear in written records (albeit with rather odd attempts at transliteration), such as parochial registers. Bill says, "it can take some patience to recognize John Mcoil vicunlay vicormett as Iain macDhomhnaill mhic Fhionnlaidh mhic Thormoid — John son of Donald son of Finlay son of Norman," though of course the effort is entirely worth it as, in this case, it provides a four-generation pedigree.

The main records to which he tried to link oral pedigrees were the census returns, which are theoretically complete.

Onto this dual peg, Bill could then hang any other information available — civil registration, parochial registers and so on. The results are astonishing — over 10,500 pedigree sheets, each neatly drawn out in immaculate handwriting, covering all the families of the islands of the Outer Hebrides (Harris, Lewis, Barra, North and South Uist and the smaller associated islands). As the 1851 census includes the elderly, many of these pedigrees go back to the late 1700s.

Bill's main clients (he makes his information available for a very modest fee) are descendants of the islands' many late 18th- and 19th-century emigrants. Some Lewis and Harris sheep farmers went as far as the Falkland Islands and Patagonia, but most Lewis people went to eastern Quebec and Bruce County, Ontario; later ones made for the Gaelic-speaking areas already colonized by their kin, while Uist and Harris people set sail for Cape Breton and Prince Edward Island, and from 1850s onwards to Australia. Judging by where they settled, Bill often has a head start working out where they would have originated. Sometimes there are clues in the emigrant communities, reminding us that our ancestors lived in extended families, and that we should always look beyond the narrow confines of our direct ancestral lines. Thus, MacDonalds on their own may be fairly ubiquitous, but MacDonalds mixed with Steeles indicate migrants from South Uist (where the surname was adopted by a group of MacLeans who wanted to disguise their identity from some vengeful Campbells: they chose Steele simply as it was the boat's skipper's surname).

However you can acquire local knowledge, be it from older relatives, local history books, websites or local archives and resource centers like Seallam!, it is an invaluable clue to unlocking your Scottish family history.

CHAPTER 3

Scotland's names

A theatrical poster of a romantic melodrama, *Bonnie Scotland*, performed about 1895, shows the idealized image of Scots people that was common around the world.

Genealogists rely heavily on names to identify people and to link them together. Thanks to strong first name patterns and the patronymic surname system, Scots' names are far more likely to identify them in terms of place and family than the names of, say, English or French people.

Variant spellings

In Scots and Gaelic, various groups of letters are interchangeable, or pronounced in non-intuitive ways. In Scots, "l" following "a," "o" or "u" is vocalized as "w," so Falkirk can be rendered Fawkirk and Goldie as Goudie. "F" or "v" at the end of a name might be dropped, so sheriff might be rendered "shirra," while "d" was often added, so Norman might become Normand. Gaelic has its own rules of pronunciation and declension. If your family is from a Gaelic-speaking area, it is worth studying the basics, using George McLennan"s *Scots Gaelic: An Introduction to the Basics* (Argyll Publishing, 1998) — the added bonus being you will then be able to speak a few words of your own ancestral tongue.

First names

When Gaelic first names were recorded in official documents such as OPRs, attempts were often made to anglicize them. Being familiar with Homer's *Iliad*, session clerks sometimes substituted Gaelic or Norse names with similar-sounding Homeric ones, hence many boys called Aonghas in Gaelic were recorded as Aeneas, and those with the Norse name Ivor became Evander.

Sometimes, several Gaelic names had only one English "equivalent," such as John. Bill Lawson found a Hebridean family with sons called Iain, Shauny, Eoin and Iagan: the registrar recorded all four as John!

There were also names that were commonly substituted not because they were actually linked etymologically but simply because they were vaguely similar. This, as with the spellings, was at the whim of the recording clerk — your ancestors seldom had any say in the matter. Some common variants are as follows, but someone recorded with one variant may easily appear elsewhere under another.

Agnes = Nancy
Mary Ann = Polly
Angus = Aeneas = Aonghas
Hugh = Hew = Ewan = Aodh
John = Ian = Iain = Eun = Eoin
Christian = Christina = Cristine = Kirsty
Alexander = Alex = Sandy = Allistair = Ally
Jean = Jane = Jeanie = Jeannie = Janet = Jessie = Jenny
Elisabeth = Elizabeth = Betty = Beatrice = Beatrix = Isabella
Morah = More Moira= Morag = Sara = Sarah
Euphemia = Erica = Afica = Effie = Oighric
Isabella = Isabel = Isobella = Bella
Margaret = Maggie = Peggy
Samuel = Sorley = Somerled
Harold = Torquil = Torkeld
Helen = Ellen = Nellie
Donald = Daniel
Patrick = Peter

These are generalizations. Local custom was often random, though more eccentric. Bill Lawson's studies of the Hebrides show that Bethag was anglicized to Rebecca in Harris, and to Betty or Betsy in Lewis, except for the Lewis parish of Lochs, where the registrar translated Bethag as Sophie. He knows, therefore, that a migrant family from Lewis who used the name Sophie was probably from Lochs.

Girls' names were often created using their fathers'. Some names, like Nicholas and Christian, were given to girls unaltered: others had "-ina" added. William's daughter might be Wilhelmina (the GROS website noted the spelling "William All-Mina" in Morton in 1769). Alexander's daughter became Alexandrina. A real Alexandrina I know of called herself Alice instead, while some girls just ended up being nicknamed "Ina." Pity poor Johnina Samuelina, who was named after both her grandfathers!

Grandfather, father and son sharing the same name: three generations of William Meikles, pictured in Falkirk in 1949. The child in the picture grew up to have two sons, the oldest also called William (courtesy of John Meikle).

James and Eleanor Ritchie (born Morgan) from the fishing community of Musselburgh, East Lothian. Her grandson, Eleanor Brown, was named after her! The eleventh son, Eleanor's parents are said to have run out of boys' names by the time he came along.

Middle names

Scots rarely used these before the 19th century. When the custom spread, Scots sometimes used the names of wealthy patrons or benefactors as middle names, but more normally used existing family first names and surnames, thereby helping identify the wider ramifications of the family tree. Walter Hooks (1847–1915), pattern-maker of Ardrossan, Ayrshire (see pp. 50–1), for example, called one daughter Mary MacClandish Hooks, the middle name being her mother's maiden name, and another Sarah Boag Hooks, Sarah Boag having been the full name of his father's third wife.

Those names were usually bestowed informally — when men appear in records such as tax lists or ships' manifests with a middle name, this will often be the father's first name, put there to tell different people apart. John Donald MacDonald and John Neil MacDonald probably weren't baptized with their middle names — they were just the sons of Donald MacDonald and Neil MacDonald respectively.

Naming patterns

The arrows indicate the person after whom the child was named.

Scots families often followed strict rules about naming children. The usual pattern was as shown on the chart below.

If this practice was followed strictly, and you know the names of all the children in the family, you can work out what the grandparents' names would have been. Unfortunately, you will seldom know for sure who the eldest son was, and the system was not followed perfectly: in some families, the eldest son was named after the *maternal* grandfather, and if a child with a particular family name died, a sibling born later might be given the same one.

Problems arose when two grandparents had the same name. If both grandfathers were called Roderick, did you name your second son Roderick, as well as the first? Sometimes no, sometimes yes, though in such cases the second Roderick might be given a completely different nickname.

Naming patterns mean that first names stayed in families, but could migrate down through female lines. Unusual first names can provide clues to ancestry — the first name Sorley is very rare in Harris, and according to Bill Lawson pretty much everyone with that name is descended one way or another from Sorley MacAulay, one of two MacAulay brothers who settled at Greosabhagh in 1780.

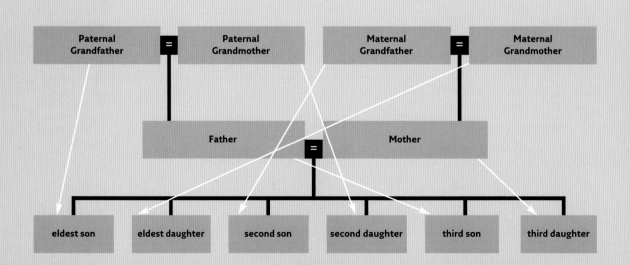

Surnames

When you encounter an ancestral surname, look it up in a reliable surname dictionary. Though far from perfect, the best starting-point is G.F. Black's *The Surnames of Scotland, Their Origin, Meaning, and History* (New York Public Library, 1946). Some areas have specialist dictionaries, such as G. Lamb's *Orkney Surnames* (Paul Harris Publishing, 1978).

It makes no sense trying to research a family line without seeing if the surname identifies a likely place or origin. You may never be able to trace back all the generations to that place, but at least you will know where the line is likely to have come from. Kinloch or Kinnock, for example, comes from Co. Fife, so a family of that name living in Inverness is likely to have migrated from the south, and any in Glasgow are likely to have moved from the east. Black is good at identifying surnames that can have more than one origin, thus helping you to not make unfounded assumptions.

Derivations

Most Scottish surnames, like so many others in the world, are from the following sources:

- From the father (patronymics – see below).
- From the occupation (metonymics), such as Mac an t-Saoir, "son of the carpenter," anglicized as MacIntyre.
- From nicknames (sobriquets), such as Cameron, from *cam shron*, "crooked nose," the nickname of a clan chief of unknown origin.
- From places. Some families named from their landholdings have earlier, known ancestry, while others come to our knowledge already identified by their place of residence, and no more, such as:

  Brodie: from Brodie (Brothac) in Moray (probably Pictish)

Colquhoun: from the Barony of Colquhoun, Dumbartonshire, descended from Humphrey de Kilpatrick

Erskine: from the Barony of Erskine, Renfrew

Forbes: from Forbes, Aberdeen

Innes: from Innes, Moray, descended from one Berowald in 1160

Menzies: from "Meyners," a Lowland surname borne by a family thought to be of Gaelic origin

Urquhart from Urquhart on the Cromarty Firth.

An extract from *The Origin of Surnames and Some Pedigrees*, a two-volume scrapbook deposited at the Society of Genealogists, compiled from entries in *The Weekly Scotsman* (courtesy of the SoG).

Patronymics

"Mac" followed by a personal name means "son of x." This patronymic is the commonest form of Scottish surname. MacLaren, for example, means "son of Laren." There are often traditions associated with the original namesake: Laren was an abbot of Achtow in Balquhidder, and the

MacArthur's original Arthur was said to be King Arthur himself — an unlikely tale! But in many cases, the namesake belongs to one of the genuine, ancient, interconnected pedigrees of the Viking and Dalriadan kings (see pedigrees on pp. 196–7 and 200–1), thus turning a mere surname into the key to a vast amount of early genealogical lore.

The Gaelic "Mac" is one of a handful of words common to languages worldwide, and may have been part of the original tongue of our earliest human ancestors. It appears, for example, in Native American tongues as *make* ("son"); in New Guinea as *mak* ("child"); and in Tamil as *maka* ("child"). When you address someone as "Mac," you're using a word that, in all probability, your 180,000 x great-grandparents would have understood. M' and Mc are contractions of Mac, found in both Ireland and Scotland. It is a myth that Scots only used Mc and the Irish Mac — the spellings are completely interchangeable in both countries.

People might use one or more patronymic. If Angus's father Donald was the son of Ewan, then he became Angus Mac Donald Mac Ewan. In proper Gaelic, the second and subsequent "Mac"s are in the genitive case, so are spelled "Mhic" and pronounced "Vic," and are sometimes transliterated thus too. So, you may find Angus mac Donald mhic Ewan, or Angus mac Donald vic Ewan, all meaning "Angus son of Donald son of Ewan." Throw in some mishearing and Gaelic renderings of the names, and you may have to spend some time deciphering them — a rental from Rodel, Harris in 1690 names Angus Mc Coill vic Ewine, which Bill Lawson translates as "Angus MacDhomhnaill mhic Eoghainn," i.e. Angus son of Donald the son of Ewen.

Sometimes, the system isn't quite so clear as this, and there are cases where someone's "patronymic" will actually be the name of the person who brought him up, not his real father — all such cases where a foster-child takes its foster-father's surname are confusing to genealogists.

Women had patronymics too: the female form of "Mac" was "Nic" or "Ni'n." Angus's sister Morag may have been recorded as Morag ni'n Donald nic Ewan.

At this point you are probably thinking that this is confusing because MacEwan is a surname, but apparently here it can also be simply a description of someone's father or grandfather. So, was Donald Mac Ewan surnamed MacEwan, or simply the son of someone called Ewan?

I'm afraid the system didn't distinguish between the two, mainly because hereditary surnames arose in an entirely informal way in the first place. The MacEwan Clan descends from Ewan of Otter, Co. Argyll, who lived in the 13th century. His sons used Mac Ewan as a patronymic that also became a fixed surname. The male-line descendants had their own patronymics — Ian son of Dougal, etc. — and at the end of their list of ancestors they might or might not add their surname. Ian Mac Dougal

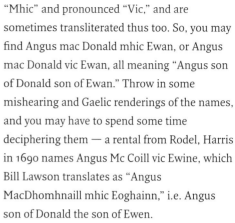

A painting by Swiss artist Johann Heinrich Fuessli (1741–1825) of Macbeth and Lady Macbeth, a Scottish name that Shakespeare made famous all round the world.

to assume that people using what appears to be a surname did so because it actually was their surname, particularly if that surname was common in the area. You just have to be prepared for the possibility that your research may reveal this not to have been the case.

Married surnames

The modern English custom of women automatically adopting their husband's name on marriage spread into Scotland by the 19th century, and was used (or imposed) almost universally in the census returns, but in many other records you'll find the older custom of women keeping their maiden name. Thus, Robbie Burns' wife was known as Jean Armour, not Jean Burns. Even when women adopted their husband's surname, they often reverted to their maiden names if widowed.

The Scottish Life Archive has rich resources for family historians. Many of its photographs depict named individuals. This picture, taken in Falkland, Co. Fife, in 1905, was taken by Andrew Venters in front of his grocery shop. The boy sucking his thumb was "W. Anderson."

Mac Ewan might be Ian son of Dougal of Clan MacEwan clan, or simply someone who, as in our example above, was the grandson of a man called Ewan.

Worse, some patronymic surnames have come to be spelled in a certain way. The Clan MacKenzie are descended from a 14th-century Kenneth (Choinnich), who in turn descended from Gilleon na h-Airde, ancestor of the O'Beolan earls of Ross. Unfortunately, some registrars, knowing this and hearing someone saying that their father happened to be called Kenneth, would put them down as "MacKenzie," when they weren't of the Clan MacKenzie at all. A man whose father was a carpenter might be recorded as the literal translation, MacIntyre, even though he was not a member of the great Clan MacIntyre.

There is no easy solution, but there are some routes through the mire. In general, it's sensible

The Ragman Rolls

The Ragman Rolls were two lists of nobles and other "subjects superior" forced to swear allegiance to King Edward I of England during his interference in the Scottish succession in 1291 and 1296. The list, published by the Bannatyne Club in 1834, is at **www.rampantscotland.com/ragman/blragman_index.htm**. Its great use is identifying early (or earliest) bearers of surnames that were often taken from the land families were then holding. Queen Victoria's prime minister William Ewart Gladstone (1809-98) did much to try to help poor Scots, through the Napier Commission, for example (see pp. 150-1). He was born in Liverpool, but his ancestry lay in Scotland. Hubert de Gledestan appears in the Ragman Roll. From him, a line comes down to the Gladstones of Arthurshiels, who settled in Biggar as maltmen. A branch of these moved to Leith, then Liverpool, producing the prime minister. Another branch ended with the mother of local genealogist Brian Lambie. She was the last Gladstone to be born in Biggar, although many Biggar people are cousins of the great Gladstone. The early Gladstones are buried on the outside wall of the old Libberton Kirk, which was rebuilt in 1810, partly over the old site, with the effect, as Brian says, "some Gladstones may now be partly inside with their feet out in the cold!"

Gaelic place names

The name of Ailsa Craig, an island in the Firth of Clyde, contains the Gaelic *creag*, meaning "rock."

Some places with Gaelic names were given new names by English-speakers — Cill Rìmhinn ("church of the king's hill") is now called St. Andrew's. However, while some names survive with their old spellings, many, as with surnames, have half-survived through anglicization (such as Bowmore for Bogha Mòr, "great rock submerged in the sea") or through direct translation, sometimes of only part of the name. Lochgilphead was Ceann Loch Gilb (where Ceann means "head"), for example. Known changes of parish names up to the 1790s are detailed in volume 20 of the *First Statistical Account* (see p. 32).

This becomes very relevant to genealogists when an ancestor gave a place of origin in a form that is no longer used. If a Gaelic place name is given, and you cannot find it, find out what it means and see if it now exists in an English translation.

Modern Ordnance Survey maps show many places in their Gaelic form, as authentically as possible. The commonest elements of place names are:

- Achadh = field, such as Achiltibuie
- Bad = place
- Baile = township, such as Ballygrant
- Caol = strait, such as Kylesku
- Ceann – head, such as Kinloch
- Cill = church or (monastic) cell, such as Kilbride
- Creag = rock, such as Craiglarach
- Druim = ridge, such as Drumpellier
- Dùn = fort, such as Dunblane
- Inbhir = mouth of river, such as Inverary
- Na = of the
- Rubha = promontory, such as Rhu
- Srath = valley, such as Strathnaver
- Taigh = house, such as Tighnabruaich

Badnaban meant "place of the women;" Cnocaneach "hill of the horses" and Badnahachlais "place of the armpit," presumably because it was in a narrow valley that really does look like one.

Anglicization

As Scots and English replaced Gaelic, Gaelic surnames were anglicized, leading to many changes in spelling that often disguised true meanings. "Mac Gille," meaning, "son of the servant of ..." often became "McIl ..." or "Macel ..." There was also a tendency (on the part of registrars) to change difficult-to-spell Gaelic surnames into more familiar, existing surnames that sounded similar, which is how some MacEahcrans became Cochranes, and some O'Brolachans are now Brodies. Some surnames were subject to (almost) literal translations — some MacIntyres ("son of the carpenter") are now called Wright, for wrights crafted things.

Nicknames

Where a surname was very common, families might add an extra nickname or "tee name." In her excellent *Scottish Family Tree Detective* (Manchester University Press, 2006), Rosemary Bigwood notes some north-east coast families being known by their surname followed by the name of their fishing boat, while in the

Hebrides Bill Lawson noted extra surnames such as Kelper (kelp harvester), Clachair (mason) and Saighdear (soldier, usually used of an army pensioner). The MacLeod descendants of John MacLeod from Muck, who settled in Harris in 1779 as a gardener, are known locally as MacLeod na Gairneileirean, or just na Gairneileirean, "the Gardeners."

Other nicknames were from characteristics, such as Dubh (black-haired) and Ruadh (red-haired). Red-haired Angus MacDougal might thus be known as Angus Ruadh Mac Dougal, or Angus Mac Dougal Ruadh. In the Lowlands, when the patronymic system died out nicknames could become people's only surnames, such as Duff (from Duhb) or Cruikshanks ("crooked legs"). Many people also became known by where they lived —

The writer Sir Walter Scott (1771–1832). His surname means literally "Scot" and was borne by a great clan on the English-Scots borders.

Cairncross, Cairns, Cladcleuch and so on. Some had interesting twists — the Caithness family aren't from Caithness, but from Kettins in the barony of Angus.

Speaking Gaelic

The language of the Picts was a dialect of ancient British, akin to modern Welsh. Gaelic, another branch of the same tongue, developed in Ireland and was spoken by Irish settlers (the Scots) in Argyll and up the west coast, especially after the establishment of the Scots kingdom of Dalriada, about the second century CE. It gradually displaced "Pictish" in the west and north. Its decline in the Lowlands was due mainly to the spread of Scots and English in the royal towns or burghs, and after the battle of Culloden in 1746 it began to vanish from the Highlands too. In the 1830s, the *Second Statistical Account* reports, for far-flung Assynt, Sutherland, that Gaelic was still spoken universally there,

"... the only medium of religious instruction. The English language, however, is making slow but sure progress. The youth of the parish are ambitious of acquiring it, being sensible that the want of it proves a great bar to their advancement in life. It is likely, nonetheless, that Assynt is one of the very last districts in which the Gaelic language shall cease to be the language of the people."

Ironically, the Gaelic School Society helped bring Gaelic to an end: once children had learned to read the scripture in Gaelic, the account says, they wanted to read more on other subjects, and to do this they needed to learn English.

The Vikings' tongue survives in many words and place names used in the areas they settled, and as a Scots/Norse hybrid, Norn, the native tongue of the Orkneys and Shetlands.

The Scots language — for a language it is — is a descendant, along with Northumbrian English, of the tongue of the Anglians of Lothian. It gradually dominated the Lowlands and then pushed northwards, though borrowing words freely from Gaelic, French, Dutch and English. It was the official tongue of Scotland until 1707. In 1773, Dr. Johnson observed that,

"... the conversation of the Scots grows every day less unpleasing to the English; their peculiarities wear fast away: their dialect is likely to become in half a century provincial and rustick, even to themselves. The great, the learned, the ambitious, and the vain, all cultivate the English phrase, and English pronunciation, and in splendid companies Scotch is not much heard, except now and then from an old lady."

By writing in Scots, Burns helped save the language from obscurity and helped restore some of its old dignity too. Later writers and poets, such as William Robertson Melvin in the 19th century and Hugh MacDairmid in the 20th century, have contributed to a limited revival. See *Scots- English English-Scots Dictionary* (Lomond Books, 1998, repr. 2001), *The Concise Scots Dictionary* (Polygon at Edinburgh, 1999) and an online dictionary, **www.dsl.ac.uk/dsl**.

CHAPTER 4

Know your parish

Your chances of success in tracing your Scottish family history, and of deriving enormous enjoyment from doing so, will be greatly enhanced by spending some time finding out about the places where your family lived.

Trying to trace a family tree without studying where people lived makes no sense. Knowing whether the parish was a Highland or Lowland one makes a massive difference in understanding the sort of people who lived there. Were your people from an isolated Highland crofting district, a coastal settlement dependant on kelp and fish, a comfortable Lowland farming community or a prosperous royal burgh? You also need to know about the place to start working out what records it is likely to have generated, and where these will be found. If the area was subject to a franchise court, its records could be searched. Which commissary and sheriff's courts had jurisdiction there? The more you know, the better.

A farmer at Stroncruby tills his field using a horse-drawn plow, while his bull grazes the pasture and a goat makes do further up the mountain, from Hume's 1774 *Survey of Assynt*, Map 11 (courtesy of Lord Strathnaver).

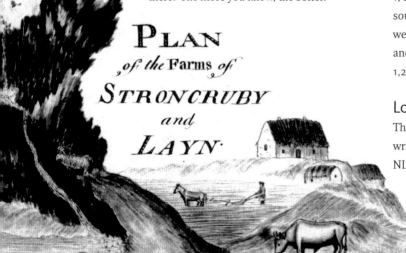

Scotland's parishes

Church reform was pioneered by St. Margaret, wife of Malcolm III Canmore (d. 1093). Up to then, priests lived under the same roofs as their lords or in monastic houses, some of which dated back to the time of St. Columba (521-97), the Gaelic missionary credited with introducing Christianity to the Picts. By 1200, however, 11 dioceses had been created across the southern feudalized areas, each run by a bishop and divided into parishes containing new churches. The system was eventually extended across the whole country, with parishes dividing as the population grew. The rather chaotic situation, with no less than 64 parishes straddling county boundaries, was rationalized in 1891, meaning that some ancestors who never moved house appeared in one parish record before 1891, and in another one afterwards.

When General Registration was introduced in 1855 each parish also became a Registration District, numbered from the furthest north (no. 1, Bressay) and working down to the furthest south (no. 901, Wigtown). Large city parishes were divided into several registration districts, and identified by the parish number followed by 1,2,3, etc. in superscript.

Local histories

The histories of many parishes have been written. Ask at the local archives, look in the NLS catalog or in *The Bibliography of Scotland* on

Some historical background

King Malcolm III Canmore and his wife, St. Margaret (both died 1093).

Kilchurn Castle, Loch Awe, Co. Argyll, seat of the Campbells of Glenorchy.

The records you will be using have been greatly influenced by Scotland's history, and in particular by King Malcolm III Canmore (d. 1093) and his immediate descendants, who consolidated royal power in Scotland.

As T.C. Smout writes in his immensely useful *A History of the Scottish People 1560–1830* (Fontana Press, 1969, repr. 1985), modern Scotland comprises 80 percent rough moor and bog, and things have improved vastly since Malcolm's day. Then, its roughly 250,000 people inhabited tiny islands of semi-cultivated land, linked by boggy footpaths, surrounded by a howling wilderness of wolves, beavers, wild boar and aurochs. Their stone-walled homes, roofed with brushwood, turf or skins, were clustered into tiny farmtowns or bailies. Though ostensibly farmers, most people still depended heavily on Stone Age skills of hunting wild animals and gathering shellfish and fruits. Their overlords, the mormaers or earls, were of Pictish origin, and their groupings and allegiances mainly tribal.

Malcolm and his wife St. Margaret were influenced by the Normans' adaptation of Roman ideas on how to run countries, and introduced similar systems of government in Scotland. Their son David I (d. 1153) spent 40 years at the English court, where he was Earl of Huntingdon. When he inherited the throne David came north with a great retinue of Anglo-Norman followers. "French in race and manner of life, in speech and culture," the Scottish kings started to transform Scotland into a modern state, using feudalism, creation of royal burghs and sheriffdoms, and church reform as their chief tools.

To feudalize a country, the king assumed full ownership of all land, and then granted parts of it to lords in return for their military support. David I started this process, leaving the old mormaers in place, but as new feudal lords. Through intermarriage, the old and new aristocracies merged into a semi-Norman, semi-native ruling class.

The Canmore kings peppered the Lowlands with royal castles, and around each created royal burghs, which were settlements of craftsmen and merchants with trade monopolies over the hinterland. The burgers were drawn mainly from immigrant Normans, Angles, Scandinavians and Flemings, and used English as their *lingua franca*, contributing to the retreat of Gaelic into the Highlands. David I planted his burghs as far south-west as Ayr and Renfrew, and as far north-east as Dingwall and Inverness, and though they later spread all over the Lowlands, they never penetrated the fastnesses of the Highlands.

The "colonized" lands were divided into counties, each with a sheriff controlling one of the castles. Sheriffs were either mormaers or Norman lords — the sheriffdoms rapidly became hereditary, but always subject to the King's good graces. The system was gradually extended into the Highlands until the whole of Scotland had been "shired." The counties remained unchanged until 1974, when they were replaced with large regions (such as Grampian and Strathclyde). These were replaced in 1996 with 32 council areas, broadly based on the old shires.

From 1286 onwards the Crown began to weaken. Barony and regality courts sprouted up, ostensibly with royal authority, but effectively tools of the excessive local power of the clan chiefs, sheriffs and feudal lords (often, of course, one and the same).

John Knox administering the first Protestant sacrament in Scotland. Although the parish system pre-dated his Church of Scotland, it was absorbed into the new reformed church.

www.sbo.nls.uk/cgi-bin/Pwebrecon. cgi?DB=local&PAGE=First. Besides providing background, histories may identify unusual local sources or actually name your ancestors.

Statistical Accounts

Read about your parish in the *Old* and *New Statistical Accounts*, on **www.edina.ac.uk/ stat-acc-scot/**.

The *Old* or *First Statistical Account* (1791–9) was the work of "Agricultural" Sir John Sinclair of Ulbster (1754–1835), MP for Caithness. In 1790, desiring "to elucidate the Natural History and Political State of Scotland," he sent a detailed questionnaire to each parish minister, asking about geography, climate, natural resources and social customs. He received all manner of different answers, including a lot of idiosyncratic notes, and published the lot.

The *New* or *Second Statistical Account* was commissioned by the General Assembly of the Church of Scotland in 1832. It included maps of the counties and took evidence from schoolmasters and doctors as well as ministers. It was published in volumes between 1834 and 1845. For Assynt, Sutherland, for example, we learn, *"There is no register of date previous to 1798. Since that period, births and marriages have been recorded with tolerable regularity, but there is no register of deaths."* The population was 1800 in 1760, 2419 in 1801 and 3161 in 1831; it was divided into 375 families, and 1400 of the population was attached to the church and parish of "Store" (Stoer).

A *Third Statistical Account* was created between 1951 and 1992 and can be inspected in libraries. A *Fourth Statistical Account of East Lothian* is on its way.

Volume 20 of the *Old Statistical Account* has a, *"List of Parishes suppressed, annexed to other parishes, or which have changed their names, with a corresponding List of the Parishes under which they are now included."*

Sir John Sinclair of Ulbster (1754–1835), who initiated the *First Statistical Account* of Scotland.

Groome and Lewis

Francis H. Groome's *Ordnance Gazetteer of Scotland* was compiled between 1882 and 1885. It is always worth checking since it states which presbytery and synod assemblies covered each parish, and will help you sort out places with the same name. It is online at **www.visionof britain.org** and at the *Gazetteer for Scotland*, **www.geo.ed.ac.uk/scotgaz/gaztitle.html**.

Samuel Lewis's *A Topographical Dictionary of Scotland* (1846) is online at **www.british-history.ac.uk/source.aspx?pubid=308**.

Obscure place names

These can present a problem if their location is not clear from the records. If even a "Google" search yields nothing, try the place name indexes in the *Register of the Great Seal of Scotland* (1306–1659); the sasine abridgments, or documents of land grants, (1781–1830), or enquire at Edinburgh University's School of Scottish Studies, which has records down to the level of individual field names. The GROS *Index of Scottish Place Names* is helpful, as is L.R. Timperley's *A Directory of Landownership in Scotland* c.1770 (SRS, 1976).

Maps

These are splendid ways of looking down on your ancestors' world to see what the terrain was like, what roads, rivers and railways there were, what other parishes were nearby — and perhaps even spot their actual houses.

All local archives and histories will help here. Reference books often say you will sometimes find detailed local maps in estate records, records of railway and canal companies, and processes of the Court of Session (as detailed in *Descriptive List of Plans in the Scottish Record Office*) — but few people have time to search

these, and many already appear in local history books. But do look at the National Library of Scotland's map collection, in Edinburgh, or at its fabulous site, **www.nls.uk/maps/index.html**. This includes the earliest surviving detailed maps of Scotland, made Timothy Pont in about 1583–96, which come with textual descriptions

A map from the surveyor's report to the Crown Commissioners on the lands of Strowan (Struan, Perthshire), one of the estates annexed or forfeited to the Crown after the 1745 rebellion.

of places (see **www.nls.uk/pont/ generalnew.html**). Of the island of Raasay, for example, Pont wrote,

"Raasa ane Ile neer the Skye upon 4 myle long perteyning to Mac-Gillichallum Rasa of the hous of Lewis of old, now holds this Ile of the Earle Seafort, it hath ane paroch kirk Kilmaluag, one castell called Breokill. hard by is Rona, a smal Ile, pertyning to that gentleman also."

You can study the subject of old maps in *A Guide to the Early Maps of Scotland to 1850* (Scottish Royal Geographical Society, 1973).

The Pont maps were saved from almost certain oblivion by Sir James Balfour of Denmilne, Fife (c.1590s–1657), Lord Lyon King of Arms, whose third wife Margaret Arnot of Ferny was a distant cousin of mine. He assembled an important collection of old manuscripts on Scottish history, which is now in the NLS.

The Ordnance Survey

One of the finest graphic sources for your family history, often showing your family's actual homes, are Ordnance Survey maps. Many, both current and historical (dating back over the last 200 years), are found in local archives.

The Survey was sparked by Bonnie Prince Charlie's rebellion, known as the '45, when King George II's generals realized they had no serviceable maps of the realm (those that existed stopped at county boundaries, so were useless for military purposes). Between 1747 and 1755 William Roy of the Royal Engineers organized a survey of Scotland, and in 1791 the creation of accurate topographical maps of all Britain began. The Trigonometrical Survey, renamed the Ordnance Survey, created maps to different scales; the most detailed (such as the 1:25,000 Explorer series) will show the shapes of fields and general shape of buildings in the countryside, and the town plans go to sufficient scale to see door steps and bay windows.

It's hard to date the maps to specific years. A map "of 1880" may have been surveyed a decade before. Some maps showing railways are actually much older maps with new railway lines engraved over the top. This is not a problem if you are aware of the issues and take time to find out the history of the particular map you are studying. For help contact The Ordnance Survey's Library (Room C454, Ordnance Survey, Romsey Road, Southampton, SO16 4GU, 0845 605 0505, **www.ordnancesurvey.co.uk**). See also **www.Old-Maps.co.uk**, where you can search and zoom in on Britain's Ordnance Survey County Series, 1:10,560 scale, First Edition maps (surveyed from 1846–99).

The Pont map showing Lochs Awe and Fyne, Co. Argyll.

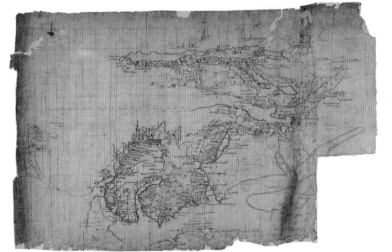

Finding Cnocaneach

I first encountered the name Cnocaneach, Sutherland, in Malcolm Bangor-Jones's *The Assynt Clearances* (The Assynt Press, 2001), which brings together information from sheriff or local court papers and the Sutherland estate papers. We had just bought the booklet in Achins' book/coffee shop at Inverkirkaig, and were scrutinizing it for more information about the MacLeods in Badnaban. This is what leapt out:

"Cnocaneach and Badnaban were held [from the Sutherland Estate] by George Ross from Easter Ross who went to work for the Custom House in Ullapool. He had removed people from Cnocaneach prior to 1812. The MacLeods, who were removed when the lands became part of Culag sheepfarm in 1812, accepted holdings in Baddidarrach but then changed their minds.

Cleared	Head of Household	Destination
1812	Alexander MacLeod	Langwell sheepfarm, Coigach
1812	Angus MacLeod (son of the above)	Badnaban
	Roderick Ross	Bad a' Ghrianan."

There were several MacLeod families in Badnaban, and Angus's was only one, but it was tremendously exciting to have confirmation of exactly where any of them came from and to discover they had come to Badnaban due to the notorious Highland Clearances (see pp. 147–50).

But where was Cnocaneach? Five minutes scrutinizing the Ordnance Survey's Explorer Series map of the area revealed "Cnoc Innis nan Each" just next to Badnaban, but that was a red herring. The correct Cnocaneach ("the hill of the horse") was a mile and a half away to the east (about 2 km).

An hour later found us panting up the track towards the hollow outlines of buildings indicated by the map. At last, we saw amidst the bracken a ruined dwelling! And then, just round a bend in the track, a derelict house, rebuilt in 1870 but on the ruins of an older one. Various walls indicated where yards and paddocks had been. The MacLeods and the Rosses had been thrown out of Cnocaneach in 1812, and here were their two ruined homes.

It would have been a tough place to live, but not nearly so much as Badnaban on the coast. The MacLeods probably went down to Badnaban in subdued silence, and as we walked back down to the loch we felt an immense sadness, knowing that the MacLeods had trudged the same path in 1812 carrying all their worldly possessions, leaving their precious crops to be eaten by the landlord's sheep and with a very uncertain future ahead of them.

This map, showing both Badnaban and Cnocaneach, was found through a search under "Assynt" at www.nls.uk/maps. The maps are accompanied by Hume's comments on the farms. Cnocaneach was described as, "*most beautifully situated upon the East side of the Hill of that name, the North and West Sides of which Hills are cover'd with fine full grown Trees, consisting of Oak, Ash, Birch, &c.*" Of Badnaban, on the other hand, Hume wrote, "*this small Farm on the South side of Loch Inver at the March with Cullack, is only a subsett, belonging to InverChirkag: it is situate near a Creak of the sea, where Boats land safely, and is occupied by two or three people who complain much of the small priviledge allowed them by their Landlord of the Hill pasture.*" The land by the farmhouses was, "*pretty much broke & interjected with Rocks and Stony Baulks.*" It was to Badnaban, in full knowledge of Hume's comments, that people from Cnocaneach were cleared in 1812. From John Hume's *Survey of Assynt*, 1774 (courtesy of Lord Strathnaver).

Mary Ann White, wife of Ally Alistair MacLeod, on the family croft at Badnaban with her grandson Murdo.

PART 2

The main records

Scotland is leading the way in making genealogical records available online to the public. With material from national and many local archives now accessible through the internet, it has never been easier to research Scottish family history. This section guides you through the many types of records that can be searched either online or in the archives, and that will reveal fascinating details about your ancestors' lives.

The impressive tombs in the Glasgow Necropolis have many elaborate memorial inscriptions of interest to family history researchers.

CHAPTER 5

General Registration

You've quizzed your elderly relatives, perhaps found some new ones and have learned about the places where your known family lived. The next step is to start original research.

General Registration records

Most developed countries have a system of compulsory civil registration (sometimes called General Registration) of births, marriages and deaths. Scottish General Registration started on January 1, 1855 (it began in 1837 in England and Wales, and in 1864 in Ireland, except for Protestant marriages that date from 1845).

Scotland's registration districts were based on existing parish boundaries, each with a local registrar, who was usually the local schoolmaster or doctor. All births had to be registered with him within 20 days, marriages within three days and deaths within eight days. The local registrars kept their own records but sent copies to the GROS in Edinburgh, where full indexes were compiled from them all.

As registration districts equated to parishes, it's easy to search for events taking place where you expect them to be. What may throw you off are events being registered in unexpected locations. Some couples married away from their home parishes, children could be born at their mother's mother's home, and some people died in hospital, or on vacation. When searching, you can nominate the registration district you want but if the search does not work then choose "all districts."

This solution can create a new problem — a massive list of possibilities. If you know the area well, you'll be able to spot local parishes easily; if not, you may be faced with a list of places you've never heard of before. ScotlandsPeople helpfully includes the registration district's county, and the GROS's official list at **www.gro-scotland.gov.uk/famrec/ hlpsrch/list-of-parishes-registration-districts.html** identifies the county or burgh in which the registration district lies and its start date. It's also easy to look them up on **www.maps.google.co.uk/**.

Access to the records

The records at the ScotlandsPeople Centre have all been digitized under the DIGROS ("Digital Imaging of the Genealogical Records of Scotland's People") project. These images can be viewed (for a fee) on the ScotlandsPeople website or at the ScotlandsPeople Centre, where

An early 20th-century photo of General Register House in Edinburgh.

you can also see images of recent records (births for the last 100 years, marriages for the last 75 and deaths for the last 50) that cannot be viewed on the website.

Alternatively you can visit or contact the local registrar who originally recorded the event — but often you won't know which to ask, hence the point of using the national indexes.

The digitized images are all you need for genealogy, but for official purposes (such as passports) you can order full certificates from **www.gro-scotland.gov.uk.**

The miraculous year of 1855

So enthusiastic were the people who introduced General Registration in 1855 that they included many details on their records that had never been recorded before. Sadly, the effort of including so much proved too complicated, so the forms were greatly simplified for 1856, though some extra information was then restored in 1861. These changes are identified below. Bear in mind that any event recorded in 1855 will be more detailed than anything before or after it. If an ancestor died or was married in 1855, you will gain useful extra information. Your ancestor may not have been born in 1855, but censuses may indicate a sibling of theirs who was; if so, it is worth getting their birth record, because it will tell you a lot about your ancestor's family.

Using the records

By quizzing your family you will usually be able to draw a family tree starting with a name, "Alexander or maybe Angus MacLeod," followed by their child with a bit more information — say, "Malcolm MacLeod, born in 1922." Then a third generation down, with much more definite information, "Flora MacLeod, born on April 22, 1951, Gorbals, Glasgow." You may think you'll save money and time if you start with Alexander (or

Angus!), but what can you really look for? Starting with Malcolm would be better. Since you can look for a birth in 1922, but as you don't know where Malcolm was born, you have no idea where to look. You're probably not 100 percent sure that the year 1922 was correct anyway; it may have been calculated from an age at death and these seldom take into account when in the year people's birthdays fell, so Malcolm could have been born in 1921 or 1923. Therefore, start with what you know for sure and seek Flora's birth certificate. Once you have this, you've established a firm foothold and can work back with confidence.

The birth record is a contemporary source providing the parents' names, probably from their own mouths — not half-remembered hearsay, then, but fact. Now, turn to the marriage indexes, seeking their wedding. Marriage records usually state ages of the couple and the full names of all four parents. Thus, following our example, once you've worked back from Flora's birth to her father Malcolm's marriage, you'll have a definite age for Malcolm and know his parents' full names, including whether the father was really called Alexander or Angus. Sometimes, admittedly, people got details wrong, or lied; if you discover discrepancies, you'll simply have to widen the period of your next search.

The next step is to seek Malcolm's birth. If his parents' names match those given on his marriage record, you'll know you have the right document.

A special feature of Scottish General Registration records, that is not found in the rest of the British Isles, is that death records state the parents' names. Admittedly, these can be inaccurate because the informant of the death may have been born years after the deceased's parents died. But usually, this extra feature is very helpful, and deaths should always be sought as a normal part of tracing your

Eleanor Conquer, born 1876 in Haddington (courtesy of the Crowley Family Collection).

Scottish family history. To help you search, all birth, marriage and death records state whether the person's parents were alive or dead at the time, and in the 19th century you can hone the search further using census returns.

Births

Births of boys and girls were indexed separately, though this is of no consequence when searching online. The indexes show:

- child's name
- registration district
- reference number. Twins are not identified explicitly in the records, but can sometimes be spotted by reference numbers that indicate their appearance on the same or adjacent pages as another child in the same district with the same surname.

- from 1929 mothers' maiden names appear, making it much easier to search for all children of a particular couple, or indeed for an illegitimate child (where the child's surname and mother's maiden surname will be the same).

Birth records always show:

- child's names. If the baby's name was changed, a diamond-shaped stamp will appear on the birth entry, with a reference to the Register of Corrected Entries (at the ScotlandsPeople Centre and website). Rarely, a birth will be registered before the child's name has been chosen; these entries should be found at the end of the list of children registered under that surname.
- date and time of birth
- address where the child was born
- gender
- father's name
- father's occupation
- mother's name and maiden name
- date of registration. Note that children were occasionally registered twice, especially if they were born some distance from home. This was technically incorrect but can be revealing, especially if the informants were different and gave subtly different information.
- informant's name and relationship (if any) to the child. This will usually be a parent but may be another close relation, or occasionally a non-relation, depending on circumstances.

Birth certificate for Alexandrina MacLeod, from family papers. She was born at "9 hours pm" on January 4, 1905 (the year is very badly written but can be confirmed from the clearer date of registration, January 16, 1905) at Badnaban, Assynt. The record includes her parents' date and place of marriage (courtesy of Mrs Moira Crowley).

It would be unwise to draw any inference from a non-relative being the informant.

- birth records for 1855 alone show parents' ages and places of birth, the date and place of the parents' marriage, the number and gender (but not names) of any children they had already and whether any of their children had died. This extra information does not appear between 1856 and 1860. From 1861 onwards just the date and place of the parents' marriage was restored to the records.

The importance of the additional information given in 1855 and to a lesser extent from 1861 onwards is immense. It provides valuable genealogical information on people who lived before 1855, and the marriage details can be linked to pre-1855 OPRs. In all cases where the couple came from somewhere else, the place of the marriage can be invaluable for working out where that was — whether in Scotland or abroad. Many Irish Famine immigrants arrived already married and had children in Scotland: a record of the latter will name the country and often the exact place of marriage back in Ireland.

Marriages

Until 1929 (when the minimum age was raised to 16), boys could marry at 14 and girls at 12 provided they had parental consent. Marriages of such young people were rare, but they really did happen. Many marriage searches fail simply because people don't search back far enough. If your female ancestor was born in 1850, then she could have married as early as 1862.

The old indexes showed males and females separately, though this is irrelevant when using the computerized indexes. The indexes show:

- name of person marrying
- from 1929, the index reference to one party states the surname of the spouse too. In addition, between 1855 and 1863, brides are indexed under both their maiden name and their new married one.
- registration district and reference number, that can be used for cross-referencing pre-1929.

The marriage records always show:

- names of bride and groom
- occupations of both parties
- whether single, widow(er)ed or divorced
- ages of both parties. If there was a large age gap between the two parties, it was not unknown for one or both to lessen the difference by lying.
- names and sometimes addresses of witnesses

The Edinburgh artist Sir David Wilkie (1785–1841) painted this depiction of _The Bride at her Toilet on the Day of her Wedding_. Not every woman would have had such a formal and elaborate wedding day, or have been able to afford the beautiful dresses shown in these old wedding photos.

A certificate, issued in 1970, for the 1935 marriage of Frederick Crowley and Lillian Watt (courtesy of Mrs Moira Crowley).

- names of parents of both parties, including maiden name of mothers. If a parent had died, the word "deceased" will usually be added. Married mothers are shown with both married and maiden names ("M.S." means "maiden surname"). If the person marrying was illegitimate, they might just state their mother's name, but many concealed the fact by making up a father's name and claiming that their mother was married to him.

- name and denomination of the minister. If the marriage had been performed irregularly, but then registered with a sheriff, then details of the sheriff's warrant will be given here.

- in 1855 alone, the records also identified whether either party had been married before. If so, how many children had been produced and of these how many were still alive. Also, the date and place of birth of the bride and groom were given, and whether these births had been registered. These details were abandoned in 1856, but the birthplace of each party was restored in 1972.

Deaths

The death indexes show:

- name
- name and number of district
- reference number
- ages (the 1859–60 indexes lack ages, but they have been added to the online version)
- from 1974 onwards the mother's maiden name appears
- married women are indexed under married and maiden surname(s). Beware that if a woman was married before, her earlier married name might be given, accidentally, in lieu of her maiden name. If she had been married more than once, one or more of her former married names might (accidentally) be left out.

Other death records

Municipal cemeteries have been operating since the 19th century. Along with crematoria, they usually keep their own records, or you can ask at the nearest archives.

Between death and burial, no small number of bodies went to the anatomy schools of Aberdeen, Dundee, Edinburgh, Glasgow and St Andrews. Registers of these cadavers from 1842 onwards are in NAS class MH1, and include name, age and last place of residence (often the workhouse or infirmary). A gory addition to your family tree, perhaps, and for pre-1855 deaths actually quite a useful one.

Transcribed monumental inscriptions from the churchyard in Robert Burns' birthplace, Alloway (*Alloway Monumental Inscriptions*, Alloway and South Ayrshire FHS, 2000), showing how inscriptions can connect families across the world.

07 Feb. 1938 aged 79 years. Their younger son JAMES died 02 Sep. 1965 aged 56 years. 'Thy will be done'
[On vase] In memory of our father HARRY WALLACE   *McLachlan*

O11   In loving memory of MARGARET FORREST HALDANE who died at Longhill 29 Jun. 1936 aged 71 years wife of JAMES BURNS Also their son JOHN died at Calgary, Canada 30 Jan. 1915 aged 25 years. The above JAMES BURNS died at Longhill 29 Jun. 1941 aged 80 years. Also their daughter HELEN BAILLIE died at Balig 27 Dec. 1947 aged 60 years

O12   In loving memory of ROBERT DAVIDSON died at Burton Smithy 08 Dec. 1936 aged 57 His grandson WILLIAM F. DAVIDSON died

The death records always show:

- name
- date, time and place of death
- cause of death, how long the deceased had been suffering, and the name of the doctor if present
- occupation
- marital status
- gender
- age, replaced from 1966 by date of birth
- place of death
- usual residence, if not the same as the place of death
- whether married or widow(er)ed
- parents' names, including mother's maiden name, and whether the parents were alive or dead
- occupation of father
- informant's name and sometimes address
- in 1855 and from 1861 onwards you will also find details of the spouse (or spouses if there had been more than one marriage). This is not given in the period 1856-60, though of course the spouse might be the informant.
- in 1855 you will learn where the deceased was born and how long they had lived in the place where they died.
- in 1855 you will find the names and ages of children born to the deceased, plus their age(s) at death, if applicable
- the period 1855-60 records where the deceased was buried

You may find a reference to the Register of Corrected Entries, that will include an entry from a sheriff court (see pp. 100-1) investigating any unusual or accidental deaths. These references are worth following up, as you may learn additional details about the deceased's family. Any unusual deaths may have been reported in local newspapers too.

District No. 573-2	Year 1968	Entry No. 9	
DEATH registered in the District of ....Johnstone..........			
in the ....County.......... of ....Renfrew..........			
(1) Name(s) and Surname	Walter Hooks.		(2) Sex M.
(3) Occupation	Iron Moulder (Journeyman) (Retired)		
(4) Marital Status	Married	(5) Date of Birth 20 / 6 / 1877	(6) Age 90 years
(7) Name, Surname and Occupation of Spouse(s)	Helen Laird Caldwell.		
(8) When and Where Died	19.68...... January Fourth. Ch. 55m. A.M. Johnstone Hospital, By Johnstone.		
(9) Usual Residence (if different from place of death)	171 Main Road, Elderslie.		

(10) Name(s), Surname and Occupation of Father	(11) Name(s), Surname(s) and Maiden Surname of Mother
Walter Hooks	Margaret Hooks
Foreman Patternmaker	m.s. McCandlish
(Deceased)	(Deceased)

Death certificate for Walter Hooks (1877–1968), showing his parents' names (courtesy of Mrs Moira Crowley).

Death traditions

Gaelic-speaking Scots believed that the soul stayed close to the corpse until after burial, so they introduced the custom of the Late Wake — watching the body constantly until burial, lamenting and singing, even dancing and playing games. Wakes were not necessarily somber or sober affairs. Anne Ross, in *Folklore of the Scottish Highlands* (Tempus, 2000), reports that, *"at the funeral of one of the lairds of Culloden the mourners were entertained so liberally before leaving Culloden House that when they did start for the Churchyard of Inverness they left the coffin behind! At another funeral a similar mistake occurred, and was only discovered when the party arrived at the churchyard and the sexton remarked, 'It's a grand funeral, but whaur's Jean?'"*

Some areas had their own death customs. In Soay, for example, a lock of the dead man's hair was nailed to the door lintel to keep the fairies out. Some clans and families had special traditions, especially surrounding portents of death. For example, the Breadalbanes knew a family death was coming when they heard a bull roaring on the hillside at night, and for the MacLachlans the appearance of a small bird foretold doom.

Lateral thinking Conquers all

Margaret Hunt Conquer

This list of deaths in a family bible came to the Crowley family from their aunt Sissy, who in turn had it from a Margaret Hunt Conquer, who died without close family in 1953. The list was intriguing because Hunt was a middle name in the Crowley family too, from Sissy's paternal grandmother Ellen Hunt, wife of James Crowley, who had married in Ireland in 1851 before the potato famine drove them to migrate to Scotland.

We used the list to look up the death records, which rapidly turned the list into a family tree. Margaret's death record gave her parents as Robert Conquer and Catherine Adelaide Hunt. Catherine Adelaide Hunt's death listed her parents as John Hunt and Catherine Kelly, proving she was a sister of Ellen Crowley, née Hunt.

It's always worth following up any new leads you find in family history, so I investigated Catherine further, finding her marriage to Robert Conquer in 1868 and her appearance in the 1881 census with a hitherto unknown sister, Charlotte. Investigating Charlotte produced a real surprise, for in the 1861 census she was living in Edinburgh with her Irish-born parents, John and Catherine — before then, we had no idea that they had come over from Ireland too.

When Charlotte married in 1868, John and Catherine were both alive, but neither were found in the 1871 census. This narrowed down the period when they must have died, and we found Catherine's death reported in 1869. This listed her parents, Hubert Kelly, a crofter, and Ellen, née Denny. These were Sissy's great-great-grandparents, and would have been born in the late 1700s. They had probably never set foot in Scotland and most likely don't appear in any Irish records either — yet through this piece of lateral genealogy their names have been found again.

The 1861 census entry revealing the unexpected presence in Scotland of the Irish-born John and Catherine Hunt.

Parish of	Quoad Sacra Parish of	Parliamentary Burgh of	Royal Burgh of	Town of	V

Road, Street, &c., and No. or Name of House.	HOUSES		Name and Surname of each Person.	Relation to Head of Family.	Condition	Age of		Rank, Profession, or Occupation.	Where Born.	
Canopate N Side						M	F			
Bothwell Close 10	1		Thomas Grant	Head	Mar	25		Shoemaker Jour	Ireland	
			Catharine Do.	Wife	Mar		35		Do.	
			Mary Jane Do.	Daur			2		England	
			James McGarva	Head	Mar	42		Do.	Ireland	
			Isabella McGarva	Wife	Mar		35	Sewer & Binder of Shoes	Do.	
			Mary McGarva	Daur	Un		16	Do. Do.	Edin. New North	
			Sarah McGarva	Daur			14	Scholar	Do. Do.	
			Elizabeth Porteous	Head	W		84		Edin. Rd Greyfriars	
			George Porteous	Son	Mar	51		Tailor Jour	Do. Wt Church	
			John Hunt	Head	Mar	60		Servant Butler	Ireland	
			Catharine Hunt	Head	Mar		50		Do.	
			Charlotte Hunt	Daur	Un		18	Shoemaker Jour	Do.	
			Patrick Monaghan	Head	Mar	46		French Polisher	Ireland	
									Do.	

Minor Registers

These tend to record people who were born, married or died abroad. If you cannot find what you want in normal General Registration, look in the minor registers — you never know. On ScotlandsPeople, select "minor records" from the drop-down county menu. If the person you expect to find does not appear, try the equivalent events-abroad records of the Registrar General in London (that effectively cover "the British"). These are indexed at **www.findmypast.com**.

The GROS Minor Records include:

- Air Register from 1948 of births (where one parent normally lived in Scotland), and deaths (of people who normally lived in Scotland) on British aircraft anywhere in the world.
- Consular Returns of birth and death from 1914 and marriage from 1917 registered with British consuls, for people "of Scottish descent or birth."
- Foreign Returns (1860–1965): births of children of Scottish parentage, "based on evidence submitted by the parents and due consideration of such evidence" and marriage and deaths of Scottish subjects.
- High Commission Returns (from 1964) of births and deaths of children "born of Scottish descent in certain Commonwealth countries."
- Marine Register (from 1855) of births on British merchant ships at sea, where one of the child's parents was usually resident in Scotland, and deaths of people normally resident in Scotland; also deaths of Royal Navy and Royal Marine personnel (including Reservists) during wartime.
- Armed Services: births include Army Returns of, "births of Scottish persons at military stations abroad" 1881–1959; Service Departments Registers from 1959 for births

of children of Scottish residents in the armed forces; marriages of Scots serving at military stations abroad; Service Returns of deaths of Scottish persons at military stations abroad (1881–1959); Service Departments Registers of deaths, "outside the United Kingdom of persons ordinarily resident in Scotland who are serving in or employed by HM Forces, including families of members of the Forces (from 1959);" War Returns of deaths of Scottish soldiers in the Boer War (1899–1902); Scottish soldiers and sailors in the First World War, except for commissioned officers, who are included in the First World War deaths at TNA, Kew

An army recruitment poster for the First World War showing young men having a wonderful time. There was no hint that the recruits might well end up in a foreign grave. The records of the unfortunate dead are part of the GROS's "Minor Records."

LINE UP, BOYS!

ENLIST TO-DAY.

Army deaths

Mr and Mrs Crowley, 415 Sauchiehall St., Glasgow, have received intimation that their son, Pte. James P. Crowley, H.L.I., aged 24 years, who was previously reported missing, was killed in action on August 16th, 1915. Educated at St Aloysius' College, Glasgow, he entered St Mungo's Academy for a three years' course as a junior student, afterwards passing through the Normal Training College, and when certificated was appointed schoolmaster at Craigton, Barra. He also was assistant master at West Calder. Previous to volunteering for active service he was assistant master at Kenmuir Industrial School, Bishopbriggs. While at St Mungo's Academy young Mr Crowley acted as editor of the S.M.A. Magazine.

Many Scots served in the British Army (see pp. 104–8), and many died on active service.

War memorials are found all over Scotland. This one, at Uig, Lewis, includes the tragic deaths of servicemen on the *Iolaire*. On January 1, 1919, the ship was carrying servicemen home to Lewis after the First World War when it struck a rock and sank just outside Stornoway harbour, drowning 205 of them within a stone's throw of safety. Scarcely a family in Lewis was unaffected. In Uig, we were told of an old lady who had died only recently, whose father conceived her before he left for the war. He survived the horrors of the trenches, but then drowned before he ever held his little daughter.

War graves of all British service personnel can be found through the Commonwealth War Graves Commission (**www.cwgc.org**), and you can also look at local war memorials and in published Rolls of Honour.

These are not just names. James Patrick Crowley, born in Falkirk in 1890, was educated at St. Aloysius's College and St. Mungo's Academy, Glasgow, before becoming a schoolmaster on Barra, where he wanted to help the local children. Jim volunteered for the 16th Battalion of the Highland Light Infantry as a private. He sent this postcard to his parents in Sauchiehall Street, Glasgow, telling of an early and unexpected danger he encountered:

"We had just left Kinghorn [Fife] when there was a terrible whistling & we were backed into the station, or rather a siding. We were scarcely there when an Express thundered past — right across where we had been just a minute & a half before … Fondest love & pray for me, Jim."

Jim was sent on the Dardanelles Campaign and, as this old photocopied newspaper cutting reveals, he was killed in action on August 16, 1915. The Helles Memorial on the Gallipoli Peninsula commemorates Jim and the 20,834 other British and Commonwealth soldiers killed in the campaign.

(and indexes at **www.findmypast.com**) and Scottish soldiers and sailors in the Second World War.

Search Tips

- Try to cross-reference between General Registration and census records. If censuses reveal an event that may have been recorded in that special year of 1855 then make it a priority to seek the 1855 record.
- Searching for the birth of someone with a common name may produce a long list of possibilities. For events from 1901 back, you can try to narrow the search by using the place of birth given in census returns.
- If an ancestor was born in the rather dry period 1856–60, see if a sibling was born in 1855 or from 1861 onwards, since then you will learn details of the parents' marriage.
- Events (especially births) taking place late in one year might be recorded at the start of the next.
- When calculating years of birth from ages stated later in life, don't forget that the year changed each January. For example, you'd think someone who died in 1950 aged 50 was born in 1900, but if they were aged 50 when they died on 7 June 1950 they could have been born any time between 7 June 1900 and 8 June 1899, so you'd need to search in both those years.
- Some ages were not given accurately, even by the people concerned. Always be prepared to widen your search by a few years either side.
- Occupations could change, but usually not by much. If the father of someone marrying in 1950 was a factory manager, and he appears on a 1922 birth certificate as a junior clerk, then you can see that the clerk could have been promoted to factory manager. If, however, you find an implausible jump from, say, road sweeper to army officer, then you may have found the wrong person.
- However, people tended to elevate their parents' status, especially after death, so a ship's mate could easily be described by their proud descendants as a ship's captain. Fortunes could go down as well as up, so an apparently implausible change from, say, gentleman farmer to road sweeper, could be explained by someone falling on hard times (or the bottle!). You need to judge each case on its own merit.
- Besides seeking Scottish death records for the useful details they provide on parents, it is good practice (and interesting) to discover your ancestors' deaths anyway. It completes their stories. Sometimes, discovering a death may alert you to a mistake you've made — if the supposed ancestor died before your genuine ancestor got married, for example, you'll know you have found the wrong person and should return to the drawing board.
- If you find several possible births for your ancestor, you can try to "kill off" the red herrings by seeking infant deaths, for many children died in their first few years. This might just leave one possibility, hopefully the right one.
- Married women's maiden names and surnames are given in the death indexes, making their deaths easier to seek than their husbands'.
- You may find conflicting information on different documents. If so, consider which is more likely to be accurate. Say someone's marriage and death records give different details about their parents. Which is more likely to be correct? The answer is the marriage, because the person themselves will have stated who their parents were, whereas on the death certificate the details will have been given by someone less likely to know the truth.

- Parents' names given in death records could be inaccurate or wrong because the informant was a child or grandchild of the deceased and may never have met the deceased's parents. Even if they had, they may just have known them as "granddad" and "grandma," so the potential for getting details wrong was enormous. If the parents are given as "unknown," this may mean that the deceased person never knew his parents, but more likely that the informant just didn't know.

- The ScotlandsPeople indexes can be slightly inaccurate and occasionally omit entries. If an entry that should definitely be there is not, it sometimes pays to search the original records at the ScotlandsPeople Centre (or try again later as the computer system is sometimes faulty).

- Not all events were recorded, but the incidence of non-recorded events in Scotland is said to be low. If you do not find what you expect, always think of variant spellings, or of widening the period or geographical area you are searching.

- When you find an entry that is right, print it out or at least make full notes of everything on the record, down to the addresses and witnesses' names — you never know when something like that will appear on another document and prove a vital clue.

- www.sctbdm.com, the Scotland BDM exchange, is a lucky dip index to some birth, marriage and death information extracted from the original records. If you find an entry of interest you can email the submitter to ask for full details.

- For 1855–75, most Scottish births and marriages are indexed on www.familysearch.org, which can be a useful (and free) shortcut to the ScotlandsPeople indexes.

Tracing living relatives

This process involves using the records in reverse, working down from a known ancestor rather than up from you. Start by seeking the births of other children of the couple from whom you want to trace down.

You can then jump forward and seek their deaths, inspecting death records of people of the right age to see which has the correct parents' names.

Once you have the right death record you can see if they had married, and if so seek the marriage record and then search for the births of children (a short-cut would be if the informant of the death was one of the person's children).

Up to 1901, use censuses to find out who people's children were. From 1928 onwards, mothers' maiden names are given in the birth indexes, so you can easily spot all the offspring

Mary Queen of Scots (1542–87). Names chosen by the royal family were promptly copied at all levels of society. Mary's own mother was also called Mary (of Guise), and she was attended by several Scottish noblewomen also all bearing the name Mary. In the ballad "The Four Marys" they are remembered as: "There was Mary Seaton and Mary Beaton and Mary Carmichael and me."

of a certain couple. Between 1901 and 1928 you may have to check all possible births in the registration district.

Adoption

Many children used to be fostered or adopted unofficially, without written records. The only clue you may have is not being able to find the child's birth registered under the names it grew up with — but you will seldom know for sure.

Nowadays, two men who think they are related through the male line (sharing the same father-to-father genealogical connection, often suggested by sharing the same surname) can have a DNA test. Their Y-chromosome signatures should be virtually identical. If they're not, this could be due to an illegitimacy, an act of infidelity somewhere back in the family tree or an undisclosed adoption.

Since 1930, adoption has been organized and recorded by the state. The child's original birth entry will be stamped to indicate that adoption had taken place, but the child's new identity will not appear. The child's new birth certificate, issued at the time of adoption, will be in the Adopted Children Register, though this will not show the original identity. The GROS will only reveal the link between new and old identities to adoptees aged 17 or over or to a local authority providing counseling. The record will also state the date of the adoption order and the sheriff's court in which the order was made. Adoptees can then apply for copies of these otherwise secret sections of the records. The amount of detail will vary considerably, but if the records reveal that an adoption agency was involved, you can contact them, as in some cases they may still know where one or both of the natural parents are now.

If the adopted person has died, their next of kin may write to any sheriff's court in Scotland and request access to the deceased person's details. The sheriff will decide the case depending on merit. Increasingly, permission is being granted for genealogical interest, although medical reasons are a surer way of securing a positive outcome.

Birthlink (21 Castle Street, Edinburgh, EH2 3DN, 0131 225 6441, **www.birthlink.org.uk**) offers counseling and help to families affected by adoption. It maintains an Adoption Contact Register, whereby adopted children, or families from whom a child was adopted, can register their whereabouts and willingness to be contacted by relatives. See *Search Guide for Adopted People in Scotland* (Family Care, 1997) and the Birthlink website for more information on this sensitive subject.

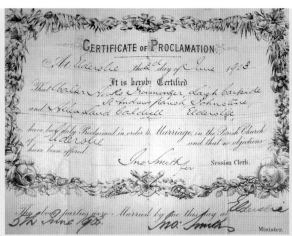

The first page of the Hooks' family bible, starting with the birth and marriage of the second Walter.

The proclamation of marriage of the second Walter Hooks and Helen Laird Caldwell.

When Walter Hooks was christened in 1904, a special picture was taken of him with his father, Walter Hooks, his grandfather, Walter Hooks and his great-grandfather — also called Walter Hooks! Because the last Walter died in 1989, this picture encompasses four generations and 167 years of Scottish family history.

Walter Hooks the first

b. about 1822/3 in Irvine, Ayr

d. February 5, 1908, Saltcoats, Co. Ayr

Walter was a pilot on the River Clyde. His work took him from his native Irvine to the harbour town of Ardrossan, five miles (eight km) away, and later to Govan by 1881, though he returned to Saltcoats, next to Ardrossan, where he died. He was named after Sir Walter Scott, said to be a relative, but more likely simply because the family enjoyed reading Scott's novels.

Walter's death shows that he complimented "the four Walters" by having four wives of his own! The death record provides his age, 85, and takes us back a generation before the photograph, to his parents Edward Hooks, a muslin weaver of Irvine, and his wife Janet Elder. Edward's own death record from 1868 names his parents as David Hooks, a tidewaiter (see p. 111), and Susan Ball. The family were pretty local to the area, for Black's *The Surnames of Scotland* refers to Adam de Huke, a tenant in Moffat, Dumfriesshire, which is only about 60 miles (96 km) south-east of Irvine, right back in 1376.

Walter Hooks the second

b. March 23, 1847

Saltcoats

d. November 16, 1915, Johnstone, Co. Renfrew

The 1851 census shows young Walter aged three (see page 56), living not with his parents but with his mother's father William Love, a weaver at Windmill Street, Ardrossan, Co. Ayr, who was born there about 1791 — an unexpected extra for the family tree. Walter started work as an iron molder and pattern maker (making molds for casting iron goods), a job that caused him to move to Paisley and later Johnstone (about 15 miles or 24 kilometers north-east of Ardrossan), where he died.

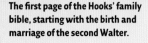

Mr W Hooks
12 Lawrence Street
Glasgow W1

30th April 1968

Dear Mr Hooks

On the occasion of your retirement I am writing to express my warm appreciation of the loyal and conscientious manner in which you have carried out your duties during the past forty years, the major part of which you have spent in a supervisory capacity.

Ancestors' occupations can be discovered from family papers. This letter of 1968 congratulates the fourth Walter Hooks on his retirement from the Prudential Assurance Co. (for which he had worked all his life, before and after his army service in the Second World War) and wishes him and his wife, "many happy years of retirement together."

Walter the fourth's grandson Scott Crowley visiting Ardrossan in 2003.

Walter Hooks the third

b. June 20, 1877
Ardrossan, Ayr
d. January 4, 1968
Walter Hooks and Helen Laird Caldwell married in 1903 at the Village Hall in Elderslie, next to Johnstone, where she was a carpet weaver and he was a journeyman (day-laboring) iron molder. Family papers include a certificate of the proclamation of their marriage and a telegram from the Queen congratulating them on their sixtieth wedding anniversary.

The death record of the first Walter.

Name, and Maiden Surname of Mother.	
Edward Hooks, Mialin Weaver (deceased)	Fatty degeneration of heart Diaphragmatic Pleurisy
Janet Hooks M.S. Elder (deceased)	Cardiac Failure As certified by Wm Turner L.R.C.P.&

Walter Hooks the fourth

b. April 7, 1904 at 6 Bankside Avenue, Johnstone
d. November 17, 1989, Glasgow

Mrs. Moira Crowley, daughter of the fourth Walter, showing the picture of the four Walters to some of her descendants. Young Matthew James, on the right of the picture, was born in 2004, 182 years after the birth of his great-great-great-great-grandfather, the first Walter, in 1822 (courtesy Mrs. Moira Crowley).

CHAPTER 6

Censuses

Hand in hand with the General Registration records are censuses. Those for 1841-1901 have been indexed on ScotlandsPeople, making them relatively easy to search.

Scotland's censuses have been taken once every 10 years since 1801 (except 1941, due to the Second World War). The most useful for genealogists are those between 1841 and 1901, which are all on **www.ScotlandsPeople.gov.uk**. The 1881 census is on the site, but instead of images of the returns you can only see a transcription (the originals can be examined on microfilm at the ScotlandsPeople Centre, and printed for a rather steep £8). The way the censuses are indexed on the site varies slightly, the indexes to 1891 and 1901 including ages, making them easier to search than the earlier ones.

The earliest Scottish census of all was compiled by the ministers of each parish in 1755 at the behest of Alexander Webster, a Presbyterian minister in Edinburgh. They submitted numbers (but not names) of the Catholics and Protestants in each parish, and how many of these were fit for armed service. The results appear in J.G. Kyd's *Scottish Population Statistics Including Webster's Analysis of Population 1755* (SRS, 1955). Further statistical censuses were compiled by enumerators, usually parish schoolmasters "or other fit persons" by order of Parliament in 1801, 1811, 1821 and 1831. Occasionally, the enumerators broke the rules and included names and other details. The best guide to these is G. Johnson's *Census Records for Scottish Families at Home and Abroad* (Aberdeen & North East Scotland Family History Society, third edn 1997). Many have been published as part of local history books (see p. 30), and some appear under the parish in the NAS catalog, while others are in local archives. Further censuses have been taken every 10 years since.

Browsing the original returns

The online version's greatest strength and weakness is that it can take you straight to the right entry. The speed is wonderful — before computerization it could take days or even weeks to find the right entry. The disadvantage is that, by not having to scroll through all the returns for the relevant village or town, you miss seeing who else was there, such as people of the same surname who could be relatives, and you do not gain a general feeling for the community in which your ancestors lived.

Browsing is worthwhile, not least because the start of each enumerator's book contains a short account of the route taken, and can include some valuable comments on his patch. Those for 1841 and 1851 had spaces for comments on the increase or decrease of the population, due, for example, to emigration, and very, very occasionally emigrants are actually named.

Of course, you need to know where to look on the census. Addresses can be found on GROS certificates or through directories (see pp. 88-9), or best of all from the online version. Once you have found the address of your ancestors you can use the reference numbers to find the right sections of the census and you can then start scrolling forwards and backwards to inspect the surrounding community.

The census enumerator would distribute forms to be filled in on census night, and then go from door to door collecting them. The forms (which have not been kept) were copied into the enumerator's book, and it is these for 1841 to 1901 that are available at ScotlandsPeople. Microfilm copies are also available in many local archives and Mormon FHCs worldwide.

Another source of Scottish census material is **www.freecen.org.uk**, containing free transcripts of parts of census returns. Its statistics section will tell you how much of each census is indexed: remember, some of these transcriptions are bound to contain errors.

The 1841 census

Most survives except for Auchinleck, and for some parishes in Fife (Auchtermuchty,

Balmerino, Ceres, Collessie, Creich, Cults, Cupar, Dairsie, Dunbog, Kinghorn, Kinglassie, Kirkcaldy and Leslie), which were lost at sea in 1910 when the records were being returned to Scotland from London.

- **address.** This may be precise, or could be a street name or just the name of the village, with each house numbered sequentially as the enumerator walked around. Double strokes indicate the break between buildings;

Crossed out?

You may see various pencil strokes made by those who compiled statistics from the returns. These strokes can make it look as if the information was being crossed out because it was wrong, but this is not so; they were just crossing off details they had counted.

Uninhabited	NAME and SURNAME, SEX and AGE, of each Person who abode in each House on the Night of 6th June. NAME and SURNAME	AGE Male	Female	OCCUPATION Of what Profession, Trade, Employment, or whether of Independent Means.	WHERE BORN	
1	James Arnott	60		Farmer	no	
	Janet do		55		no	
	James do	35		Ag. Lab.	no	
	David do	20		Ag. Lab.	no	
	Edward do	15			no	
	Mathia do		25		no	
	Elisabeth do		25		no	
	Mary do		20		no	
	James Thompson	12		Linen H.L.W. Ap	no	
	Janet Speedie		10		yes	
1	Inhabitants					
	Robert Taylor	55		Farmer	yes	

The 1841 census for my five x great-grandfather James Arnott, who died before 1851. He was a farmer at Pitversie House, Abernethy, Perthshire, aged 60. This means he was aged 60–4, so was born about 1776–81. He was not born in Perthshire. His sons James and David were "agricultural laborers," presumably working for their father. The double dash below James's daughter Mary indicates the end of the family, but not of the inhabitants of the farmhouse, for included was James Thompson, 12, "Linen H.L.W. Ap," i.e. "linen handloom weaver apprentice," and after him (also a separate "household") was a 10-year-old Janet Speedie, presumably a young relation they were looking after.

single strokes indicate the break between different households in the same building.

- **name of each person in the household.** Middle names or initials were not supposed to be recorded.
- **age.** The ages of those under 16 were recorded precisely, but the ages of those over 16 were rounded down to the nearest round five years. Thus, people aged from 50 to 54 were all to be recorded as 50. Luckily, some enumerators failed to heed this and wrote down the exact ages. There were two columns for ages, one for males and the other for females.
- **occupation**
- **whether the person was born in the same county.** Usually "Y" for yes and "N" for no, or "NK" for not known, "I" for Ireland, "E" for England and "F"(foreign) for everywhere else.
- **relationships were not stated.** They can often be inferred, but should not be assumed. Two 50-year-olds of opposite sexes and a 20-year-old could be husband, wife and child, but they could also be brother, sister and a child of one of their cousins, or one of many other possible permutations.

1851–1901

The returns survive almost entirely, except for the 1881 records for Dunscore and half of Dumfries. They include people on board ships in Scottish ports from 1861, and people on Scottish ships in English waters in 1871 and 1881. They give:

- **address.** Households are divided by // and buildings by /. From 1861 onwards the existence of uninhabited houses is noted, which can be useful if you are tracing the history of a building.
- **name of each person in the household.** Initials or middle names were often recorded.
- **relationship to the head of household.** Usually wife, son or daughter, but also step-

child, in-laws, servants and, if you are very lucky, parents or grandparents. Sometimes, the terms "in-law" and "stepson/daughter" were used interchangeably.

- **marital condition**, whether married, single or widowed.
- **ages** were recorded precisely, as far as the person giving the information was willing or able to tell the truth.
- **occupation.** In 1891, extra columns asked whether the person was an employer, employee or worked alone. This is good for seeing how people's careers developed or declined, but an abrupt change in occupation may alert you to a mistake.
- **place of birth**, recorded by parish and county. If the person was born outside Scotland, then maybe only the county or country would be given. If luck does not strike with the first census return you examine, try another. In the case of immigrants it is worth looking through the pages surrounding your family to see where others came from, as people often migrated and settled in groups.
- **physical and mental condition.** In 1861 onwards blindness, deafness and dumbness was noted. From 1871 it was also noted if you were an "imbecile," an "idiot," a "lunatic," or just "feeble minded."
- **language.** Ability to speak Gaelic and/or English was noted from 1891.
- **living conditions.** From 1861 the number of rooms inhabited by the family that had one or more windows was noted. I have always thought this rather misleading, as it takes no account of rooms without windows.
- **education.** In 1861 the number of children aged between five and 13 was noted specifically, and if they were attending school they were described as "scholars."

1911 onwards

Due to confidentiality rules, the 1911 census is not due to be released until 2012. Later censuses will presumably be released at ten-yearly intervals.

Using censuses

Censuses have two main uses. First, they provide valuable coordinates on families, stating who was related to whom, how old people were and where they were born. They create bridges from General Registration to parochial registers and on many occasions will provide clues to finding elusive General Registration entries. They may flag-up a member of the family who was born in that

William Robertson Melvin, pictured on the left with his son Alexander. He was editor of the *Fraserburgh Herald* and an authority on Burns. William was thought to have been born in Aberdeenshire, and this is confirmed from the 1881 census, that shows him with his parents at 19 High Street, Fraserburgh, Aberdeenshire (courtesy of Mrs H. Weaver).

The original 1881 census entry for the Melvins at 19 High Street, Fraserburgh, which you can see at the ScotlandsPeople Centre but not online.

| ₀: 650179 | Census Place: New Monkland, Lanark, Scotland | | | | | | | Hu |

AD, STREET, ODRESS &c.	GIVEN NAME	SURNAME	RELATION to Head	CONDITION as to Marriage	AGE	SEX	OCCUPATION	BIRTHPL
elling: 1 No mmo Lane	William	WATT	Son	N/A	4	M	Scholar	Airdrie, La Scotla
elling: 1 No mmo Lane	Maggie	WATT	Daughter	N/A	1	F	Scholar	Airdrie, La Scotla
elling: 1 No mmo Lane	Robert	WATT	Head	Married	32	M	Engine Smith	Carluke, L Scotla

An example of the 1881 census transcript, which is all you can see on the ScotlandsPeople website.

Censuses can show you what you thought you knew, and can contain surprises. The 1851 census shows Walter Hooks (misindexed under Hook) living at Windmill Street, Saltcoats, Ardrossan, Co. Ayr, but instead of his parents we have his maternal grandparents, William and Jane Love.

magical year of 1855, enabling you to seek a detailed GROS record for them.

Secondly, they are fascinating documents of social history, showing many aspects of families at home and how they made their livings. Scrolling through census returns, especially in small settlements, can give a great sense of the reality of extended families, and indeed of communities where most people were interrelated. The returns don't state how households were related to each other, of course, but once you know who was living in the village, you can use OPRs and General Registration to find out what the relationships were.

As with all records, censuses are subject to the foibles of their creators. The enumerators could make mistakes. Imagine the man traipsing around in the sleet and semi-darkness, venturing into the squalid tenements leading off the wynds or alleys of Glasgow or Edinburgh, trying to make any sense out of the poor families crammed into every conceivable space. Imagine the poor themselves, afraid these new-fangled records would lead to forced repatriation to their home parishes (or, in the case of the Irish, to their country of origin).

Imagine young Jamie being asked to say how old his deaf granny was, and where she was born: how should he know? Imagine Laird Robertshaw, interrupted during his venison by some impertinent clerk at his door, who had the temerity to ask how old he was. Small wonder censuses are not always razor-sharp in their accuracy, or that they contain the odd wry comment. Rosemary Bigwood noted that one household was described as "wild couple — very" and a visitor was recorded as an "unwelcome guest."

Luckily, you can usually compare the answers given in several censuses to see what the "consensus" view was. Later censuses tend to give more accurate answers, presumably since people had grown used to them.

Although you may not need to look for your family in all the censuses, it's interesting to do so — you may find extra clues, new family members, and see what they were up to. However don't be too upset if some people just cannot be found.

Problem? Watt problem?

The 1881 census of 1 Nimmo Lane, Airdrie (New Monkland), Co. Lanark, shows William Hamilton Watt with his parents Robert Watt (born about 1849 in Carluke) and Jane Hamilton. Their 1874 marriage shows Robert's parents as James Watt, a deceased colliery manager, and Jane Miller. Married women were indexed under maiden and married surnames, so it was easy enough to find the death of Jane, widow of James, a coal pit manager — she died in Glasgow in 1894. But searching for James's death between 1874 and 1849 produced too many possibilities, and we did not know his age or where he had died. To narrow the search down, we sought the family in the intermediate censuses but, because the surname was so common in the area, we could not definitely identify the right Watts family.

The solution came by using testaments: there was just a chance that, as a pit overseer, James may have had enough money to justify a testament (see pp. 91–5) — and so he had. It stated that he died in Airdrie on December 8, 1864. His death could be found easily, naming his parents as John Watt and Janet Crawford and giving his age as 54.

James's earlier census entries still could not be found, so we searched for other children born to him and Janet Miller. Robert's birth in Carluke was not registered, but James and

Janet did have a son, Andrew, born there in 1847. He turned up, aged 13 (stated, presumably incorrectly, to have been born in Midlothian) in the 1861 census for Meadowside Farm, Airdrie, with his mother's parents John and Janet Miller. There was no sign of the rest of his family. Andrew appeared in 1871, though, with his widowed mother Janet who was then running a dairy in Airdrie, and siblings including ten-year-old Archibald, born in Airdrie.

This showed that the Watts family must have been in Airdrie in the 1861 census. Giving up on the indexes, we searched manually through the returns at the ScotlandsPeople Centre, and lo and behold, there they were (including 11-year-old Robert) at 9 Burnbank, Airdrie. Their surname was written without the first "t" being crossed, so they had been indexed in ScotlandsPeople as "Walt."

The 1861 census told us that James Watt had been born about 1812 in Crawford, part of the parish of Crawford and Leadhills, Co. Lanark. His birth was not registered there but that of a sister, Margaret (daughter of John Watt and Janet Crawford) was, confirming the family was there in 1806. A transcribed memorial inscription from the churchyard records a "William Wat in Lidhills" who died on July 22, 1705, the earliest trace found so far of this family line.

Part of the 1861 census entry for the WATT family, indexed as WALT, of 9 Burnbank, Old Monkland Eastern District.

CHAPTER 7

Church registers

Registers of baptisms, marriages and burials have been kept in various forms in Scotland since the 1500s. Before the mid-1800s, they are the most useful records we have for tracing back Scottish family trees.

The early General Registration records of marriages and deaths should tell you the names of your ancestors who were born just before 1855. The death record of a 100-year-old just after 1855 would give you the names of a couple who had children in the 1750s! The censuses will tell you where people who were born before 1855 originated. If you know that naming patterns were adhered to firmly, you can often speculate on the names of yet earlier generations. These several sets of coordinates together should point your research firmly towards the religious registers of a specific area.

John Knox delivering his thunderous sermon at St Andrews in 1559, calling for reform of the church.

Old Parochial Registers

Scotland's parishes have been recording the births or baptisms, marriages and sometimes deaths or burials of their inhabitants in their Old Parochial Registers (OPRs) since 1551, when James Hamilton, Archbishop of St. Andrews, ordered that registers of baptisms and marriages should be kept and preserved. The registers were kept by the kirk session clerk — he was usually the school master or sometimes the minister himself.

All the surviving OPRs were deposited at New Register House between the 1820s and 1855 (the odd one, or section of one, turns up in other records, but the vast majority were collected in that period). These have all been indexed, and these indexes are most easily searched on the ScotlandsPeople website. Microfilm images of the original entries can also be examined at the ScotlandsPeople Centre, the Scottish Genealogy Society Library and at Mormon FHCs worldwide.

The online OPR indexes are of course tremendously helpful. Besides looking for individuals, you can undertake searches to find all the children of one couple (though success depends on the parents being recorded consistently: children of "Alexander and Jeanne" will not appear in an index search if the original records record "Alex. and Jane"). It's up to you to work out variant spellings, but mercifully the spellings Mac, Mc and M' have

[... James] Good lawful daughter to James Good in Barrshian... oning was baptized Aprile 9th 1704

Lamson — James Lamson lawful son to James Lamson in Shaw was baptized April 9th 1704

Cochranne — Mary Cochranne lawful daughter to Alexander Cochranne in Parkhead was baptized April 9th 1704

Something — George Something lawful son to What-ye-call-him in Mains of Barskimming was baptized April 9th 1704

Reid — Agnes Reid lawful Daughter to James Reid in Auchinbay was baptized April 23d 1704

Culloch — Jean McCulloch lawful Daughter to James McCulloch in Someplace was baptized April 3d 1704

been grouped together. Using the indexes without paying to view the images of the original register keeps the costs down but takes away some of the flavour of the hunt, and means you will not spot interesting extra details, or indeed errors in transcription.

Defects in the OPRs

One of the reasons why General Registration was introduced into Scotland in 1855, however, was because a system that relied on people attending the Church of Scotland was doomed to failure. The *Statistical Accounts* comment repeatedly on the failure of people to have their children's births recorded in the OPRs. Indeed, by 1850, an estimated two-thirds of all Scots were not recorded in the OPRs at all.

Registers were not always kept perfectly: "*Any person that wants a child's name in any of the three preceding pages may scarcely expect to find it in the proper place,*" wrote James Whyte in the Dunnings register in 1794, "*they being wrote by Mr King, late schoolmaster depute here without any regularity or order.*" A singular example of irregularity comes from Ochiltree in 1704:

"*Something — George Something lawful son to what-ye-call-him in Mains of Barskimming was baptized April 9th 1704.*"

Another message of mixed doom and optimism comes from the 1833 *Statistical Account*. For Selkirk, it comments, "*Unluckily, the register of births is not as complete as could be wished, for the circumstance that people belonging to the Succession church, who are here pretty numerous, have a seeming reluctance to enter the births of their children ... there is also a register of deaths kept, not by the session-clerk, but by an individual merely for his own amusement. It commences in 1742 ...*"

Survival rate is poor — think about what an 18th-century kirk was like! You can imagine how much damage damp and mice could make, to say nothing of the occasional fire or theft. Also, some OPRs were sent to courts as legal evidence and never returned.

Thus, only 21 OPRs survive before 1600, starting with Errol, Co. Perth (from 1553), then 127 more up to 1650; 266 more to 1700, and so on. Those for Skye and the Orkneys only begin in the 1830s, and in plenty of parishes you will be disappointed to find registers that only go back to the late 1700s. Sadly, in a lot of cases, the start-date of the OPRs will set a cap on how far back you will be able to trace your family tree. But many of the later chapters of this book identify records that could take you further back, while DNA and the origins of surnames can open up some surprising extra avenues into the past, so read on!

Some OPR entries appear in kirk session records (see p. 68) rather than in the parish registers themselves. Those identified as such by the 1970s were included in the OPR indexes; those that have come to light since are not, so might be chanced upon in the kirk session records (CH2). These will be on ScotlandsPeople by 2010 so hopefully these random entries will be much easier to find than before.

You can see what OPR material survives, and where gaps may exist in the registers, using the GROS's *List of the Old Parochial Registers of Scotland* at **www.gro-scotland.gov.uk**.

Perils to avoid

Using the OPR indexes is easy, but do bear in mind how few ancestors may actually appear in this source. Not finding ancestors in the OPRs may mean simply that the OPRs for their parish have not survived, or that there are gaps in them, or it could mean that your ancestors never attended the Established Church. Their records might appear in the registers of other denominations, which are not indexed on ScotlandsPeople. Also, the session clerks often charged a small fee for making entries, putting

off the poor or stingy, and between 1783-92 Stamp Duty levied an even less palatable 3d (three pennies) tax on each entry.

So, if your family was from X and does not appear in the OPR indexes under that place, but people of the right name appear in the OPRs of Y, you may have found useful evidence of their having moved from Y to X. But it is just as possible that the family living in Y is a red herring, and you may have to spend some time exploring the records of both X and Y before working out which of these possibilities is the correct one.

Searching the originals

Often it makes little sense to think of Scottish families as single strands stretching back into the past. Most people tended to live in communities of extended families, and while online indexes are a good way of establishing the bare bones of pedigree, they are a terrible way of learning about extended families, and can often cause genealogical problems by deterring you from examining the original registers themselves.

You may find the originals confusing to use, not least when the births/baptisms, marriage proclamations and even some burials are mixed up together, or when a list of marriage

Graves facing the sea at Stoer, Assynt. Gravestones can be an essential source for family history information.

Baptismal customs

Baptism often took place quickly after birth — if the child died unbaptized it could not be buried in consecrated ground, with dire consequences for its soul. Another danger awaited unbaptized babies in rural areas — fairies might come for it. Despite these perils, it could take a family weeks or even years to take their child to the font, especially if going to the kirk was a long trek away. Sometimes, families had all their children baptized together years after the eldest had been born. In other cases baptisms were not late, but missed being recorded until the mistake was realized later. This can be a problem when using the originals, but it is not a problem for the computerized indexes.

This baptismal entry from Torthorwald in 1773 includes a comment: *"Andrw. /S/ Samuel Murrah laborer Torw. Born Jany. 26 Baptized Decr. 31. Note: Andw Murrah was born with an eye tooth come a considerable length but disappeared afterward in the Gum."*

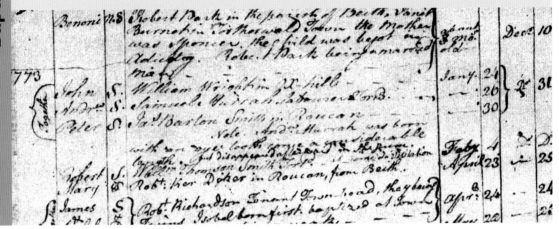

proclamations appears upside down at the back of a volume (and hence a long way further along the film). But using originals will alert you to some of the records' shortcomings and help you place what entries you have found in their proper context.

OPR births/baptisms

The OPR indexes give the child's name, parents' names, date, name and number of the parish, and a volume and microfilm frame reference. There were no hard-and-fast rules governing what the session clerks recorded in the OPRs themselves, so the records will include all or some of the following:

- child's name
- father's names
- father's occupation
- mother's names (including maiden name)
- residence
- date of baptism. Sometimes the birth date is recorded too, or just the date of birth and not of baptism. If only one date is given, assume it is baptism, not birth. The OPR indexes give B for birth and C for christening (i.e. baptism).
- witnesses. These were usually close relatives, though there were no firm rules. Although witnesses' relationships to the child will very seldom be stated, their names provide vital clues, perhaps by linking a family in one parish to that of the same surname in another. Some of the Dundee registers state after whom the child was named. Some OPRs will state that the baptism was witnessed by a non-Presbyterian congregation (indicating that it was a nonconformist baptism).

Illegitimacy

A record firmly amended to make it clear that the parents were not married and the child was not "lawful" but "natural."

As in most countries, illegitimacy has always been widespread and common in Scotland, despite the church's efforts to stop it. Almost 10 percent of children born in the mid-1800s were illegitimate (falling to about six percent by 1900), the highest incidences being in the cities and among itinerant farm laborers. In the countryside, it was sometimes deliberate — David Moody (in his *Scottish Family History*, Batsford, 1988), suggests that as, in some areas, "a farm worker was hired on the understanding that he could provide family labor ... pre-marital pregnancy would be seen as an insurance policy against infertility."

Often, having a child together was a precursor to a couple marrying. In such cases, you may find both parents named on the birth record — and indeed the birth may even have been registered under the father's surname. Usually, however, the birth will be under the mother's maiden name. The father's name may never be found or, in extreme cases, one may be made up. The Livingston register for 1807 records:

"Born to Hellen Baxter in the Village of Livingston on 28 Decr 1805 and Baptized on the 26th Feby. 1807 named Helen Baxter. N.B. This Child at the time of its Baptism could not find a Father. Her Mother gave it to a Packman which she said came up to her on the road from Edinr. though the Father was suspected to be nearer the doors. But a confession from the time it was born to this day could not be extorted from the Mother." (Livingston, 1807; OPR 669/1, Fr 358).

If you cannot find your (apparently legitimate) ancestor born under their expected surname, then look under the mother's maiden name instead, which from the mid-1800s onward you're likely to know from the child's marriage or death record. If for some reason you don't, you could find the child in a census and seek the birth record of a younger sibling who may have been born after the parents married.

Cases where the mother did not marry the father are harder to solve. Sometimes the waters are muddied deliberately, such as when the "parents" named on a census or marriage certificate turn out to be an illegitimate child's maternal grandparents. Such deceptions are often discovered only after some painstaking detective work among the records.

A child's unusual middle name was often the father's surname. A search of censuses for the area where the birth took place might reveal a likely man with this surname, who you may be able to identify as the father. Absolute proof may not be possible — there are many cases where the mother herself never knew the father's full name, perhaps due to rape or simply a drunken fumble behind the tavern. In some cases, it is possible to gain clues from DNA by looking for exact matches of male Y-chromosome signatures, which will at least suggest a surname of the father of the illegitimate child. But that's usually as far as one can go towards actually identifying the specific man concerned.

Sheriff courts and kirk sessions heard many cases involving illegitimacy, often brought by women seeking child support from the father. Sometimes, you'll find a GROS birth entry annotated with a reference to the Register of Corrected Entries — this may then refer you to a sheriff court case.

The kirk sessions often went to great lengths to find the fathers of illegitimate children. Pre-1855 cases may be solved thus, but involve an initial complication whereby the OPR birth will often name the mother but not the child. Your initial search under the child's name may therefore draw a blank, but a subsequent search for an unnamed child of the right surname may reveal your ancestor. The child's given name may then be confirmed in the kirk session minutes.

In the vast majority of cases, children born illegitimately to couples who later married acquired the father's surname, but on an entirely informal basis. Don't expect to find a record of a change of name.

OPR marriages

Scottish weddings could be (and sometimes remain) rowdy affairs, mixing pagan and Christian customs freely. The custom of processing sunwise (*deiseal*) round the marriage venue was a pagan one. So was the lengthy wedding feast, strung over several days when copious quantities of cold mutton and fowl, scones, cheese and oatcakes were munched, whisky knocked back and the wedding reel danced till everyone was beyond exhaustion.

When seeking marriages, don't be too narrow-minded about when they may have taken place. Up to 1929, if they had parental consent, girls could tie the knot at the age of 12 and boys at 14. They may then have had a long string of children (not all of whom may have survived) before your ancestor was born. At the other end of the spectrum, people could be quite old when they married. Often, men whose wives had died in childbirth would marry again quickly for the very practical necessity of having someone to look after their children. Marriages in extreme old age are not unknown (for it was no fun on your own in an unheated, turf-roofed hut in winter). In the 18th century, Donald MacLeod (d. 1781) the "Old Trojan" of Bernera, Lewis, married his third wife when he was 75 and had nine children by her before he died aged 90. So, if you just know someone's date of marriage, you must be flexible about when they

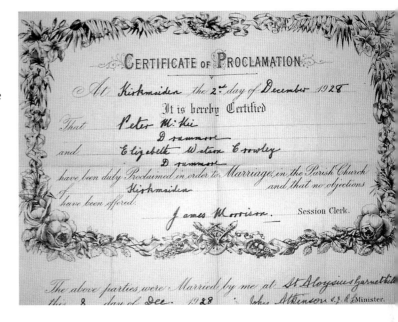

Proclamations continue to this day, and certificates for them can turn up in family papers, such as this one from December 2, 1928, to which is added confirmation of the marriage, six days later (courtesy of Mrs Moira Crowley).

Proclamations did not always result in routine marriages, as the Strontian registers for 1833 reveal: "Donald Cameron (Woodend) to Mary Cameron (Aharkile). N.B. There has been something very odd about the above parties. They fast contracted and then split. Then agreed and with much regularity married, were not married passing 5 days when lo the weaker vessel set sail and steered her course for her mammy."

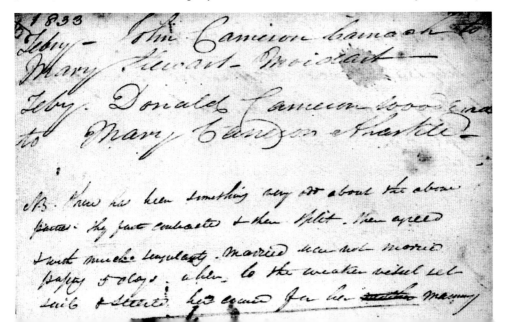

April 4th 1801.

Arnot | James, in this Parish, and Janet McCash in the Parish of Newburgh gave up their names for pro= clamation in order to Marriage

— May 15th —

Livingstone James, in the Parish of Newburgh, and Christia...

clamation in order to Marriage and being procla= ed three several times, were married the 14th of Mar...

Arnot | April 4 | James Arnot Farmer in the Parish of Abdie and Janet: McCash in this Parish, gave in their names for proclamation in order to marriage, an being thrice proclaimed, were married the 14th inst.

Living= stone | May 16 | James Livingstone Merchant in this Parish, & Christian Williamson in the Parish of Abdie, gave in their names for proclamation in order to marriage and were married on the 20th Instant.

A search for the marriage of my five x great-grandparents on ScotlandsPeople reveals two entries, which are the proclamations for their marriage in each of their home parishes. The entries themselves give different degrees of information, emphasizing that both are always worth examining. Note that only one entry states when the marriage itself took place:

"**Abdie: April 4th 1801** Arnot James in this Parish and Janet McCash in the Parish of Newburgh gave up their names for proclamation in order to marriage
Newburgh: April 4, James Arnot Farmer in the Parish of Abdie and Janet M.Cash in this Parish gave in their names for proclamation in order to marriage and being thrice proclaimed, were married the 14th Inst."

may have been born — it could have been anything between 12 or 75(ish) years earlier!

(Ir)Regularity

Scottish marriages fall into two sorts, regular and irregular.

Regular marriages were preceded by the proclamation of banns in the parish churches of both parties, with at least two witnesses present. Proclamations were supposed to be made on three consecutive Sundays, though in the 1700s this could be reduced to three proclamations on the same Sunday. The purpose was to make public the couple's intention to marry, so that reasons why they should not could be aired. If one of them was

under age and had no parental consent, or was already married, or if they were more closely related than first cousins, then someone in the congregation was likely to stand up and say so. A pand, pawn or consignation of money was sometimes handed over to the session clerk, redeemable provided no child had been born within less than nine months of the wedding!

The proclamations were entered in the OPR. Session clerks seldom bothered recording the date of the wedding itself — if only one date is given this will usually be that of the proclamation. The wedding generally took place within six weeks of the proclamation. It could be performed anywhere — in church (usually in the bride's parish) or, more normally, in the bride's family home. There had to be a priest present — from the 1712 Toleration Act, Episcopalians could use their own ministers, provided they said prayers for the Royal Family. From 1834, the Marriage (Scotland) Act allowed ministers of all denominations, even Catholics, to perform marriages, provided the proclamations had been read in the parish church.

The OPR will always record:

- the names of the parties
- the date of the proclamation
  OPRs may also include:
- parish(es) of residence
- marriage date
- witnesses (sometimes they listed their places of residence and occupation, useful details not least because they were often close relatives of the happy couple).

If the parties lived in different parishes, it is worth examining both registers, as one may give more detail than the other. If the marriage did not take place, this may be noted in the register against the proclamation, and you may find subsequent wrangling in the kirk sessions or a local court. However, some records of proclamations do not note the subsequent failure of the parties to marry, so what you think is evidence of an ancestor's marriage may be nothing of the sort.

But none of the formality of proclamations and wedding ceremonies was actually necessary under Scots law.

Irregular marriages were often of the sort termed "clandestine" or "inorderly" marriages, performed by a non-Establishment minister before witnesses, but without a church proclamation. Even such formality was unnecessary, though, for a marriage could be created by people simply living together, often after a betrothal or "hand-fasting." Such unions were termed variously "marriages by

Divorces

In the Middle Ages, if your spouse turned out to be impotent, mad, a bigamist or a disturbingly close relative, you could attend a Catholic church court and ask for your marriage to be annulled. From the Reformation onwards, Protestants did not see marriage as a sacrament, so the commissary court of Edinburgh allowed marriages to be fully dissolved on the foregoing grounds, and also if your spouse had been unfaithful or had simply run off. Its divorce records run from 1566. For the period 1658–1800, see *The Commissariot of Edinburgh — Consistorial Processes and Decreets, 1658–1800* (SRS 1909).

The Court of Session (cataloged on the NAS website) took over all divorce proceedings from 1830–1983, and from 1855, marriages recorded by GROS that ended in divorce are annotated and cross-referred to the Register of Corrected Entries. From 1984 divorce cases were heard in sheriff courts and can be found in the GROS Register of Divorces at ScotlandsPeople.

declaration" (*De Praesenti*), in which no promise had ever been witnessed; "cohabitation with habit and repute;" "promise with subsequent intercourse" (there would have been witnesses to the promise, though presumably not to the subsequent intercourse); and "consent before witnesses." These latter types of marriage are legal phrases imposed on what normal Scots people were doing — courting, rolling in the heather and setting up home together.

Needless to say, the Established Church of Scotland took a very dim view of such activities, not least because they dispensed with the church's involvement. Until 1834, despite such unions being legal, the kirk sessions often summoned wrong-doers and fined them before acknowledging the marriage — the union may then appear in the OPRs, possibly identified as "irregular." Some irregular marriages were investigated in the law courts, and may turn up in their records. After 1855, if a couple who had married irregularly wanted legal recognition of their

Graves

Graves and accompanying Monumental Inscriptions (MIs) were often placed inside churches, but this "Romish" practice was discouraged in the 17th century. Instead, you sometimes encounter *caibeals*, stone enclosures built in the churchyard to house a wealthy family's graves.

A family's specific burial place, whether inside or outside the church, was known as a lair. The MIs in lairs provide names and dates, and sometimes contain other useful details of the relationships within a family. Records of lair ownership might be found in kirk session records such as sextons' or beadles' books, or even in special lair books. Of course, only the better-off could afford a proper gravestone engraved with MIs. Poor people might simply mark their graves with wooden crosses.

The wind and rain has rubbed many MIs away, but the kirk session records, local archives and the library of the Scottish Genealogy Society contain notes on or transcriptions of many that are no longer legible. Notable are the transcriptions made by Robert Monteith in 1704 and 1713 as part of his *Theatre of Mortality*, which was republished in *Collection of Epitaphs and Monumental Inscriptions, chiefly in Scotland* (D. MacVean, 1834). The NAS has S. Cramer's extensive collection of MIs from all over Scotland (cataloged in RH4's appendix 13). Some are in *The Scottish Genealogist* (1891, pp. 19-32 and 171-6).

If you are faced with a partly illegible gravestone that has not been transcribed, try looking at it when the sun is low in the sky, for the shadows may help you make out what it says.

Finally, don't forget that Dissenting congregations sometimes created their own graveyards — details of these are in D.J. Steel's *Sources for Scottish Genealogy and Family History* (1970).

The magnificent tomb of Alistair Crotach MacLeod, Chief of Harris and Skye, contemplated by relative Scott Crowley, whose grandmother was a MacLeod of Assynt. Scott commented afterwards that seeing this tomb made the MacLeod chiefs, and his connection to them, seem far more real than they had before.

Dunchraigaig Cairn in Kilmartin Glen, Argyllshire, taken just before Halloween. This burial mound is about 4,000 years old and like all other such sites it was believed to be a gateway to the underworld. It's really not hard to see why. Evidence of ancient burials, in the form of burial mounds, chambered tombs and cairns, can be found in many parts of Scotland. They are often linked to standing stones, and indeed many Neolithic stone circles seem to have been chosen later as burial places for Bronze Age chiefs. They seem to exert an irresistible draw on us now — though we cannot trace our family trees so far back, we know perfectly well that, one way or another, these are our ancestors.

union, they might approach a sheriff court and obtain a warrant for the marriage to be recorded by the local registrar, and this will be noted on the GROS record.

The number of people marrying "irregularly" was considerable, perhaps as much as a third in the mid-1800s, falling to less than 10 percent by 1914. Besides the morally lax, irregular marriages were favored by members of dissenting congregations, because they dispensed with church interference. Many irregular marriages did not, obviously, appear in any records.

Marriage contracts

Marriage contracts were sometimes drawn up to formalize the financial relationship of newly-weds from moneyed families. The bride's father would settle a tocher or dowry on his daughter, that would remain hers should her husband die, and the husband might settle money or land (that could in turn involve a sasine — see pp. 132–3) on his wife and any subsequent children. In older contracts there might be provisions forcing the husband to return the dowry to the bride's father if the marriage did not result in a child within a year and a day. These contracts might record a marriage that does not appear in surviving OPRs. They are sometimes found in family papers, notaries' records or deeds, or might be mentioned in testaments. NAS class RH9/7 contains 306 Marriage Contracts (1591–1846 and 1605–1811).

OPR burials

If parochial records are anything to go on, our 17th- and 18th-century Scots ancestors were remarkably long-lived, for virtually none of them seem ever to have died! This is largely the fault of old Archbishop Hamilton's 1551 orders creating OPRs, for he did not include recording

Gretna Green

The famous Border Marriage Houses (Allison's Toll Bar; Coldstream Marriage House; Gretna Hall; Lamberton Toll; Sark Toll Bar and Springfield) were mainly used for run-away marriages by English people avoiding the strictures of Hardwicke's 1754 Marriage Act, but inevitably include plenty of Scots' names too. Details of surviving records are at **www.gro-scotland.gov.uk/famrec/hlpsrch/summrar/index.html**.

of burials. Although the General Assembly issued subsequent instructions to do so in 1565 and 1616, very few session clerks took any notice and relatively few pre-1855 deaths were recorded.

Most evidence of deaths comes indirectly in the kirk session records by showing payments made for digging the grave or hiring the parish mortcloth. This was a black cloth for draping over the coffin — some parishes had several, of differing qualities and costs, and I expect it must have been quite a big deal whether you got the cheap one or the expensive one.

Some reports of deaths could offer splendid detail, such as this reference to events in Eshaness, Shetland:

Recording the gravestone of Ally Alistair MacLeod at Lochinver, Sutherland.

"James Robertson born January 1785 died 16th June 1848 aged 63 years. He was a peaceable quiet man; and to all appearances a sincere Christian. His death was very much regretted which was caused by the stupidity of Laurence Tulloch in Clotharter who sold him nitre instead of Epsom salts by which he was killed in the space of 3 hours after a dose of it."

Other records of the Established Church

The Church of Scotland was organized by a hierarchy of assemblies, with the parish ministers and the kirk sessions at the base of the pyramid.

Parishes were grouped together under a presbytery, an assembly of the local ministers and an elder from each parish that exercised powers similar to an Episcopalian bishop. The presbyteries oversaw church schools, the maintenance of the kirks and manses (the ministers' houses) and the appointment of ministers, and dealt with moral cases too serious for the kirk sessions, such as witchcraft and incest. Presbytery records mention all sorts of people, though in many cases you won't know if your people are mentioned unless you look. Some

The manse (minister's house) at Uig, Lewis, designed by the great Scottish architect Thomas Telford (1757-1834). In poorer areas, the manse is often the only large house for miles around. This one, Baile-na-Cille, is now a splendid guest house (www. bailenacille. com).

have been published: see D. and W. Stevenson, *Scottish Texts and Calendars* (SHS, 1987).

Above the presbyteries were the synods, all answerable to the General Assembly that met in Edinburgh. Their records are all at the NAS in class CH. You will find reports from individual parishes on all sorts of matters, making them potentially useful sources to explore.

Kirk sessions

The kirk sessions comprised the minister and the ruling elders, who were appointed either by the session itself or elected by the congregation. Though technically a mere member of the sessions, the minister (or 'teaching elder') was in practice its head, with the casting vote. The deacons, who dealt with church funds, were not necessarily members.

Presbyterianism sought to control people's morals in what would now be considered an absolutely intolerable fashion. So, following the decrees of John Knox (c.1510-72), considered to be the father of the Church of Scotland, the kirk sessions reproved and corrected faults of *"drunkenness, excess (be it in apparel or be it in eating and drinking), fornication, oppression of the poor by exactions, deceiving of them in buying and selling by wrong mete or measure, wanton words and licentious living ..."* The earliest kirk session records are for St. Andrews, going back to 1559 — most start much more recently. Most kirk session records are at the NAS, with microfilm copies in local archives as appropriate, although some records are still with their original churches. The NAS holdings are being digitized and should be searchable on ScotlandsPeople by 2010. In the meantime, they are listed in the NAS catalog under CH2, searchable by the name of the parish. The records include minutes, accounts, records of the care of the poor, testimonials and communion rolls.

Sean Connery of Glenbucket

007 star Sean Connery's male-line ancestry has been fairly well explored so, when I was asked to look into his Scottish roots for *The Sunday Mail*, I decided to follow the route up from his maternal grandmother, Ellen Forbes Ross, who was born in 1884 at Brae of Cuttalich, Grantully, Perthshire.

Using General Registration and census records, we found that her father was John Forbes Ross, a farm laborer, born at Mortlach in 1864, son of James Ross, also a laborer, whose baptism appears in the OPRs of Mortlach in 1824. James's father William Ross, who was Sean's three x great-grandfather, was baptized at Glenbucket, Co. Aberdeen, in 1789 and appears as a crofter, farming two acres (roughly 8,000 meters squared) in Glenbucket in the 1851 census, and later as a pauper of Mortlach in the 1871 census — small wonder, as two acres was scarcely enough to support anyone.

Through Genes Reunited, I was able to find a four x great-granddaughter of William's daughter Ann. Ellen Sutherland is thus Sean's fourth cousin twice removed. Ellen lives in Cardiff and works selling make-up, hence the *Sunday Mail*'s inspired headline. She told the newspaper, "I knew about my Glenbucket ancestry and have visited the graveyard [but] I had no idea Mr. Connery is related to the people buried there."

William Ross's father William was one of the sons of an earlier William who died in 1771. In John Henderson's *Aberdeen Epitaphs & Inscriptions*, I found a memorial inscription from Glenbucket that reads:

"Erected by John Ross in memory of his father William Ross, who died at Uppertoun 10th October 1771 aged 58 years. His wife Isabella Michie who died 26th August 1787, aged

65 years.

The above said John Ross died at Sunnybrae, 4th August 1830, aged 82 years, and his wife Isabella Reid, died 7th June 1783 aged 36 years.

Isabella Atkinson Dawson, wife of William Ross, their grandson, died 27th October 1851 aged 35 years."

This MI enabled me to go even further back, finding that Isabella Mitchie's mother was the daughter of Helen Gordon. Glenbucket Castle was the seat of the Gordons of Glenbucket, of whom the most famous was "Old Glenbucket," John Gordon, Laird of Glenbucket, who was active in the 1715 uprising and one of the leading Jacobites supporting Bonnie Prince Charlie in the 1745 rebellion, after the failure of which he was forced to flee to Norway. I don't know the exact connection between Sean and "Old Glenbucket," but the resemblance is striking!

From blusher with love

Family tie: Sean and Ellen's ancestors are buried at Glenbucket

By HEATHER GREENAWAY

SIR SEAN CONNERY has a secret long-lost cousin — an Avon lady from Cardiff.

Avon lady is Sean's secret Welsh cousin

Licensed to sell: Avon lady Ellen Sutherland

Licensed to thrill: Superstar Sean Connery

Robert Burns in the records

On January 25th each year, Scots all around the world get together to drink whisky, eat haggis and listen to bagpipes, because it is Burns Night, the anniversary of the birth of Scotland's best-loved poet. Burns' work brings Scottish family history to life, and the Scottish records shed some interesting light on his own amorous liaisons.

Robert, or Robbie, Burns won the hearts of Scots at home and abroad by his sense of fierce independence and pride in his Scottish roots, his fondness for a wee dram of whisky, the straightforward simplicity with which he portrayed normal Scottish life and his love of the old Scots tongue (as opposed to English, the "Dei'ls tongue" — in which this book is written).

Failed farms

Burness and its variants Burnes, Burns and Burn all mean the same thing: someone who lived by a burn or stream. Robbie spelled his surname Burness until he went to Edinburgh in 1786, when he started using the Ayrshire spelling, Burns. As far back as records go, Burns' ancestors were farmers in Glenbervie, Kincardineshire. In 1745, the year of the great uprising, his grandfather Robert Burness took out a seven-year lease of Falside, Kinneff, but failed to make enough money and retired to live with his daughters at Denside.

His son William Burness left Kincardineshire, going to Edinburgh to help landscape The Meadows there. In 1750 he traveled west to Ayrshire, working in a succession of gardening jobs until, in 1756, he took out a seven-year lease at Alloway, built a cottage and established a market garden. Robbie was born there on January 25, 1759. After nine years trying to eke a living out of the poor soil of Alloway, William took out a 12-year lease for a 90-acre farm (36 hectares), called Mount Oliphant, near Alloway. It was here that young Robbie started his own dismal career as a farmer, toiling on the "churlish and ungrateful" soil, but always with some small book of Scottish ballads in his pocket to read in spare moments. He received very little formal education, but was, through his own efforts, vastly better read than many who had spent years in the church.

In 1777, William took a seven-year lease at Lochlie in Tarbolton, an equally barren farm where, in the midst of a long and furious rent dispute with his landlord, he died in 1784.

Robbie worked for a while as a flax dresser in Irvine, and then became a farmer in Mossgiel, Mauchline, still in Co. Ayr, all the time busily composing poetry. A true ladies' man, he was a co-founder of the Tarbolton Bachelor Club, that required members to have both a "frank, honest, open heart" and be "a professed lover of

LEFT: **A picturesque 19th-century illustration of Robbie Burns romancing one of his country lasses.**

MIDDLE: **Burns' wife, Jean Armour, with whom he had nine children, but very few grandchildren.**

RIGHT: **An old watercolor of the cottage in which Robert Burns was born and grew up in Kirk Alloway.**

one or more of the fairer sex." He met Jean Armour in Mauchline in 1785 and she became pregnant. Robbie promised to marry her, but her father refused his consent. Jean was humiliated, and he, bitterly, contemplated emigrating to the West Indies ("farewell dear old Scotland, and farewell dear, ungrateful Jean"). To fund his trip, Burns decided to publish his poetry. *Poems, Chiefly in the Scottish Dialect*, was first published in Kilmarnock in 1786.

Robbie and Jean were forced to do public penance on the "creepy chair" or stool of repentance at Mauchline in 1786, before being absolved of their sins. Their twins Jean and Robert were born and Mr. Armour issued a writ of damages against Robbie, who fled to Edinburgh. Here, the "Ploughman Poet's" witty irreverence towards all institutions, from state and church to nagging wives alike, made him the toast of the city.

While Robbie enjoyed his fame and short-lived wealth, he continued a spasmodic affair with Jean, finally marrying her informally about in April 1788. On August 5th the Mauchline kirk session gave them a formal rebuke before recognizing their marriage. But success had chilled his muse, and the financial needs of his farmer brother, his widowed mother and his sisters forced him to take a job as an excise officer, living first on a leased farm at Ellisland, north of Dumfries, and later moving to Dumfries itself.

Later work included 176 Scottish songs, either of his own composition or improved from old ballads, that appeared as part of James Johnson's *Scots Musical Museum* (Edinburgh, 1787–1803), others, including *Ye Banks and Braes o' Bonny Doon*, in George Thomson's *A Select Collection of Scotish Airs* (London, 1793–1818), and the great poem *Tam O'Shanter*, which he wrote for Francis Grose's *Antiquities of Scotland* (London, 1789–91).

Burns had been plagued with illness all his life and it finally got the better of him in the form of rheumatic fever. He died in Dumfries on July 21, 1796, aged only 36. His funeral was attended by 10,000 people and his memory has never faded — more than the patrician Walter Scott, Burns' work captured the spirit of the ordinary Scot, and that was where his genius lay. Burns Night has become a celebration of Scottishness worldwide — his Scots version of *Auld Lang Syne* is sung throughout the world on the Scots' great New Year festival of Hogmanay. The Homecoming Year of 2009 is a fitting tribute to his memory.

Descendants

Robbie had numerous affairs, having a child each by three women, and four by Jean Armour before they were married in 1788, after which she produced five more. Out of all his children by Jean, only two left descendants. One

James Brown, the "missing link" between Andrea McLean and Burns. The portrait is by Robert Gemmel Hutchinson RSA of Biggar, who lodged for a time with the Browns (courtesy of Biggar Museum Trust).

JAMES BROWN, St. B1819 Darvel 2000.1 Came to Biggar 1849 PA14 Died 15.12.1905 By R. Gemmel Hutchison J. B's GRANDMOTHER WAS MARY, SISTER OF JEAN ARMOUR

line died out in 1937, meaning that all Robbie's and Jean's descendants living today come from only one of their offspring, James Glencairn Burns. There are many descendants, however, of his two illegitimate daughters, Elizabeth Paton and Elizabeth Park. In all, a total of some 300 descendants are known, while an impressive 3,000 descendants of Robbie's earliest known ancestor, Walter Burness (d. 1670), have been traced.

Robbie's eldest son Robert (1786-1857) was educated at Glasgow University but ruined his career in the London Stamp Office through gambling, ending up as a maths and classics teacher in Dumfries. Two of Robbie's sons, William and James, had successful careers as officers in the East India Company's army, and their illegitimate brother, another Robert, became a merchant in London, benefiting more from the fame than the retrospective wealth of his father.

The Burns' Family Tree

Much information about Burns' family tree was published in Charles Rogers' *Genealogical Memoirs of the Family of Robert Burns and the Scottish House of Burnes* (Edinburgh, 1877), covering six main branches of the family and descendants through female lines, especially Begg, Caird, Elles, Falconer, Gleig, Holland, Hudson, Hutchinson, Keith, Ley, Major, Reith, Stuart, Watson and Whish. A detailed pedigree by John Burness is at **www.burness. ca/burns.html** and includes genealogies for families of Robbie's wife Jean Armour and mother Agnes Brown.

A GMTV Burns connection

In 2006, I was asked to trace the family tree of GMTV (Good Morning Television) weather-presenter, Andrea McLean. Her ancestor Archibald McLean was from the Isle of Tiree, Co. Argyll — solid McLean territory — but the 1851 census shows him as a day laborer in Glasgow, his family being one of 49 households crammed into 109 Oswald Street. Archibald's son (and Andrea's great-great-grandfather) was Charles McLean, who by 1871 had become a plumber, employing two men. He was married in Biggar in December that year to Mary, daughter of James Brown of Biggar and his wife Janet Gordon.

When the film about Andrea's family was broadcast, I was contacted by Brian Lambie of Biggar, with extraordinary news: "Old Jimmy Brown was Mary (or Helen?) Armour's grandson, and her sister Jean married Robert Burns." I was later able to confirm that Charles McLean's father-in-law James Brown was born in Loudoun in 1819, son of James Brown from Mauchline (b. 1796), who was the son of "Old Jimmy" Brown who, on April 19, 1793, married Helen Armour. Helen was baptized at Mauchline on March 10, 1773, daughter of James Armour (a builder in Mauchline) and Mary Smith, while Helen's sister Jean, baptized there on February 16, 1765, was indeed the future wife of Burns.

Andrea McLean is Robbie Burns' six x great-niece by marriage!

Your family and Burns

Burns' poetry captures life in the late 18th-century Lowlands so well that it makes evocative reading for anyone with ancestry there. If your family is from Ayrshire, it can become highly relevant, not least because of the number of people he mentioned. In "The Twa Herds," for example, he writes about some of the local ministers, including Rev. Alexander Moodie of Riccarton, who were involved with secessionist church groups:

"What flock wi' Moodie's flock could rank? —
Sae hale and hearty every shank!
Nae poison'd soor Arminian stank
He let them taste;
Frae Calvin's well, aye clear, drank, —
O, sic a feast!"

The *Burns Encyclopaedia* at **www.robertburns.org/ encyclopedia/** identifies many of the characters in the poems. You never know — your ancestors may be included!

"The Ploughman Poet," Robert Burns.

More about Burns

Should auld ac-quaintance be for-got, And nev - er brought to min'? Should auld acquaintance

A songsheet for Burns' famous song, "Auld Lang Syne."

For general information about Burns and his work, see **www.robertburns.org/**, which includes *The Complete Works of Robert Burns online* and the *Burns Encyclopaedia* along with advice on haggis-making and hosting Burns Suppers.

Burns' birthplace in Kirk Alloway is now part of the Burns National Heritage Park (Murdoch's Lone, Alloway, KA7 4PQ, 01292 443700, **www.burnsheritagepark.com**). It is a lovingly preserved area encompassing a fascinating museum, the impressive Burns Monument, the old kirk where Tam O'Shanter espied the witches cavorting with the Devil, and the Brig O'Doon over which he achieved his narrow escape from them. The Burns family's longhouse is a fine example of how farming families lived in 18th-century Ayrshire, they at one end of the building, and the animals at the other (a plastic chicken and cow there now add to the atmosphere).

CHAPTER 8

Religious denominations

From the days when the Picts worshipped the sun, the moon and perhaps their own forbears, down to the secessions and disruptions of recent times, religion has played an important, sometimes overbearing part in our ancestors' lives.

The Presbyterian Church

Modern dissent from the Catholic Church started in 1517, when the German Martin Luther made his first "protest" against it. The English King Henry VIII broke from Catholicism when the pope refused him a divorce. The Reformed religion, as honed by the ideas of John Calvin in Geneva, was formally adopted in England by Henry's son Edward VI, whose Scottish chaplain John Knox (c.1510–72) met Calvin, and then returned, full of fire, to Scotland.

Knox preached his sermon "vehement against [Catholic] idolatry" in St. John's, Perth,

in 1559, inciting the congregation to tear down the ornaments there and then to sack the local monasteries. When the Regent, Mary of Guise, sent in the army, Knox raised his own force as the "Faithful Congregation of Christ Jesus in Scotland," which received widespread support. The Calvinistic idea that the laity were equal to the clergy appealed to the freedom-loving burghers, while the minor lairds, impoverished by the heavy tithes they had to pay to dissolute Catholic clergy, were also ready to lend their support.

To plant the new faith firmly, a group of Protestant lords signed a Covenant to "apply our whole power, substance and our very lives" to protecting Protestantism, and in 1560 Parliament declared Scotland a Protestant state under the reformed Church of Scotland (CoS). Despite this rapid advance, it took until 1690 for the actual form of Protestantism to be decided,

The Protestant reformer John Knox reproving the lords and ladies of the Scottish court who all seem rather scared of him.

during which period the Church varied between different forms of episcopacy (governed by bishops) and presbyterianism (governed by assemblies or courts).

King Charles I's misguided attempts in 1638 to force the Scots to use the English Prayer Book, together with his imposition of unpopular taxes, provoked the nobility, burghesses and ministers to sign the National Covenant, swearing to protect their church against what they perceived as "Popery." A General Assembly of the Church of Scotland abolished the bishops altogether. Both sides, King and Covenanters, resorted to arms, and from this came the Civil War. In 1643, the Covenanters entered into a Solemn League and Covenant with the Westminster Parliament, promising military help against Charles if England became Presbyterian. The Westminster Confession of that year, a gathering of 100 English and eight Scottish Presbyterian ministers, decided what form Presbyterianism should take throughout Britain. Ironically, although England's flirtation with Presbyterianism petered out after 1660, the Westminster Confession's blueprint has remained in force in Scotland to this day.

Charles II restored the Scottish bishops in 1660, but integrated them with presbyteries and synods, and in 1690 William III ratified the new constitution of the Church of Scotland, doing away with bishops for ever. Thus, in 1690, there emerged what Smout called,
"the classic Presbyterian church of the 18th and 19th centuries, with its elders, deacons, and ministers, its kirk-sessions, presbyteries, synods and General Assembly, its frequent but not invariable association with Sabbatarianism [observing Saturday as the holy day] and Puritanism, and its convictions of ecclesiastical parity."

Clergy

Ancestors among the clergy are generally well recorded, not least in terms of who their parents were. It was not unusual for sons of clergymen to follow the same occupation, so sometimes several generations can be traced through clergy records alone.

Established Church ministers from the Reformation onwards are covered by H. Scott (ed.)'s *Fasti Ecclesiae Scoticanae: The Succession of Ministers in the Church of Scotland from the Reformation* (Edinburgh, 1915–28, repr. 1961). This details their careers, parents, children, testaments and so on, and is arranged by synod, presbytery, then parish. To work out which synod and presbytery you need, see Groome's *Gazetteer* (p. 33) and the *Statistical Accounts* (p. 32). Details of many itinerant preachers and catechists who were sent to the Highlands and Islands between 1725 and 1876 by the Royal Bounty Committee are in NAS CH1/2/29/3. Details of Theological Colleges and student societies are in CH3/119, CH3/273, CH3/281, CH3/305 and CH3/885.

Episcopalians

By 1690, virtually everyone belonged to the new Church of Scotland, not least because it was backed by the law. However, around that year 500 clergy left their parishes and formed the Episcopal Church in Scotland, adhering

J.K. Rowling's clerical ancestry

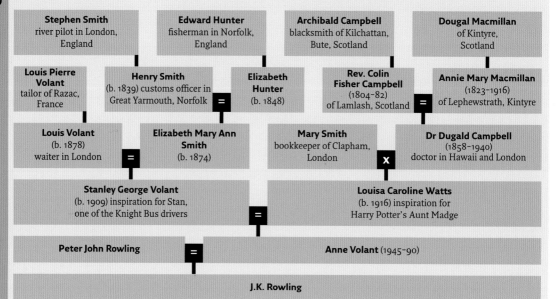

Colin, born 16th March 1850, died 16th Oct. 1861 ; Anne Elizabeth, born 31st Jan. 1852 ; Catherine Isabella, born 7th April 1854 ; Angus, born 23rd Feb. 1856, died 13th May 1916 ; Dugald, born 25th Jan. 1858 ; Alexander Hall, born 27th Feb. 1860 ; Colin, born 2nd Jan. 1862, died 14th June 1863 ; Maria Margaret, born 28th May 1864 (marr...

How the newspapers reported my discovery of J.K. Rowling's Scottish roots.

Detail of the entry for Colin Fisher Campbell in *Fasti Ecclesiae Scoticanae for the Synod of Argyll, Presbytery of Kintyre and Parish of Kilbride*, listing his children including Dugald, J.K.R.'s mystery great-grandfather.

Stephen Smith
river pilot in London, England

Edward Hunter
fisherman in Norfolk, England

Archibald Campbell
blacksmith of Kilchattan, Bute, Scotland

Dougal Macmillan
of Kintyre, Scotland

Louis Pierre Volant
tailor of Razac, France

Henry Smith
(b. 1839) customs officer in Great Yarmouth, Norfolk **=**

Elizabeth Hunter
(b. 1848)

Rev. Colin Fisher Campbell
(1804–82)
of Lamlash, Scotland **=**

Annie Mary Macmillan
(1823–1916)
of Lephewstrath, Kintyre

Louis Volant
(b. 1878)
waiter in London **=**

Elizabeth Mary Ann Smith
(b. 1874)

Mary Smith
bookkeeper of Clapham, London **X**

Dr Dugald Campbell
(1858–1940)
doctor in Hawaii and London

Stanley George Volant
(b. 1909) inspiration for Stan, one of the Knight Bus drivers **=**

Louisa Caroline Watts
(b. 1916) inspiration for Harry Potter's Aunt Madge

Peter John Rowling **=** **Anne Volant** (1945–90)

J.K. Rowling

There used to be a big mystery in the family tree of Harry Potter author J.K. Rowling. Her grandmother Louisa Volant was born in London in 1916, the illegitimate daughter of Mary Smith, a secretary. Nobody knew who Louisa's father was.

A few years ago, the magazine *Family History Monthly* asked me to trace J.K. Rowling's family tree. I was able to get in touch with J.K. Rowling's aunt Marion, who was a daughter of Louisa's, via www.genesreunited.com. Marion told me Louisa never knew her father, but thought he was called "Dr. Campbell." Using directories, I found there was only one Dr. Campbell in the whole of London at the time, and he lived a short bus journey away from Mary Smith. Mary Smith was probably his secretary, and I am sure he was J.K. Rowling's long-lost great-grandfather.

Dr. Dugald Campbell, to give him his full name, was certainly an exciting ancestor. As a young doctor, before he worked in London, he had sailed to Hawaii. There he founded a clinic at a place called Waimea. It is still running to this day, and the people of Waimea continue to be very grateful to him for it. There are stories of him galloping around the island on his horse, organizing paper-chases and teaching the islanders to play cricket.

J.K. Rowling already lived in Scotland before I found that Dr Dugald Campbell, her long-lost great-grandfather, was a Scotsman. He was born at Lamlash on the Isle of Arran, on the west coast of Scotland. Maybe a love of Scotland, and of adventure, had been in J.K. Rowling's blood all along.

doggedly to the old structure of ministers governed by bishops. It only retained any real footing in the north-east, and many of its early registers have been lost or remain in private hands. The NAS has microfilms of some registers in class RH4/179–185 and appendices 51–7. For others, look in the NRA. For ministers see D.M. Bertie's *Scottish Episcopal Clergy 1689–2000* (Edinburgh, 2000).

Cameronians

Not all Presbyterians approved of Charles II's hybrid Church of the 1660s. The hard-core Covenanters formed dissenting groups. In the 1680s, many Covenanters followed the preacher Richard Cameron, and became Cameronians, and later (1743) Reformed Presbyterians. They remained outside the 1690 settlement, regarding it as too liberal, even refusing to swear loyalty to a non-Covenanting king. In 1876, most were united with the Free Church of Scotland, and thus most records, such as they are, are in NAS class CH. A few congregations remained independent, the last of the Cameronians, and retain their own records.

The Secession Churches

Since 1690, the Church of Scotland has seen several substantial secessions (splits). The main difference between the Church and the Secessionists is one of personal responsibility. While the Church of Scotland assumed a broad, paternalistic responsibility for its members, the Secessionists, as David Moody puts it,

"believed that each man stood before God with no intermediaries, either secular or religious. Independent and egalitarian... he or she would have to some extent lacked the communal support of the parish... such self-confidence would often be a reflection of social status: independent tradesmen and hand-loom weavers could have

afforded the luxury of integrity more than farm-workers in thrall to an estate."

In 1733, a group led by Ebenezer Erskine left to form the Associate Presbytery. This split into the Burghers and Anti-Burghers, each of which formed "Auld Licht" and "New Licht" factions, the former adhering to the original obligations of the Covenant, the latter being more moderate. In 1760, the Relief Presbytery split from the Church of Scotland, later absorbing both the Associate Presbytery's New Licht groups.

The Free Church of Scotland (or "Wee Frees") broke from the Church of Scotland in "the Disruption" of 1843. The Free Church spread rapidly, appealing as much to independent-minded Highlanders as to industrial workers, and just by 1851 the Free Church had 889 chapels. In 1893 yet another secession created the Free Presbyterian Church of Scotland, sometimes called the "Wee Wee Frees," a body so austere that it was once jocularly said of them that, "they disapproved of sex because it might lead to dancing."

Further reading

- Diane Baptie, *Records of Baptisms, Marriages and Deaths in the Scottish Secession Churches* (Scottish Association of Family History Societies, 2000).
- A. Drummond and J. Bulloch, *The Church in Victorian Scotland 1843–74* (Saint Andrew Press, 1975).
- A. Drummond and J. Bulloch, *The Scottish Church 1688–1843* (Saint Andrew Press, 1973).
- W. Ewing, *Annals of the Free Church of Scotland 1843–1900* (Oliver & Boyd, 1914).
- J. Lamb (ed), *Fasti of the United Free Church of Scotland 1900–29* (Edinburgh, 1956).
- W.D. McNaughton, *The Scottish Congregational Ministry 1794–1993* (Glasgow, 1993).
- D. Scott, *Annals and Statistics of the Original Secession Church to 1852* (Edinburgh, 1886).
- R. Small, *History of the Congregations of the United Presbyterian Church 1733–1900* (David M. Small, 1904).

While these secessions were erupting, moves were afoot to unite their different branches. In 1847, the United Presbyterian Church of Scotland was created by unifying the United Secession Church and the Relief Church. In 1900 it merged with parts of the Free Church (the parts of the Free Church that did not join remain independent to this day), having also absorbed the Associate Synod, Burghers and Anti-Burghers and Reformed Presbyterian Kirk. In 1929, this in turn merged back into the Church of Scotland itself!

Besides being bewilderingly complicated, these secessions caused the OPRs of many parishes to become quite thin. Luckily, this is not universally true, because some dissenters still registered births and marriages in the OPRs, and sometimes their denomination will be stated. But if your family doesn't appear in the OPR you expect, it could well be because they had become nonconformists. After 1855 you can tell which denomination by seeing where they married, or look in Groome's *Gazetteer* or the *Statistical Accounts* to see what nonconformist chapel was nearest your ancestors' home.

Seeking their records is harder. Many just don't survive. Of those that do, some are indexed in the IGI (**www.familysearch.org**) and many are in NAS in classes CH3 and CH10-16. As the United Presbyterian Church's registers include many records of its earlier constituent parts, it's worth searching its collection in CH3 first. Some surviving registers are in local archives (sometimes with microfilm copies in NAS). Look at **www.nas.gov.uk/ researchers.asp** under "organizations," and select "nonconformist and other churches" — or just ask locally.

Most dissenting congregations have published biographical details of their clergy. A good place to start is the New College Library, Mound Place, Edinburgh, EH1 2LX.

Quakers

Sometimes misnamed Anabaptists, the Society of Friends was founded by George Fox (1624-91) as a breakaway Protestant group during the English Civil Wars (1642-8) and reached Scotland soon afterwards. Known as Quakers, their refusal to take oaths aroused the hostility of the state and many migrated to the Quaker colony of Pennsylvania, while most of those left behind eventually joined less demanding denominations, so many people may have unsuspected lines of Quaker ancestry.

The serious and sombre members of the General Assembly of the Kirk or Church of Scotland in 1787.

The Society of Friends was run by a hierarchy of meetings with Yearly Meetings at Aberdeen and Edinburgh, replaced in 1786 by the North Britain Half Years Meet and renamed the Scotland General Meeting in 1807. Most of their fabulously detailed records are at the NAS in H10, including a list of all Scottish Quaker births, marriages and deaths up to 1890.

Methodists

John Wesley (1703-91), an Anglican clergyman, founded Methodism as an evangelical preaching movement within the Church of England in the late 1730s, later splitting off to form a separate church. Wesley traveled extensively in Scotland, and the oldest Wesleyan church is in Victoria Street, Dunbar, founded in 1757.

Early Methodists appear in the OPRs, but later the congregations started keeping their own registers. These were the personal property of itinerant ministers who traveled in large circuits to visit their flocks, so family events may be scattered through several sets of records without much clear geographical logic. The following examples from Dundee are fairly typical:

"Hodge William 30 Aug 1831 2 Nov 1831 [son of] James Hodge [living in] Dundee Blacksmith [and] Elizabeth Doo dau[ghter] of John & Charlotte Doo" and

"Hodge James Stewart 11 Mar 1837 9 Apr 1837 [son of] James Hodge Dundee Blacksmith [and] Elizabeth Dow dau of John Dow & Charlotte Curd"

This illustrates a point to remember in all Scottish research — however useful one birth or baptism entry (such as that for William Hodge) may be, always seek records of other siblings, for that of his brother James Stewart Hodge gives their mother's mother's maiden name.

Wesleyan registers are scattered between university and local archives, and are best sought through **www.scan.org**. Dundee's registers, in Dundee Archives, are online at **www.fdca.org.uk/methodists.htm**.

The Wesleyan Historical Society has Minutes of Conference from 1752, including brief obituaries of ministers. For early to mid-19th-century ministers, see Rev. William Hill, *An Alphabetical Arrangement of all the Wesleyan Methodist Ministers, and Preachers on Trial, in connection with the British Conference* (London, 1885).

Catholics

Scotland was Catholic until Knox's time, when it changed, lock, stock and barrel, to Presbyterianism. Yet Catholicism was not eradicated at the Reformation. Despite opposition from church and state, many families refused to abandon "the Old Faith." It survived mostly in "seigniorial" form, with landed families maintaining a chaplain and encouraging (or coercing) their people to be Catholic too.

Catholic families were particularly drawn to the Stuart cause in the 1650s and again in 1715 and 1745, and the Stuarts' downfall was often theirs as well. Maybe Catholicism would have died out altogether had it not been rejuvenated by two important 19th-century influxes of Catholics, the masses of poor Irish flooding into Edinburgh and Glasgow in the wake of the Potato Famine, and to a much lesser extent the arrival of Italians.

Surviving Catholic registers are cataloged in M. Gandy's *Catholic Missions and Registers 1700-1880* (M. Gandy, 1993) in six volumes covering England, Wales and Scotland, and his *Catholic Parishes in England, Wales & Scotland: An Atlas* (M. Gandy, 1993). The NAS has photocopies of (apparently) all surviving Catholic registers in RH21, arranged by diocese. The earliest, for Braemar, starts in 1703, but most are 19th century. Baptism registers usually name

The '15, the '45 and the last of the Stuarts

A Hanoverian aristocrat comes to grief at the hands of Jacobites at the Battle of Culloden on April 16, 1746. About 1,300 men were killed in the battle, which decisively ended Jacobite attempts on the throne.

The rebellions that rocked Scotland during the 18th century had their roots planted firmly in the events of 1688. King James VII and II, who succeeded his brother Charles II in 1685, was a Catholic. In 1688 he was deposed by a cabal of Protestant nobles, who offered the throne to his daughter Mary and her husband William of Orange, who also happened to be the son of James's sister Mary. James fled to France, where his son James, "the Old Pretender" (1688–1766), grew up in exile.

William and Mary were childless, so were succeeded by her sister Anne, who also failed to produce surviving heirs. When she died in 1714, her nearest heirs were Catholics in France, so the government offered the throne to her more distant Protestant cousin George I of Hanover (grandson of Anne's great-aunt Elizabeth Stuart). The exiled Stuarts had meanwhile cultivated supporters termed Jacobites (after Jacobus, the Latin for James), who were mainly Catholics

and Protestant Scots whose ancient loyalty to the House of Stuart overrode all other considerations. George I's accession in 1715 was answered with a Jacobite rebellion, which saw uprisings in Northumberland in England and in the Highlands, the latter led by the Earl of Mar. The English rebels marched to Preston, where they surrendered, while Mar fought an indecisive battle against government troops at Sheriffmuir, near Stirling. The Old Pretender arrived by sea, realized the situation was hopeless, and sailed back to France again, taking Mar with him.

The leaders of the '15 (as the rebellion became known) who were caught were executed — many captured soldiers were sent to the American colonies and Jamaica, effectively as slaves. There remain in the Caribbean today pockets of desperately poor white descendants of these and other contemporary deportees.

Back on the Continent, the Old Pretender and his son Charles Edward Stuart (1720–88) — Bonnie Prince Charlie or the Young Pretender — continued to hanker for their lost throne. In July 1745, Charlie landed in Scotland and, dressed in Royal Stewart tartan, raised the Stuart standard again. He gathered an enthusiastic army, many, but not all, being Highlanders. Initially, all went well — the Jacobites captured Edinburgh and defeated the government troops at Prestonpans. They marched south to Derby in England, but the promised French support never materialized, and even the English who were sympathetic to Charlie were terrified by the advancing Highlanders. The Jacobites lost their nerve and returned to Scotland. On April 16, 1746, the Duke of Cumberland's 9,000 government troops fought Charlie's 5,000 Jacobites at Culloden Moor near Inverness, soundly defeating them. Bonnie Prince Charlie spent several months on the run in the Highlands and Islands before escaping to France, dying years later in Rome as an embittered alcoholic. His brother Henry, a Catholic cardinal, lived his last years considering himself the rightful king of Scotland and England, but he eventually made peace with his cousin King George III and sent the Crown Jewels back to London.

The story ends with a series of would-be kings claiming descent from Bonnie Prince Charlie, such as the brothers John Carter Allen and Charles Manning Allen, born in the late 18th century, who changed their names to John Sobieski Stuart and Charles Edward Stuart. They claimed that their father Thomas Hay Allen was actually Bonnie Prince Charlie's son; there is no evidence that this was so. More recently, a Belgian called Michael Lafosse claimed descent from a hitherto unheard-of marriage between Bonnie Prince Charlie and the Countess de Massillan. He started calling himself "Prince Michael of Albany" but could not produce hard evidence concerning the alleged marriage.

"Prince Michael" and I found ourselves guests on Ruby Wax's BBC1 television show *Ruby* a few years ago, and I was placed in the awkward position of having to say whether or not I believed his claims — my honest answer was "no." In June 2006, the *Sunday Mail* reported that Michael faced deportation for having used a false birth certificate to obtain British citizenship, and shortly afterwards we heard that he had fled back to Belgium to live with his mother. But the amount of support and publicity he received shows how potent, and romantic, the story of the exiled Stuart kings of Scotland remains.

Bonnie Prince Charlie (1720–88), Charles Edward Stuart, "the Young Pretender."

The most English of superstars traces his roots back to David Livingstone's Scottish sidekick, a Jacobite rebel and a major decorated at Dunkirk

Hugh's who

The *Sunday Mail* reports of my investigations into Hugh Grant's ancestors, that had originally been commissioned by the magazine *Family History Monthly*.

Though actor Hugh Grant might seem quintessentially English, his name is Scottish. Hugh's most curious Scottish ancestor must be his two x great-grandfather Dr. James Stewart (1831-1905). The son of a dispossessed tenant farmer from Perth, James qualified as a doctor at Glasgow University before falling under the influence of the great missionary and explorer David Livingstone and, in 1861, setting sail for Africa with Livingstone's wife. James explored much new territory along the Zambesi, and later founded a mission, Livingstonia, on the western shore of Lake Nyasa, now in Malawi. Apparently, he was the first white man ever to set foot on the northern shore of that great lake.

James Stewart returned to Scotland to serve as Moderator of the General Assembly of the Free Church of Scotland, but died back in South Africa, having written *Dawn in the Dark Continent* (1903), detailing the successes of the missions there to date. He was described in his lifetime by Lord Milner as "the biggest human in South Africa."

Hugh's paternal grandfather, Major James Murray Grant DSO (1899-1974), served in the Seaforth Highlanders. When the Highland Division was stranded near Dunkirk in 1940, James, taking Burns' phrase "do or die" to heart, refused to surrender, but was captured. He proceeded to tunnel out of the prisoner-of-war camp with his bare hands.

The forenames "James Murray" indicate descent from the Jacobite Grants of Glenmoriston, an offshoot of the Grants of Freuchie, who suffered severely at Culloden in 1745. Coincidentally, through his English mother, Hugh is a seven x great-grandson of William Drummond, fourth Viscount Strathallan, the commander of the Jacobite forces who was slain at Culloden.

---

godparents, who were often close relations. Death registers tend to be better kept than those of Presbyterians, because the priest was always called to give the Last Rites. For example, the NAS guide records that, "*John Carley, a married man, was suddenly suffocated in an old coal pit at Campsie by Damp Air,*" on June 27, 1815.

Kirk session and other Church of Scotland records sometimes state the numbers or names of Catholics in given parishes. For example, the General Assembly papers at NAS (class CH1) includes a list of Catholics during 1708-28, sometimes including the name of the nearest Protestant relative who was held responsible for their behavior.

Catholic priests between 1732 and 1878 are covered by *The Innes Review* (Scottish Catholic Historical Association, vols 17, 34 and 40) and C. Johnson's *Scottish Catholic Secular Clergy, 1879-1989* (John Donaldson Publishers Ltd, 1991). You can look further in the Scottish Catholic Archives, Columba House, 16 Drummond Place, Edinburgh, EH3 6PL, 0131 556 3661, **www.catholic-heritage.net**. Since Catholicism was outlawed, several Scots Colleges were established on the Continent to train priests — for the records of Douai, Rome, Madrid, Valladolid and Ratisbon see *Records of Scots Colleges* (New Spalding Club, 1906).

Irish Catholics

Throughout the 18th century, Irish landlords had been exporting grain and forcing their tenants to grow potatoes for themselves. In common with many a poor Scottish family, the Irish peasantry therefore subsisted on boiled potatoes, mixed where possible with milk or fish. When, in 1845, a disease called *phytophthora infestans*, or "potato blight," swept the land, it was a true disaster. Combined with heavy rains, it destroyed up to 40 percent of the crop, and the following year up to 95 percent of the potatoes came out of the ground as rotten slime. For many peasants, the choice was starvation or emigration. Those who could afford it sailed to the Americas, but for the poorest the passage to mainland Britain was safer and cheaper. By December 1846, Scotland had acquired a population of 26,335 Irish refugees, many of whom trudged to the Grassmarket, West Port and Cowgate areas of Edinburgh, where they lived crammed into the city's narrow wynds and closes. Anti-Irish rioting led, in June 1847, to many being sent back to Ireland, but even when conditions in Ireland eased later that year, emigration had become a normal aspiration for the young, and the exodus to countries including Scotland continued for the rest of the century.

For details of tracing Irish immigrants back to Ireland, and research in the Emerald Isle, see my book *Tracing Your Irish Family History* (Firefly, 2009).

Italian Catholics

Famine and corruption at home also drove Italian migration. The first Italians to arrive in Scotland were known as Ciociari, as they were from the Ciociaria region in southern Lazio. They sold statuettes or food, specializing in fish-and-chip shops that also sold ice cream,

and by 1914 they numbered about 4,000, a third of them in Glasgow but with sizeable communities in Greenock and Edinburgh and others spread further afield. Most other Italian immigrants were from Tuscany and Lazio — the former tended to settle in Glasgow, and the latter in Edinburgh.

The Scots-Italians suffered badly in the Second World War by negative association with Mussolini's Fascist movement, and newer arrivals who were Italian-born were interred on the Isle of Man and in Northern Ireland for the duration of the conflict.

Scots-Italian descendants have made a particular impact in TV drama, including Daniela Nardini (from Largs), one of the stars of *This Life*; Tom Conti (from Paisley), co-star of *Shirley Valentine*; Peter Capaldi (from Glasgow), the abusive spin-doctor in *The Thick of It*; GMTV presenter Carla Romana (from Glasgow); and radio satirist Armando Iannucci (also from Glasgow).

As with all immigrant communities, genealogical problems are caused by anglicization of Italian names. A few years ago I

St. Patrick's church in Edinburgh, one of many new Catholic churches built due to the influx of the Irish in the 19th century.

Glaswegian siblings Jim and Sissy Crowley and some children enjoying Italian ice creams in July 1910 (courtesy of the Crowley Family Collection).

investigated a plaster sculptor named Mark Brown, earlier recorded as Stark Brown. He was clearly of Italian origin, and it was his Edinburgh Catholic Church wedding record that gave away his original identity — Eustachio Bruni.

For more information on the Italian community see **www.members.lycos.co.uk /scots_italian**.

Irvingites

Catholics are not to be confused with the Catholic Apostolic Church, a spiritualist prayer movement started in the 1820s that came to be known as Irvingite after Rev. Edward Irving (1792–1834), who visited Scotland in 1827 and 1828, preaching the imminent Second Coming of Christ. This denomination attracted many converts, but most fell away after its founders died and, of course, Christ never turned up. Registers of the Irvingites' Edinburgh congregation 1833–1949 are in NAS RH4/174.

Huguenots

This is the term given to Flemish and French Protestants who fled Catholic persecution in France in the 16th and 17th centuries. Pre-1707 Scotland required no form of registration comparable to the English practice of

naturalization, making Huguenot origins hard to detect, though in many cases French-sounding surnames and occupations — many were weavers and silk-makers — give the game away. A group from Flanders settled in Canongate, Edinburgh, in 1609, and many more came after the Revocation of the Edict of Nantes in 1685 — with virtually all settling in burghs. What may fairly be called a bible for researchers here is D. Dobson's *Huguenot and Scots Links, 1575–1775* (Genealogical Publishing Co., 2005).

Jews

Scotland is virtually unique in having no history of medieval violence against Jews. There were Jewish moneylenders in Scotland by 1190, and later there were small Jewish communities in the royal burghs, especially Aberdeen and Dundee, that had close trade links to the Baltic ports. In 1691, David Brown, a Jew, made an application to trade and live in Edinburgh. Other relatively prosperous Jews came from Germany and Eastern Europe during the 18th century, but later that century and in the early 19th century there was a spate of pogroms (persecutions) in Eastern Europe. These forced many poor Jews, particularly those from Lithuania, to seek refuge in Edinburgh, Aberdeen, Ayr, Dundee and

Greenock, and particularly in the Gorbals of Glasgow, where numbers may have reached 20,000.

There are now only 6,400 practicing Jews in Scotland, but many families with roots in those cities have Jewish ancestry. Broadcaster Jeremy Isaacs, guitarist Mark Knopfler, and novelist Muriel Spark are all from Scots-Jewish families.

Garnethill in Glasgow is Scotland's oldest synagogue, built in 1879. Its Historical Database of Scottish Jewry contains information on some 16,500 people, and it is also home to the Scottish Jewish Archives Centre (Garnethill Synagogue, 129 Hill Street, Glasgow, G3 6UB, 0141 332 4911, www.sjac.org.uk). See also the Jewish Genealogical Society of Great Britain on www.jgsgb.org.uk.

Jewish origins can often be found through families with Jewish names, or in censuses indicating origins in "Russia" (which then covered the Baltic States, the Ukraine and most of Poland). Finding precise origins abroad is often a matter of luck, but much can be learned from the records here. When I traced the ancestry of GMTV weather presenter Andrea McLean I found her three x great-grandparents (and one of their sons) living at 5 Bedford Row, Gorbals, Glasgow, in the 1901 census, recorded as:

"Dishkin, Abraham, head, 64, synagogue beadle, Russia FS [foreign subject]
Dishkin, Ettie, wife, 53, Russia, FS
Dishkin, Hyman, son, 24, cigarette packer, Russia FS."

In all probability, Abraham and Ettie's parents never left Russia, yet their names are recorded in Scotland in Abraham and Ettie's death records. Abraham's death record (January 8, 1917) names his parents as David Dishkin, furniture dealer, and Rachel Dishkin formerly Yelin, both deceased. As Abraham was born in Russia about 1837, David and Rachel are likely to have been born at the very start of the 19th century.

Garnethill Synagogue, Scotland's oldest and home to the Scottish Jewish Archives Centre.

Writer Muriel Spark, who is of Scottish Jewish descent.

Testaments, deeds and other useful records

Scotland's archives contain a wealth of other records that can be used for genealogical research. Many are couched in rather arcane and frankly frightening terminology, but the matters they deal with are simple enough — death, debt, buying, selling and so forth. And many are becoming much easier to search than ever before.

Deeds

A major source of Scottish genealogical information, albeit mainly focusing on the better-off, are deeds. Deeds are written agreements made between two or more parties and cover a wide range of social interactions, from the purchase and sale of practically anything (though particularly land), disposal of property after death, marriage contracts, loans, tacks (leases of land) and a vast amount more.

In the Middle Ages deeds were drawn up by notaries, who were so notorious for forging false documents that, in the 1500s, it became common practice to register deeds in a court. By being registered, they were thus preserved for us to use now.

Searching for deeds from 1809 onwards is quite straightforward. Those concerned with heritable rights (i.e. land ownership) in royal burghs could be registered there, but all others had to be registered in the local sheriff court (see pp. 100–1) or the Court of Session's Register of Deeds (they are also called Books of Council and Session).

Before 1809, the situation was rather chaotic, as a deed could be registered in practically any court save those of baronies. Deciding where (and indeed whether) to look can be a matter of guesswork. The deeds registers of royal burghs are not too arduous to search. The sheriff courts had registers of deeds from the 1500s, albeit with some gaps, though these can often be filled by searching their warrants instead. Minute books can be used to make up for the lack of indexes. Commissary courts (see p. 100) held registered deeds, except for those of Wigtown

From the Index to the Register of Deeds, 1666, vol. 6, HMSO, 1921.

300

REGISTER OF DEEDS, 1666.

Name and Designation.	Granter, Grantee, or Principal Party.	Nature of Deed.	Date of Recording. 1666.	Office.	Vol.	Page.
M'LELLANE, Thomas, son of William M'L. of Collin	G.	Bond	27 Mar.	Dur.	12	379
,, William, of Airds	G.	,,	31 Aug.	Mack.	16	946
,, ,, of Collyne	G.	Bond of Corrob.	22 Feb.	Dal.	15	902
,, ,, ,,	G.	Bond	15 Mar.	,,	16	117
,, ,, ,,	G.	,,	30 ,,	Mack.	15	724
,, ,, ,,	G.	,,	9 June	,,	16	196
,, ,, ,,	G.	,,	6 Aug.	,,	16	810
,, ,, ,,	G.	,,	31 ,,	,,	16	946
,, ,, son of Robert M'L. of Ballmangane.	G.	,,	21 June	Dur.	13	130
M'LEOD (M'LEOID, M'LEWD, M'CLOUD, M'GLAUD).						
,, Alexander, son of John M'L. of Drynoch (bis)	Ge.	,,	24 May	Dal.	16	479
,, Hew, of Cambuscurrie	G.	,,	24 June	,,	17	290
,, John, of Rasay	G.	,,	23 Mar.	,,	16	174
,, Neill, of Assin (Assint)	G.	,,	18 Jan.	,,	15	627
,, ,, ,,	G.	,,	17 Feb.	,,	15	868
,, ,, ,,	G.	Bond of Corrob.	17 ,,	,,	15	868
,, ,, ,,	G.	Bond	20 ,,	,,	15	891

(and warrants alone survive for Aberdeen and the Isles), and franchise courts held registers of deeds up to their abolition in 1747.

Types of deed: There were many types of deed, ranging from income guarantees for widows and children to settlements of disputes.

Debt looms large, with many sorts of bonds or promises to repay borrowed money. If a debt was finally repaid, there may be a bond of discharge confirming the fact.

Probative writs were documents containing something the holder wanted to go on permanent record, such as evidence of a loan. A bill was a note written by one person promising to pay money to another. Protests (abbreviated to "Pro") were written evidence that someone had asked for a loan to be repaid. Other forms of deed that can be more genealogically useful include factories, whereby a relation or outsider was appointed as a factor to manage an estate for an absent owner. Contracts made through deeds include apprentice indentures, business partnerships, arrangements for joint ownership of ships and cargoes, and contracts of excambion, whereby two parties swapped pieces of land.

Deeds in the Court of Session: The Court of Session, the highest civil court, has a Register of Deeds in NAS class RD. Up to 1660, some deeds are in the Acts of the Lords of Council (*Acta Dominorum Concilii*) 1501–14 (CS5), in the *Acta Dominorum Councilii et Sessionis* (CS6, 1532–59) and in the Acts and Descreets (indexed in CS7, 1542–81). Somewhat overlapping this is the Calendar of Deeds 1554–95. The period 1596–1660 is not indexed, and there are five separate clerks' offices through which deeds were registered, making the search rather hard. From 1660, the registers stop being in Latin and

Robert Lister MacNeil, an American citizen who returned to his ancestral roots, reclaimed the deeds to the island of Barra for the MacNeils when he bought Barra and Kisimul Castle in 1937. Traditional MacNeil lands, they had been sold in 1838. Robert's son is the current Chief of the Clan MacNeil.

are in three clerks' series: Dalrymple (DAL, RD2), Durie (DUR, RD3) and Mackenzie (MACK, RD4). Annual indexes to the main parties cover these for 1661–1702, 1705–7, 1714–15 and 1750–2. From 1770–1811 there are annual indexes to grantors (but not the recipients, making them much less useful). Then, from 1812, all deeds are in RD5, indexed annually. Some archives and Mormon FHCs have some of these indexes on microfilm, and for the years lacking indexes, a manual search can be made through the minute books to the clerks' registers.

Wadsets: Any bond concerning land, perhaps offering it as security for a loan, is termed an heritable bond, of which most were wadsets or mortgages. The lender or wadsetter would acquire the land itself or just the right to collect rent from it for the duration of the loan. The borrower would receive from him letters of reversion, promising to restore the land once the loan had been repaid. The wadset and its termination would both be accompanied by a sasine (see pp. 132–3), as both involved land

Debts

Debts generated some useful records, especially diligences, which were legal mechanisms for creditors who had been authorized by the courts to regain their money. Diligences took several forms: letters of horning allowed the creditor to poind or seize the debtors' goods; letters of apprising (also called letters of adjudication) were claims made on the moveable estate; and letters of inhibition could be taken out to prevent the debtor selling land until the debt was paid. There are General and County Registers of Diligence in NAS class DI. Similar registers were kept by regalities.

If your ancestor eventually went bankrupt, he will appear in the Court of Session records. Sheriff court records include some registers of sequestrations, particularly claims for *cessio bonorum*, by which the debtor would surrender their entire estate and thus be protected from further action, including imprisonment. If the debtors did come clamoring for you to be thrown into jail, you could always take sanctuary in the Palace of Holyroodhouse — those who did so are registered in NAS RH2/8/17-20.

---

118   MELROSE REGALITY RECORDS

market cross of Melrose ; witnesses, James Penman, glover, portioner of Melrose, and John Sheill, weaver.

November 22. HORNING—John Hounam in Darnick *against* Robert Edgar in Melrose for 73 l. 5 s. Scots and 10 l. 14 s. of expenses contained in Decreet by the bailie of regality of Melrose, 27 November 1697. Dated Edinburgh, 27 September 1698.

Executions : 2 November 1698, by James Blaikie, messenger, against him personally ; witnesses, John Lourie and Robert Blaikie, residenters in Melrose. 22 November 1698, at the market cross of Melrose ; witnesses, as above.

1699.
April 11. HORNING—John Donaldsone in Gallasheills *against* Andrew Dasone in Melrose to fulfil conditions of Tack by complainer to him, 4 May 1695, of his houses and yards in Melrose (reserving the malt kiln, barn and steep), and these two acres and a half of land in the Annay of Melrose with the teindsheaves and pertinents, as then possessed by said Andrew Dasone himself, for nine years for 31 l. 6 s. 8 d.

Letters of horning, from Melrose Regality Court, published in C.S. Romanes' *Selections from the Records of the Regality of Melrose and from the Manuscripts of the Earl of Haddington*, vol. 3, 1547–1706, SHS, second series, vol. 13, 1917 (courtesy of SoG).

---

transfer. Wadsets can create confusing situations, as both the lender and borrower might describe themselves as being "of" the place concerned at the same time.

Directories

Directories started in England in 1677 as lists of prominent merchants. Edinburgh's first one appeared in 1773 and Glasgow's in 1783. There were some national directories, such as the *Universal British Directory 1793-98*, although its coverage of people was limited to the most important residents and businessmen. They proliferated in the 19th century and flourished until the spread of telephone directories after the Second World War. They generally listed tradesmen, craftsmen, merchants, professionals, farmers, clergy, gentry and nobility but as time passed coverage grew broader.

From the mid-19th century onwards directories usually comprised four sections: commercial (tradesmen and professionals listed alphabetically), trades (individual alphabetical lists for each trade or profession), streets (tradesmen and private residents listed house by house) and "court" (originally the heads of wealthier households, but this rapidly became an alphabetical listing of the heads of all families save the poor). They provide a snap-shot of the communities in which ancestors lived, including useful historical sketches and descriptions of the places concerned. By searching a series of directories, you can work out when ancestors lived and died. Bear in mind, though, that

Clergymen, such as Rev. Mr Morrison with his splendid beard, are among the people who are well recorded in directories.

directories were usually printed a year or so after the data had been collected, so were always slightly out of date. Directories also provide addresses for manual censuses searches. They are found in most good libraries and local archives, and some have been published on CD.

Newspapers

Newspapers started as propagandist newsbooks during the English Civil Wars (1642–9). Regular newspapers first appeared in London in the early 1700s, followed rapidly by the *Edinburgh Evening Courant*, published three times weekly from 1718, the *Glasgow Journal* in 1741 and the *Aberdeen Journal* in 1748. Although it is now a daily newspaper, *The Scotsman* first appeared as a weekly in 1817 (and is searchable to 1900 at **www.archive.scotsman.com**). The first daily paper, *The Conservative*, was established in 1837.

Newspapers provide valuable background detail on your ancestors' individual stories — announcements of evictions, clearances, sailing of emigrant ships, the establishment or closure of factories and so forth. Many were produced by religious denominations, and can be found in denominational archives. Some carried announcements of births, baptisms, marriages, deaths, obituaries and burials. Although they very seldom include the illiterate poor (for obvious reasons), poor people may be mentioned retrospectively, for example as parents of people who had risen in the world. This is especially true for emigrant families, when the poor Scottish grandparents of a prosperous colonial businessman or farmer might be described in some detail in his obituary in a colonial newspaper.

You will also encounter advertisements concerning bankruptcy, business partnerships being made and dissolved, and even notices placed by husbands disclaiming financial responsibility for wives who had eloped. Trials, crimes and inquests into unusual deaths were reported in the past with as much detail and relish as they are today.

Local newspapers can be found in local archives and some have been indexed by volunteers. The *Wigtown Free Press*, for example, has personal name indexes from 1843, published by the Dumfries and Galloway Regional Council Library Service, 1982. J.P.S. Ferguson's *Directory of Scottish Newspapers* (NLS, 1984) lists all known Scottish newspapers, but more useful now are the online catalogs to the vast collections of local and national newspapers at the NAS (**www.nls.uk/collections/newspapers/ indexes/index.cfm**) and the British Library in London (**www.bl.uk/catalogues/newspapers**). Use their online catalogs to identify the papers most likely to help.

OBITUARY.—The death took place on Tuesday, 13th inst., of Mr Alexander Macleod, Badnaban. He had been a sufferer for many months and was 79 years of age. Mr Macleod was the last surviving member of the family of the late Alister Macleod, whose memory is still fragrant among the older generation. Mr Alexander Macleod was of the old school, hard-working, and a faithful attender and supporter of the Free Church, of which his father was a member and precentor. He is survived by a widow, who is herself an invalid, and a family of eight. The funeral, which was largely attended, took place on Friday to the family burying ground at Inver, Mr John Macrae, Free Church missionary, conducted the services. The chief mourners were:—Mr James Macleod (son), Messrs George Ross and Roderick Macleod (sons-in-law), Messrs Hugh and Angus Ross (grandsons), and Mr George Macleod (nephew). Sympathy is extended to Mrs Macleod and family in their bereavement.

Here is the newspaper obituary in August 1940 of Ally Alistair MacLeod of Badnaban, crofter, full of useful genealogical information (though his date of death is wrong — he died on the 14th). A precentor led the singing, for Ally Alistair's precentor father could also sing — what a wonderful extra detail for the family's history!

Old prints can provide amusing windows into the past. Here, kilted soldiers in the Napoleonic Wars are tricked into bending over so the local women can answer the age-old question, "what's he wearing underneath?"

For information on middle and upper class families, such as appointments of officers, officials and suchlike, you can also search the *Edinburgh Magazine*, founded in 1739 and renamed the *Scots Magazine* in 1817. There is a card index to its birth, marriage and death announcements from 1739 to 1826 at Lord Lyon's office.

Poll Books and Electoral Registers

Elections to burgh councils and parliament generated lists of electors can be useful in piecing together details of an ancestor's life — their appearance in a list of 1844 but not 1845 suggests a death in about 1843/4. Someone's new appearance may suggest the year when they reached voting age or attained the necessary property-based qualifications. Modern electoral lists are useful tools for tracing forward to find living relatives.

Very few men could vote before 1832, and those that could are usually better recorded elsewhere (in sasines, testaments, burgh records and so on). But the Reform Acts, from 1832, gradually increased the electorate on the basis of property qualifications, and these are noted in the pre-1918 records, making them interesting to study for that reason alone. Subject to strict property restrictions, women could vote from 1882. Full voting rights for people aged 21 or more came for men in 1918 and women in 1929, reduced to 18 in 1971. Surviving records are in local archives, and some are in the NAS — those for burghs are in class B and those for the shires are in the sheriff court records.

Tax lists

The Exchequer dealt with the state's finances. Its records are in NAS class E, although some early records are published by HMSO, such as *The Exchequer Rolls of Scotland 1264–1600* and *Accounts of the Lord High Treasurer of Scotland 1473–1566*.

The records include various tax lists. These will not state relationships, but they can be useful for picking up traces of your family and surname, and a succession of tax lists may show a change in first name that may suggest, say, the death of a father and the advancement to taxable status of his son.

Hearth tax: Also called Hearth Money, this was raised between 1691 and 1695. Collected by heritors (see p. 143), it was payable by all householders with hearths save the poor, or people such as blacksmiths and bakers who used hearths for their work. Useful for tracing the histories of buildings, the records (not all of which include names) are in NAS E69 and local archives, and some are published, such as those in D. Adamson's *West Lothian Hearth Tax, 1691* (SRS). His pages for "the Toune of Borroustouness" start with a contemporary preamble stating that 241 hearths of the poor people had been exempted, so were not listed.

The list of taxable hearths includes such details as:

"Keingloss house   10*
James Hunter in the Parke   1*
William Hay, a smidie   1*
Alexander Cornwels airs [heirs]   3d"*

Poll tax: This "head tax" was raised annually between 1694 and 1699, excepting the poor and children under 16 if their household's tax bill was under 30 shillings. Records are divided between NAS E70 (under "pollable persons") and local archives. Where records survive they are useful in identifying all taxable people in the family.

18th-century assessed taxes: Various odd taxes were raised from 1747 onwards, including Carriage Tax, Servants Tax, Window Tax (1748-98) and Dog Tax (1797-98), and are in NAS E326. They all sound quite exciting, but the records are sparse and few include many names. They inspired Robbie Burns' poem *The Inventory*, listing all such taxable items, such as,

"... Wheel carriages I ha'e but few,
Three carts, an' twa are feckly new;
An auld wheel barrow, mair for token,
Ae leg, an'baith the trams, are broken ...

... I've nane in female servan' station,
(Lord, keep me aye frae a' temptation!) ..."

Worth a search, however, because they include many names of small farmers, are Farm Horse Taxes (1797-8, E326/10), continued in the Consolidated Assessed Taxed records (1798-9, E326/15) that survive for various counties.

Income tax: Records from 1799 list those earning £60 a year or more, but survival is very poor (mainly Midlothian and some burghs). See the NAS catalog under E327/78-121.

Testaments, inventories and latterwills

Wills and testaments are documents marking the end of people's lives. They provide useful details of what people owned, and to whom they were related. The people generally identified in these records were spouses and children, but you may also find parents, brothers and sisters, nieces and nephews, grandchildren and so on.

These documents were generally made for people with something worth leaving (and hence inheriting), or people in debt. The poor tended not to bother, but this is not always so — if your family were illiterate laborers they probably won't appear here, but once in a while

Poll tax payers in Easter Muress in the Presbytery of Kincarden, with and without social pretensions, from *List of Pollable Persons within the Shire of Aberdeen*, 1696 (Aberdeen, 1844).

EASTER MURESS.

	£	s	d
John Farquharson, tennent ther, but he classing himself in an higher capacity, his poll is £3, and the generall poll of 6s., both is	£3	6	0
Item, His wife and sone, Ludovick *in familia*, their poll is	0	12	0
Item, John Catanach, his servant, his fee per annum 20 merks, the hundred pairt whereof and generall poll is..	0	12	8
Item, Janet Gordon, his servant, her fee 8 merks per annum, the fortieth pairt whereof and generall poll is	0	8	8
Item, Elspet Catanach, his servant, her fee 10 merks per annum, the fortieth pairt whereof and generall poll is	0	9	4
Item, John M'Fersone, tennent ther, and his wife, their poll is	0	12	0
Item, Alexander M'Fersone ther, and his wife, their poll is..........................	0	12	0
Item, Findlay Morgan ther, and his wife, their poll is................................	0	12	0
Item, William Morgan ther, and his wife, their poll is	0	12	0
	£8	18	8

A painting by Scottish artist Sir David Wilkie (1785–1841) showing a family attending the reading of a will. Everyone is waiting to find out what they are set (or not) to gain.

they might. As wills and testaments are so easy to search now, it is always worth a look. Even if you don't find your ancestors, you may find people of the right surname who may turn out to be relatives, and indeed who may even have left legacies to your direct forebears.

Testaments were created in court after someone's death, appointing executors and cautioners and recording an inventory of the movable estate (anything from clothes and money to animals and vehicles) of the deceased (who was called, in Scots, the *umquhile*). This will tell you much about the deceased's life, the tools of their trade and the fruits of the labor, and what they were worth (though there was an understandable tendency to undervalue things, to keep the taxable value down). The inventory also included debts owed to and by the deceased, sometimes including (and thus identifying) relatives, clients or the deceased's landlord. You may find an eik, a codicil or supplement, usually an extra inventory added to the original when further goods or money (or debts) had been discovered.

The executors, appointed by the testament, were the people chosen to distribute the *umquhile*'s estate as instructed. Although it will seldom be stated, executors were usually close relatives, though an executor *qua creditor* was

simply someone to whom the deceased owed enough money. Cautioners (also, usually, relatives) were also appointed, to make sure the executors did their jobs properly.

Sometimes, the deceased had written a "latterwill" (also called will or "legacie"), stating how their estate was to be distributed and appointing executors. If so, the court would produce a "testament testamentar." If the deceased had not left written instructions, then the court would produce a simple testament dative, appointing executors.

Latterwills could include instructions regarding burial, but their main purpose was the disposal of the estate. Since 1868, Scots have been able to bequeath both their moveable possessions and heritable possessions (land, buildings and minerals in the ground). Before 1868, and unlike the rest of the British Isles, heritable possessions passed down through the family according to strict and generally unalterable rules: where there was one, the eldest son succeeded to the land, regardless of the father's wishes. The latterwill, therefore, could only be used to bequeath moveable possessions and even this power of disposal was limited.

Movable possessions left over after tax (cases where tax exceeded value are described *debita bona excedunt*) were called free gear. This was divided, a third to the spouse (*jus relictae*), a third to the children (*legitum*) and a third to the *deid's part*. If, on the other hand, the spouse had died, or there was a spouse but no children, then half the estate became the *deid's part*, and if there were no spouse or children, then there was *na division* and everything was the *deid's part*. It was the *deid's part* alone that could be bequeathed by a latterwill.

If there was no will, the *deid's part* was shared between the spouse and children; in the cases of *na division*, the siblings or other relatives could claim shares from the executors.

Searching the records: All testaments are indexed up to 1901 on ScotlandsPeople, which almost entirely supersedes the old published indexes and greatly simplifies the work of searching. The site's only drawback is with married women: when a woman is recorded "Jean Hamilton wife of Robert McKenzie," the old printed indexes would index her under Hamilton and McKenzie, but ScotlandsPeople will have her as Hamilton alone. In its favour, the site allows you to see all results for a surname for free, making it easy to find ancestors, and to spot collaterals anywhere in Scotland. When researching the unusual surname Hooks, for example, the site revealed a branch of the family I had never encountered before.

How to search

Under "wills and testaments" on the ScotlandsPeople site, you can select name, dates and court. To find out which court you need, choose "click here for more information" and then scroll down to the link to the courts map. This is actually a map of Scottish counties, but by clicking on it you are told which commissary and sheriff courts covered the county. You can then select the one that you want.

The system has its faults — according to the site, Dornoch sheriff court, covering Sutherland, only runs from 1799 up to 1824, yet in fact the testamentary documents revealed by specific searches run (as you would expect) up to 1901.

You can search by surname, title, place and occupation (there are no testaments of genealogists, I see, but several of heralds). You can limit results for common surnames by adding a forename or time-span, but don't forget that, while most testaments were made within a year of death, some could take years to be started or completed. You pay to view digitized images of specific documents.

The records, which start in 1513, come from Scotland's 22 commissary courts, of which the main one was that of Edinburgh (with records dating from 1514). The Edinburgh Commissary Court heard local cases, and also appeals from the others and cases for people who had died outside Scotland, or whose families came from all over the realm, who simply liked the social caché or convenience of having the business transacted in Edinburgh.

The Commissary Courts (Scotland) Act of 1823 abolished these courts and transferred their work to the sheriff courts. The period 1823-30 was one of somewhat confused transition, Edinburgh not ceasing to function until 1830. Some testaments in this period may appear in both a commissary and a sheriff court (and will thus appear twice on ScotlandsPeople). The Edinburgh Sheriff's Court also registered testaments for some Scots who died elsewhere.

The ScotlandsPeople search result for testaments by anyone called Hooks.

Forename	Date	Description	Type	Court
Alexander	14/06/1766	merchant in Wigtoun	Eiks (2)	Wigtown Commissary Court
Alexander	27/08/1825	victualler in Glasgow, spouse of Margaret McLeod	No Date of Recording. Mutual Settlement dated 27/08/1825	Glasgow Sheriff Court Wills
Alexander	01/09/1827	victualler at Glasgow	Inventory;	Glasgow Sheriff Court Inventories
Elizabeth	07/11/1901	or Shennan, Danevale, Parish of Crossmichael, Stewartry of Kirkcudbright, widow, d. 06/09/1901 at Danevale aforesaid, testate	Inventory only	Kirkcudbright Sheriff Court

Note that inventories for people dying outside Scotland are not online, but are in the Edinburgh Register of Inventories, SC70/10.

Other commissary court records: Sometimes, although a testament was never registered, you may find that the process of obtaining one had been started. The old commissary court records include edicts. These were published in the deceased's parish, announcing someone's death and the intention of the relatives or creditors to register a testament, asking anyone with claims on the estate to come forward.

Edicts curatory and edicts tutory concerned the appointment of guardians for children whose fathers had died: tutors looked after pupils (boys under 14 and girls under 12) and curators looked after minors (from those ages up to 21). Commissary court records can also include "processes" or records of testamentary cases, some of which, again, were never completed, and petitions made by heirs needing to auction (or *roup*) of goods immediately, in order to pay for the funeral or other pressing expenses, before the testamentary process was completed. When such records are found, they can be rich extra information for the family tree.

Some are easy to look for, especially those in Argyll, for which see F. Bigwood's *Argyll Commissary Court: A Calendar of Testaments, Inventories, Commissary Processes and Other Records, 1700-1825* (F. Bigwood, 2001: Flat B, The Lodge, 2 East Road, North Berwick, EH39 4HN).

Testaments after 1901: ScotlandsPeople does not currently include testaments after 1901. For 1902-59, search in the printed annual calendars of confirmations and inventories, copies of which are in the NAS's Historical Search Room and in larger Scottish libraries. After 1959, the series continues on microfiche in the Legal Search Room. These include Scots living outside Scotland. After 1985, and up to 10 years ago, all testaments, inventories and confirmations from sheriff courts can be viewed on microfilm (SC70/17). For testaments within the last 10 years, contact the Sheriff Clerk's Office, Commissary Section, Sheriff Court House, 27 Chambers Street, Edinburgh, EH1 1LB, 0131 225 2525, cru@scotcourts.gov.uk. Testaments for First and Second World War servicemen, plus a few pre-1914 and some for the period 1919-38 too, are in NAS SC70/8-10.

Entries in the Calendar of Confirmations and Inventories for 1883, including Rev. Colin Fisher Campbell, J.K. Rowling's Scottish great-great-grandfather.

CAMPBELL, Christina.

Value of Estate, £75, 13s. 1d.

11 September. — Confirmation of Christina Campbell, wife of John Campbell, Farmer, Sallachary, Kilmartin, who died 5 May 1883, at Sallachary, intestate, granted at **Inveraray,** to the said John Campbell, Executor dative *qua* husband.

CAMPBELL, Rev. Colin Fisher.

Value of Estate, £1,466, 2s. 11d.

1 February.—Confirmation of Rev. Colin Fisher Campbell, Minister, Parish of Kilbride, Island of Arran, County of Bute, who died 31 July 1882, at Lamlash, Arran, testate, granted at **Rothesay,** to Rev. Archibald Alexander Campbell, Minister, Parish of Crathie, Aberdeenshire, Executor dative *qua* next of kin.—Will or Deed, dated 1 June 1876, and recorded in Court Books of Commissariot of Bute, 31 January 1883.

CAMPBELL, David.

27 April.—Confirmation of David Campbell of Crofthead, Parish of Kilmaurs, who died 6 March 1883, at Crofthead

2. Cash in National County Savings Bank with interest thereon till date of affidavit per Bank Book No. 92486 £ 101. 1. 4

3. Principal Sum due under Promissory note granted by John Thomson Wearper Glasgow dated 26th November 1863 and payable on demand 100. —. —

4. Cash due to deceased by the River Carl Navigation Trust per Certificate of debt dated 6th June 1850 for one hundred and thirty six realised at four shillings per pound 27. 4. —

Part of a page from an inventory in a testament showing the sort of detail you may find.

Interpreting testaments: Not all the immediate family might be mentioned in a testament. If, for, example, goods or even property had already been settled on daughters when they married, they might not be mentioned in their father's testament. Eldest sons might not be left any movable goods because they were set to inherit the land. Also, be careful how you interpret not finding an ancestor's testament. You simply may not have looked under the right spelling. Surname spellings were standardized in the old printed indexes up to 1800, but not the online version. Also, many Scots who died outside Scotland had wills proved in their country of settlement and left no trace of testamentary process in Scotland.

Most Scots' houses were so small that they never owned enough moveable goods to warrant making a testament. Not even everyone of means had one, and some records do not survive — a fire at the Aberdeen Commissary Court means that its testaments go back no further than 1722. The digitized records include some warrants of testament, which were created prior to the testament itself. Normally of no use, some have been digitized where groups of testaments have not survived — but not all. If your missing testament was likely to have been at Aberdeen, Brechin, Kirkcudbright, St. Andrews, Stirling or Wigtown, and you are fairly sure there would have been one, it may be worth seeing what warrants are cataloged for

that court under class CC in the NAS catalog and searching them.

James Watt's testament

It was known (see p. 57) that James Watt, colliery overseer, died between 1849 and 1874. It was hoped that he may have had enough money to justify a testament. A search of testaments under "James Watt" in that period produced 45 "hits," which are free to examine. They included this:

33	Watt	James	29/ 04/ 1865	inderground overseer at Beueside near Airdrie, co of lanark	Glasgow I Sheriff Court Inventories	SC36/ 48/52	VIEW (PAID) (3 pages)

I paid my £5 and, after a wait, was able to view the document.

James's testament comprised an inventory and the appointment of William Watt, collier of Braeside, who, "*has entered or is about to enter upon the management of the deceased's estate as Executor dative qua next of kin of his said Father, nominated and appointed by the Commissary of the County of Lanark upon the 3rd day of February annent 1865.*" He was described as "*James Watt, Underground Overseer sometimes residing at West Meadowland, thereafter at Braeside near Airdrie in the County of Lanark,*" who had died, "*at Braeside aforesaid on the 8th day of December 1864.*" His "household furniture, body clothes and other effects" were valued at £20-19-6 (20 pounds, 19 shillings and six pence). He had life assurance with the Royal Insurance Company, taken out on October 29, 1857, payable three months after death, worth £100 with a premium of £4, less three months' interest, making the "Sum of the Inventory" £132-13-6. According to www.measuringworth.com/calculators/ppoweruk, that's about £9,228 in modern money. It's not an earth-shattering amount of information, but it adds a little more color to what we knew about James before, and was very helpful simply in identifying his date of death.

To learn more about Scotland's legal system, see G. Watson's *Bell's Dictionary and Digest of the Law of Scotland* (Edinburgh, 1882), D.M. Walker's *Legal History of Scotland* (Edinburgh, 1988–2001) and A.D. Gibb's *A Student's Glossary of Scottish Legal Terms* (Green, 1971).

High Court of Justiciary: This was the highest criminal court in Scotland, presided over by the Lord Justice General. Its cases often concerned crimes punishable by death or transportation that were too serious to be heard in the smaller "inferior courts," such as sheriff courts. It also heard appeals from these inferior courts.

Originally, the court just sat in Edinburgh, but from 1672 it also made two-yearly journeys, called justice ayres, to sit and administer justice around the country.

The paper trail may start in the kirk sessions, with "rogue money" raised from the parishioners for the expense of apprehending a villain. The Lord Advocate then decided whether to bring cases to trial (it was his junior, the Procurator Fiscal, who brought prosecutions to the sheriff courts). The Lord Advocate's records are well cataloged in the NAS website under NAS class AD. For example:

Ayr, one of the destinations of the coincidentally-named justices ayre. The Northern Circuit took the court to Perth, Aberdeen and Inverness, the Southern to Dumfries and Jedburgh, and the Western Circuit encompassed Stirling, Glasgow and Ayr. Argyll and the Isles had its own hereditary justiciarship until 1747, when Inverary became a further port-of-call in the Western Circuit. Cases were of two types: solemn trials were heard before judge and jury, and summary trials were heard by the judge alone.

Inland Revenue records: From 1796 you can also search Inland Revenue records in NAS class IR. These records were created for tax purposes and record how estates were actually distributed, and thus who was liable to pay tax on them. While not desperately easy to search, they can provide useful extra information; more details are given in the NAS guide.

Scotland's Courts

The new cataloging and indexing of Scotland's court cases means that a random search may reveal ancestors involved in all sorts of hitherto unsuspected shenanigans.

Ref No	Title	Date	Access Status
AD14/41/287	Precognition against Archibald MacPherson, for the crime of sheep-stealing	1841	Open

And in genteel Kirkintilloch:

| AD14/48/468 | Precognition against Andrew Watson for the crime of assault with intent to ravish | 1848 | Open |

Precognitions were the evidence given before the trial. The accused was summoned to court by an indictment (or "dittay") if he was in prison, or by criminal letters (or "libel") if the accused was at liberty. The trials themselves were in the High Court of Justiciary and its circuit courts, recorded in NAS class JC, again well cataloged. For example:

| JC26/1895/61 | Trial papers relating to William Crowley for the crime of bigamy at George Street, City, Glasgow. Tried at High Court, Glasgow | Feb 26, 1895 | Open |

The records are incredibly easy to search, and you never know what will turn up.

Incidentally, those awaiting trial, transportation or death might also be found in prison records, in NAS class HH (Home and Health Department records). Class HH11 covers the Edinburgh Tolbooth Warding and Liberation Books (1657-1816), some of which have been published in *Book of the Old Edinburgh Club* (vols 4-6, 8-9, 11-12 for 1657-86). HH12's Miscellaneous Prison

Records include details and even photographs of the unfortunate inmates at Greenock Prison (HH12/56/7; 1872-88), as you can see below.

Court of Session: This was Scotland's principal civil court, that grew originally out of the King's Privy Council. The Court of Session (CS) heard its own cases and also appeals from inferior courts, such as the sheriff courts. The records are in NAS class CS, amply cataloged online. For example:

CS258/13409	Janet I Low or Crowley v John H Crowley: Divorce	1946	Open

NAS's HH12 class includes photos of some of the miscreants, along with a description of their appearance and a note of where they were born.

Affairs of State

Lords admit the protestation.

The Lords, having on 12th October last granted a commission to the provost and bailies of Culros, Sir George Colvill of Cleish, Sir George Preston of Valafield, Mr Robert Colvill of Kynneddir, and James Aitkin of Middle Grange, or any three of them, for the trial of Margaret Huttoun, spouse of Edward Ezat, burgess of Culros, by an assize for witchcraft, ordaining them to report before pronouncing sentence, and their report being this day produced, showing that the said Margaret was convicted of the said crime at a justice court held by the said commissioners at the burgh of Culros on 25th October, ordain the said justices or any three of them to pronounce doom against her according to the laws of the kingdom and see the same put to execution.

"A Committee to meet with the borrowis and coalmaisters."

Sederunt :—Chancellor ; General ; Argile ; Mar ; Cassills ; Wems ; Angus ; Yester ; Elphinston ; Balmerino ; Balcarres ; Clerk Register ; Treasurer Depute ; Wauchtune ; Sir John Smith.

Margaret Hurroun of Culross, convicted of witchcraft, makes her unwilling way into history in the *Register of the Privy Council of Scotland* (vol. 8, 1554–1660, second series).

The Privy Council existed formally between 1489-1708 to help the king administer justice. The Register of the Privy Council of Scotland contains published abstracts, indexed, for 1545-1691, about all manner of business concerning many ordinary people.

Much information on Scotland's people lies in Parliamentary Papers, in the form of testimonies from named people, professional and ordinary, in reports on such matters as farming, prostitution, education and the poor — sadly, this is mostly hidden because it is unindexed. See J.A. Haythornthwaite's *Scotland in the Nineteenth Century: Analytical Bibliography of Material Relating to Scotland in Parliamentary Papers 1800-1900* (Ashgate, 1993).

Engraving of the judges of the Court of Session, second division, March 1832, showing the Rt. Hon. David Boyle, Lord Justice Clerk, flanked by (left) Lords Armadale, Woodhouse, Glenlee and (right) Meadowbank, Robertson and Gilling (from *The History of the Speculative Society 1764–1904*, T. & A. Constable, Edinburgh, 1905; courtesy of SoG).

Cases contain much genealogical information. In 1770, a boundary dispute between Harris and North Uist reached the Court of Session, where evidence was heard that,

"Rory MacLeod, grieve in Bernera, aged 54 years, depones that his grandmother by his mother's side was Mary MacLeod, alias Ninhormoid vic Ean vi Gillichalum [ie, daughter of Norman, son of John son of Malcolm], who died fifteen or sixteen years ago, above 100 years old; that upwards of thirty years ago she told the deponent that she could herd cattle when Sir Norman Macleod went to the battle of Worcester [1651]."

You will find processes, which are the writs and pleadings in the case, and productions, the evidence presented (cataloged separately under CS96). I have referred to CS cases elsewhere where they may prove useful to your research.

The record of a court of session case brought in 1812 by Mary Hogg, mantua maker of Edinburgh, against the musician Nathanial Gow for breach of promise.

Franchise courts: These courts resulted from landowners or officials being granted special jurisdiction over certain lands, often in the wilder areas where nobody else was available to maintain law and order. They included regalities, which have pretty much all the Crown's powers except trying treason; stewartries and bailiaries, which were royal lands in which the (usually hereditary) steward or bailie wielded the exclusive power normally held by a sheriff; baronies, presided over by the local laird, and birlaw courts that comprised an estate's tenants, with rather limited powers.

The franchise courts were abolished in 1747, save for the baronies, some of which continued on a reduced scale. Background research into your ancestral parishes will tell you if your ancestors may have been subject to a franchise court. If so, you can see if any relevant court records survive (including registers of deeds for all except the baronies) — some are at NAS (RH11), others are in sheriff courts or landowners' family papers (some of which are in GD), and a few are published (especially by SHS).

Admiralty courts: Admiralty courts dealt with civil and criminal law on the seas, from wrecks to mutinies and piracy to prizes. Scotland had a Lord High Admiral until the 1707 Act of Union, after which there was a Lord High Admiral of Great Britain.

Lawyers

Tarbolton, Ayrshire. *Born* 16 August 1887. On Recruiting Staff: Lieutenant Territorial Force Reserve in Great War.

PATERSON, JOSEPH   23 May 1808

Apprentice to George Robinson.—Youngest son of George Paterson, Merchant in East Sheen, Surrey. *Born* 1778. *Died* 16 February 1832, unmarried.

PATERSON, ROBERT

See WALLACE, ROBERT PATERSON.

PATERSON, THOMAS   14 July 1859

Apprentice to Adam Paterson.—Son of John Paterson, Agent Royal Bank of Scotland at Dalkeith. *Born* 11 July 1834. *Married* (1) 16 July 1902, Mary Campbell Craig (*died* 8 May 1905); and (2) 30 January 1907, Alice (*died* 14 March 1923), third daughter of John Mortimer, Elland, Brodie, Forres. *Died* 13 May 1911.

PATERSON, TOM SMITH   12 March 1893

Apprentice to A. W. Black and A. L. Menzies.—Son of John Thomas Scott Paterson, Farmer, Plean, Bannockburn. *Born* 23 July 1869. *Married* 21 July

Details of Patersons who became Writers to the Signet.

The law was a popular choice for younger sons of landed families who had to earn a living, and for sons of merchants wanting to join the Establishment. Lawyers are easy to trace from 1848 onwards in the *Scottish Law Lists* (first published as *Index Juridicus*).

Writers (the equivalent of modern solicitors) were lawyers who pleaded cases in the inferior courts, such as sheriff courts. Some can be traced through apprenticeship records (see p. 121).

Writers to the Signet ("W.S.") were lawyers who had joined the College of Justice (founded by King James V in 1531/2). H. McKechnie's *History of the Society of Writers to H.M. Signet* (Signet Library, 1890) lists many members between 1595 and 1890, with details of apprenticeships and usually fathers' names, and is followed by *The Register of the Society of Writers to the Signet* (1983).

Strictly speaking, **Advocates** were writers who could plead at the Court of Session and House of Lords. Sir F. Grant's *Faculty of Advocates 1532–1943* (SRS) contains useful details of their family origins. However, the term "advocate" was also used by writers in Aberdeen — see J. Henderson's *History of the Society of Advocates in Aberdeen* (New Spalding Club, 1912).

Judges (or "senators") who sat in the Court of Session are listed in G. Brunton and D. Haig's *An Historical Account of the Senators of the College of Justice* (Edinburgh, 1832).

Notaries Public (who, before the Reformation, were generally clerics) were found in the burghs. Their records are in NAS class NP. There are incomplete registers of admission of notaries 1563–1903, and warrants of admission in NP2–NP6, some giving ages and fathers' names. They recorded such things as sasines (see pp. 132–3) and deeds.

T. Maley and W. Elliot's *Selkirk Protocol Books 1511–47* (Stair Society, 1993) reveals much interesting detail about the doings of my own Paterson ancestors. My 18th-century five x great-grandparents were John Paterson and Elizabeth Scott of Selkirk. It is interesting to read that back on Apri 7,l 1535, Robert Patersone, Bartholomew Andersone and Archibald Broun "asked instrument" — in other words, wanted a notary's record — that Alexander Scot of Paliss near Ashkirk had forgiven "all charges, debts or harmful words against him by the said Robert, Bartholomew and Archibald" and had promised "never to repeat the same in law or outside the law." On another occasion, April 6, 1536, Thomas Scott and [blank] Patersone met about noon at the "mercat cross of the burgh of Selkirk" to ask pardon from John Scott "regarding the slander on the same Thomas and [blank] Patersone regarding sheep stealing."

Every port would have an army of workers like these girls who would gut the catch before it was packed.

The main Admiralty court sat in Edinburgh; for this see S. Mowat and E. Graham's *The High Court of Admiralty of Scotland, 1627–1750* (2005) on CD from Early Scottish Maritime Exchange ESME **www.maritime-scotland.org.uk**. Under this sat several smaller Vice Admiralty courts, scattered around the coast at Caithness, East Fife, Kirkcudbright, St. Andrews, Logan and Clanyard (Wigtownshire) and Inverary. The latter was the Court of Argyll and the Isles, with jurisdiction from Dumbarton Castle right up to Cape Wrath, whose deeds, processes and bonds of caution 1685–1825 have been so admirably covered by Frank Bigwood's *The Vice-Admiral*

Fishing has always been a crucial part of life for many Scots. These fishermen in the 1930s or '40s are gaffing or hooking halibut using a mechanical line-hauler (on the right).

Court of Argyll (Frank Bigwood, 2001), now available on CD (along with many of Argyll's other court records). The processes, for example, contain a case from 1752 when the sailors of the *Betty* of Airth, carrying wood from Norway to Glasgow, mutinied at Inverary and refused to sail further. The master, John McConochy, had them summoned before the Vice-Admiral court, where they were ordered to complete the voyage to Glasgow, the court also helping master and crew agree in advance a fair wage for them.

The records are in NAS class AC. From 1830, these courts' civil powers were removed, taking away some of their general appeal for researchers whose ancestors made their living on the waves.

Commissary courts: In the Middle Ages, the commissary courts of Scotland's Catholic bishops had the authority to register testaments, grant probate and try cases of irregular marriage, legitimacy, annulment, slander and any contract made under oath. Three years after episcopacy was scrapped in 1560, the commissary courts were revived to act as civil courts responsible for the same matters. They continued thus until their work was taken over by sheriff courts in 1823. The main commissary court was in Edinburgh with subsidiary courts, one for each medieval diocese, and thus with some rather quirky boundaries and detached parts.

Sheriff courts and other courts of other local officials: In the early days, sheriffdoms were hereditary, but after 1747 most officeholders were trained lawyers, termed sheriff deputes.

Through sheriff courts, sheriffs exercised considerable power in running the county. This was increased in 1823, when they were given control of the local commissary court business,

Known as "the Exemplification," this is the formal letter sent to the Parliament of Scotland by the English Government to announce that the Articles of Union had been approved by the English Parliament in 1707. The Union led to many functions of government being transferred from Edinburgh to London and thus caused some important changes in the nature of the resulting records.

and in 1830 when they took over the Admiralty courts. They continue to this day.

Sheriff court records are all at NAS in class SC, except those for Orkney and Shetland, which are still in those islands. Each sheriff court had a repertory of different records, of which the most useful for us are registers of deeds, protests, services of heirs (see p. 129) and commissary records. These divisions are indicated in the NAS catalog.

Besides the sheriffs, there were several other wielders of local power. Commissioners of supply were appointed from among local landowners between 1667 and 1889, to collect cess (land tax). You may encounter their records at the NAS and in local council records. From the 18th century each county had a lord lieutenant who oversaw the raising of militias, and whose records sometimes turn up in sheriff court or burgh records. Justices of the peace were instituted by James VI in 1587, and abolished in 1975. They exercised criminal and civil authority in the shires, with a brief covering poaching, local crime, vagrancy, debt, raising

local militias, recruiting for the army, looking after roads and bridges, debt, licensing those making spirits and tracking down those without licenses. Their records are divided between the NAS (class JP) and local archives. Searching the records is usually a "lucky dip," but elsewhere in this book I have identified circumstances in which their records may come in useful.

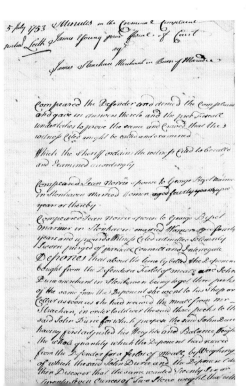

Minutes from a sheriff court held in 1753, hearing a case against a merchant, James Strachan, for giving short measure. The procurator fiscal of the court is named, as are people complaining against the defendant, making these very interesting family history records.

PART 3

How they lived

Scotland in the past was a predominantly rural country, and most of our Scottish ancestors earned their living off the land. Others, however, were prosperous merchants or craftsmen living in the towns or burghs. This section will give you an understanding of the ways your ancestors lived, and will also point you in the direction of the many records that were created by what people did.

A piper and bandsman of the Seaforth Highlanders.

CHAPTER 10

What people did

Knowing what ancestors did for a living makes them easier to envisage as real people, rather than just names. In many cases their work, whether in a high-flying profession or in subsistence farming, generated records that you can use to find out more about them and who their ancestors were.

There are several published biographical dictionaries for many of the highest skilled trades (such as clockmakers) and the professions. For architects, for example, there is H.A. Colvin's *A Biographical Dictionary of British Architects 1600–1840* (Yale University Press, third ed., 1995), A. Felstead, J. Franklin and L. Pinfield's *Dictionary of British Architects 1834–1900* (Mansel Publishing, 1993) and the *Dictionary of Scottish Architects* at **www.codexgeo.co.uk/dsa/index.php**.

If your ancestor had a distinctive job, it is worth exploring the catalog of the NLS to see what may be available. In many cases D.R. Torrance's *Scottish Trades, Professions, Vital Records and Directories* (Scottish Association of Family History Societies, 1998) is helpful for finding records here and elsewhere.

Old occupational terms can be confusing to modern ears. A shoemaker is obvious, but cordiners (the Scots form of cordwainer) were so-called because they made boots and shoes from superior leather, originally leather from Cordoba, Spain. Another uncommon term is hecklemakers, who made heckles, which were toothed combs that were used to separate flax to make fibres for spinning. A list of what old occupations mean is at **www.scotsfamily.com/occupations.htm**.

Agriculture

See chapters 12 and 13 on landowners and tenants.

Armed Forces: the Army

In ancient Scotland men were summoned to arms, whether by the king, his feudal lords or

Neil Kennedy, laborer from Kilmanmay, Inverness, aged 23, described as 5'6" high with a fair complexion, fair hair and blue eyes, enlists in the Northern Fencibles, commanded by the Duke of Gordon, on April 9, 1793 and is sworn in on May 10 to serve King and Country.

the clan chiefs, by men running from settlement to settlement carrying a burning cross. The names of the men who responded to this call are not recorded. Similar militias were raised in the wars of the 17th century but for them NAS Exchequer series E100 contains 4,800 rolls, the earliest starting in 1641. These contain so many names that you can seldom be sure an "Alexander MacGregor" is the one you need. Later militia lists for the Napoleonic Wars can include useful details of payments to militia men's families — see the NAS Military Source List at **www.nas.gov.uk/guides/**.

C. Dalton's *The Scots Army*, 1661–88 (repr. Greenhill Books, 1989) transcribed some rolls, the focus being mainly on officers. It includes officers' commissions found in State Papers: for 1688-1714 see Dalton's badly-named *English Army Lists and Commission Registers, 1661–1714* (Eyre & Spottiswoode, 1892-1904).

The yeomanry or volunteer corps could be raised by the justices of the peace in case of invasion. From 1797, the Scottish Militia Act arranged for militias to be raised by a ballot of able-bodied men aged 18 and 45 (with some exceptions — those who did not want to serve could pay for someone else to go in their stead), except schoolmasters and men with more than two children aged under 10. Their records, in local archives, are best sought using A. Morrison's *Some Scottish Sources on Militias, Fencibles and Volunteers* (A. Morrison, 1996) and J. Gibson and M. Medlycott's *Militia Lists and Musters, 1757–1876* (FFHS, 1994). They are worth a shot if you are stuck, as the records (attestations) list age, occupation and birth-parish, and sometimes include personal remarks. Wives of enlisted men sometimes applied for dependant allowances, giving children's names and ages.

From 1707, many Scotsmen served in Scottish regiments of the British Army. Army records are

A kilted soldier of the Queen's Own Cameron Highlanders.

in TNA, Kew, in department WO (War Office). For sons of crofting or cottar families, joining the army meant escape from the tedium of subsistence farming and the tyranny of landlords, and provided a guaranteed pension and a chance to see the world. In the Napoleonic Wars of the late 18th century up to 1815, great numbers of young Scots were enlisted. In the Highlands, chiefs wishing to demonstrate their loyalty to the Crown went to great lengths to encourage their tenants to join up — the Duchess of Gordon went among her clansmen with six pipers, offering a guinea and a kiss to each recruit. The Countess of Sutherland pretty much ordered 500 young men from her tenantry to join the Sutherland Highlanders — they obeyed, little suspecting she would repay their loyalty with the Highland Clearances.

A piper and officer of the 92nd Regiment of Foot.

The specifically Highland regiments start with the Black Watch, created in 1739, followed by Loudoun's Highlanders in 1745, and Montgomery's (77th) and Fraser's (78th) Highland Regiments in 1757, and so on, officered by junior kinsmen and tacksmen (see pp. 137-8) of the chief. The idea was to drain potentially troublesome young warriors away from the Highlands, and harness their energies in Empire-building. After Culloden, the only Scots allowed to play bagpipes and wear tartan were those in the Highland regiments — ironically, as these were raised on a geographical basis, they thus preserved clan identities at the very time when the Government was trying to stamp them out. Numbers involved were substantial: 65,000 Scots were soldiers in 1763, mostly Highlanders. Between 1797 and 1837 Skye alone provided some 700 officers, 10,000 men and 120 pipers to the British Army, and half the farms there were rented by officers on half pay.

Besides the regular regiments, there were fencible (homeland defence) regiments of full-time volunteers raised by landowners between 1759 and 1799, some serving in Scotland or England but more often in Ireland (see **www.regiments.org/regiments/uk/lists/fen1793.htm**). Records are in J.M. Bulloch's *Territorial Soldiering in the North-East of Scotland During 1759-1814* (New Spalding Club, 1914).

The army took Scots all over the British Empire. When their service ended, many chose to remain where they were stationed. As regiments were often recruited in specific places, knowing a soldier-migrant's ancestors can help pinpoint their place of origin. Equally, ancestors who you know merely as farmers may have spent their youth in uniform, serving in Africa or India — local histories will indicate which local regiment(s) there were and a speculative search may reveal your forbear. Regimental museums are worth exploring — details can be found online and are listed in T. and S. Wise's *A Guide to Military Museums and Other Places of Military Interest* (Athena, 2001), and *Exploring Scottish History* (M. Cox, ed., Scottish Library Association, 1999). A visit to the National War Museum in Edinburgh Castle is also worthwhile. A good summary of the Highland regiments is in the back of F. Adam, *The Clans, Septs, and Regiments of the Scottish Highlands,* (1908, rev. ed., Sir T. Innes of Learney, 1970).

Officers: Until the 20th century, officers — from generals down to second lieutenants — were almost entirely from the middle and upper classes. C. Dalton's *George the First's army 1714-27* (Eyre & Spottiswoode, two vols, 1910-12) covers the period to 1727. From 1740 there have been regular *Army Lists*, with basic details of all officers. TNA has much documentation on officers, the main being "services of officers on

A Scotsman at war

Allen Holford Walker (1890–1949) was the maternal nephew of John McAusland Denny of Dumbarton, MP for Kilmarnock and a colonel of the 91st Argyll and Sutherland Highlander Regiment. Allen joined this regiment as a junior officer in 1909, and in May 1915 he sailed with his men for Flanders

Allen kept and illustrated a diary that displays a considerable sense of humor, despite the dangers and physical hardships endured as his regiment approached and finally garrisoned the Front Line near Festubert and Le Plantin. For example, on June 15, 1915 he wrote: *"Saw some signal bombs fired. One rather humorously never burst & fell on or near Lumsden's head. The other burst & stars fell among the horses & caused a stampede. We have been told to hold ourselves in readiness to move at 6 a.m. tomorrow."*

Soon afterwards, however, Allen was wounded. His granddaughter Siân Ahlås told me that, preparing for an attack on German lines, Allen *"had instructed his troops to attack anyone wearing trousers, as his Scottish Regiment were all kilt wearers. However, he apparently tore his kilt and had to wear his tartan trousers. Unfortunately, an over zealous soldier came across him in the dark and duly attacked!"*

Allen became one of the pioneers of tank warfare, a key factor in the eventual British victory over Germany.

(Top) **Allen Holford Walker, and his sketch of a Sutherland Highlander.**

(Bottom) **Allen (left) and Archie (right) with their brother Leslie. Miraculously, all three survived the First World War (pictures courtesy of Mrs. Siân Ahlås).**

the active list" in series WO 25 and 76, partially indexed, dating back to 1829 and in some cases to 1764, including age and place of birth. Records of WW1 officers are indexed at **www.catalogue.nationalarchives.gov.uk**.

Other ranks: Non-officers' service records from 1760 to 1854 are indexed at **www.catalogue. nationalarchives.gov.uk**, through which the records themselves can be sought. Because records are generally arranged by regiment, it is best, for soldiers after 1854, to try to discover their regiment from a mention elsewhere, such as the birth record of a child, or pension records. Besides service records, you can also use muster rolls, pay lists (a few of which go back to 1708) description books (some back to 1754) and records of casualty, desertion, attestation, discharge, prisoners of war and pensions, which were paid through Chelsea (London).

Army births, marriages and deaths: see p. 45. Do bear these in mind — a family you may have encountered as civilians may well have started with the marriage of a soldier — anywhere in the world.

First and Second World War: many Other Ranks' service papers were blown up, but some two million are still extant so it's always worth searching for an ancestor here. The many published memorials include the *National Roll of the Great War 1914-18* (National Publishing Company, 14 vols, 1918-21), containing information on about 150,000 men. All British Army First and Second World War armed forces deaths are indexed by the GRO, London, online at **www.findmypast.com**. Deaths, war graves and war memorials are indexed by the Commonwealth War Graves Commission at **www.cwgc.org**.

Scotsman James H. Petrie, pictured here, wrote home from the Western Front in the First World War, "observe the beautiful countryside around. We drill ankle deep in mud."

Medal rolls: these tell you by implication the campaigns in which men served, and are in TNA series WO 372. Those for the First World War, partially substituting those service records that are lost, are online at **www.documentsonline. nationalarchives.gov.uk**.

The Royal Air Force

This was formed in 1918 by amalgamating the Army's Royal Flying Corps and the Navy's Royal Naval Air Service, founded in 1912 and 1914 respectively, all with records in TNA. See W. Spencer, *Air Force Records for Family Historians* (PRO, 2002) and the RAF Museum for more information.

Royal Marines

Established by Charles II in 1665 to serve as soldiers on navy ships, they fall into three divisions: Chatham, Plymouth and Portsmouth. Records are in department ADM at TNA, in whose Research Enquiries Room is a card index to most attestation forms (ADM 157/1-659). See G. Thomas, *Records of Royal Marines* (PRO Publications, 1994). Also useful is the Royal Marines Museum, Eastney Barracks, Southsea, PO4 9PX, 0239 281 9385, **www.royalmarinesmuseum.co.uk**.

Royal Navy

For the 17th century, see J. Grant's *The Old Scots Navy 1689-1710* (London, 1904) and the Admiralty Court records (see p. 98). From 1707, many Scotsmen appear in the (British) Royal Navy's records at TNA in department ADM (Admiralty). See B. Pappalardo, *Tracing Your Naval Ancestors* (TNA, 2003) and N.A.M. Rodger, *Naval Records for Genealogists* (PRO Publications, third ed., 1998) and if possible visit the National Maritime Museum, London.

Officers: commissioned officers (from admiral down to lieutenant) between 1660 to 1845 are outlined in:

- J. Charnock, *Biographia Navalis, or Impartial Memoirs of the Lives and Characters of Officers of the Navy of Great Britain* (vols 1-4 and supplemental vols 1-2 by R. Faulder 1794-98).

- J. Marshall, *Royal Naval Biography* (Longman, Hurst, Rees, Orme & Brown, 1823-35).
- W.R. O'Byrne, *A Naval Biographical Dictionary* (John Murray, 1849, repr. 1861).
- *Navy Lists*, published from 1782.
- *The Naval Who's Who 1917*, covering many First World War officers.

Officers' service papers and other records are at TNA.

Ratings: until 1853, non-officers were only employed, sometimes against their will, per voyage, so can be very hard to locate in ships' musters — if you can't guess the ship, you may not find them. From 1853 to 1923 they appear in "continuous service engagement books," fully indexed in ADM 188/245-7 and now indexed on **www.nationalarchives.gov.uk/**, which give dates and places of birth. Muster rolls in ADM 36-9 (1740-1808, with a few back to 1688) can lead you from ship to ship, and will tell you age and place of birth from 1764, together with other details such as tobacco and clothing allowances. Pay books, seamen's effects and papers, medal rolls, description books and pension records can also be consulted at TNA. Pensions were paid through the Chatham Chest (records from 1653-7 and 1675-1799) and then through the Royal Naval Hospital, Greenwich.

The Merchant Navy

The term "merchant navy" covers all the British ships not in the Royal Navy. The best guide is C. and M. Watts, *My Ancestor was a Merchant Seaman* (third ed., SoG, 2004). Records are in TNA department BT (Board of Trade). There are some muster rolls from 1747, but most are from the mid-19th century. Records are generally arranged by port, making them very hard to

Lochinver was one of several Highland port-towns developed in the 19th century to promote fishing as a way for people cleared from their farms to make a living. William Young, the Sutherlands' estate factor, hoped Lochinver would be the "metropolis" of Assynt.

Trinity House

A.J. Camp, *The Trinity House Petitions: A Calendar of the Records of the Corporation of Trinity House, London, in the Library of the SoG* (SoG, 1987) details applications made to the Trinity House charity from 1787–1854 by needy ex-sailors and their families from both the Royal and Merchant Navies.

search except between 1835–1857, which are indexed in the "registers of seamen," BT 120, 112, 119 and 114, leading straight to crew lists (BT 98), which give age and place of birth. BT 114 can also be used to look up "seamen's tickets" (1845–53) which include date and place of birth. After 1857, searching reverts to being very hard, until 1913–41, which is covered by a Central Index Register of Seamen at TNA.

A great deal of merchant naval material, including many post-1861 crew lists, can now be found at the Maritime History Archive, Newfoundland, Canada (**www.mun.ca**), which offers an online search service. Those who died at sea between 1852–1889 are indexed in BT 154.

Further records to search include ships' log books. Many boys and men were trained for the merchant navy by the Marine Society, whose indexed registers 1772–1950 are at the National Maritime Museum, Greenwich. Medals awarded to merchant seamen who served in the Second World War (some 100,000 of them) are now searchable online at **www.documentsonline. nationalarchives. gov.uk**.

From 1845 (and compulsorily from 1850), new merchant navy captains (masters) and second-in-commands (mates) could obtain a "certificate of competency." Including year and place of birth, the records are indexed in BT 127. Other records of them include a list covering 1868–1947, giving date and place of birth, in Lloyd's Marine Collection at Guildhall Library, London.

Between 1752–1796, bounties were paid to encourage "buss fishing," which entailed catching herring using vessels with proper decks, weighing between 20 and 80 tons. E508/49/9–96/9 at the NAS contains records of the payments, listing the whole crew, their parish of birth, height and hair color. Similar bounties for whaling 1750–1825 are in

Bringing the whales ashore at Olna, Shetland, in 1911. Today it is a very small rowing boat to be dragging such a large catch.

E508/47/8–130/8, with ship owners identified in E5021.

David Dobson's *"The Mariners of ..."* series, published in St. Andrews in various volumes covering much of the Scottish coast, reports several sources' details of mariners such as: *"LOVE, John, master of the* Happy Return *of Greenock, 1710 (CTB.24.297),*

LYAL, Robert, master of the brig Sisters *of Greenock, 1786 (SRO.CE60.11.10),*

MCALLISTER, John, skipper, son of John McAllister shoemaker, burges of Dunbarton, 1784 (DnBR)."

Clergy
See chapter 8.

Coalminers
Many records of the old mining companies that were nationalized under the National Coal Board are in NAS class CB. These include some wages books and pay books (mainly 20th century) and some records of company-run insurance plans.

Customs and Excise
Ancestors involved with the sea may appear in Exchequer records of customs dues collected at ports, dating from the 1300s. Various accounts are in NAS E71–E74 (1498–1707). Collectors' quarterly accounts (E504, 1742–1830) list ships entering or leaving port, naming the master and owners.

Customs officers were also called "tidewaiters," for they waited on the tides that brought in ships bearing taxable goods. Their reports are in NAS CE51–87, and mention many names of local people in the ports. If your ancestor was a customs officer, then more can be found on them in NAS class CE3 (catalog) and CE12 (establishment books), both 1707–1829, and E502 (salaries).

1764, Oct. 20.—From collector and comptroller. We have received your letter of the 15th ult., acquainting us that your honours had received undoubted information that large quantities of rum and tea were to be smuggled from the Isle of Man, at Troon, Heads of Ayr, or Turnberry, when the nights were dark and favourable for the purpose, and therefore directing us, and all the officers under our direction, to exert ourselves upon that occasion, and to inform you of our proceedings.

We beg leave to acquaint your honours that, in obedience to your said order, we and all the other officers have used our utmost endeavours to disconcert the smugglers in the execution of their intended fraud, and that notwithstanding thereof, no seizure has been made by any of us since the receipt of that order, excepting four kegs of rum, by John Harper, tidesman; that the said four casks of spirits are part of a wherry, and of a boat's cargo, directly from the Isle of Man, and landed at the Troon yesterday, and the whole of the spirits and a parcel of tea, &c., conveyed into the country before the said John Harper, and Robert M'Clure, and Andrew Crawfurd, tidesmen, could make up to the smugglers. That John Harper was cut and much abused by sundry cadgers and carriers, supposed to have come from Glasgow and the country adjoining, whose names are unknown to him and the other tidesmen. That the said officers were so much obstructed in the execution of their duty, and threatened by

Excise officers, including Robert Burns, collected dues and sought out those trying to evade paying them. Details of salaries are in NAS E502; also useful are J.F. Mitchell's notes on excisemen 1770–1830, on microfiche in the NAS searchroom. Burns' own poem about excisemen tells us exactly what they were there to prevent:

"The De'li cam fiddling thro' the town,
And danced awa wi' the Exciseman;
And ilka wife cried 'Auld Mahoun,
We wish you luck o' your prize, man.'

We'll mak our maut, and brew our crink,
We'll dance, and sign, and rejoice, man;
And mony thanks to the muckle black De'il
That danced awa wi' the Exciseman."

Doctors
In the Middle Ages, Scotland boasted a rabble of chirurgeons, apothecaries and barbers (who doubled, terrifyingly, as surgeons). Later medics

Life as a tidewaiter was seldom dull, as is revealed by these reports from Irvine, Co. Ayr, published in James Paterson's History of the County of Ayr, with a Genealogical Account of the [landowning] Families of Ayrshire, *two vols (Thomas George Stephenson, 1853; courtesy of SoG).*

who had studied the subject often appear in the university alumni lists, and those who were qualified can be sought in the records of the Royal College of Physicians of Edinburgh (9 Queen Street, Edinburgh, **www.rcpe.ac.uk**), dating from 1681; the Royal College of Surgeons of Edinburgh (Nicolson Street, Edinburgh, EH8 9DW, **www.rcsed.ac.uk**), from 1505; and the Royal College of Physicians and Surgeons of Glasgow (234–42 St Vincent Street, Glasgow G2 5RJ, 0141 227 3234, **www.rcpsglasg.ac.uk/ archives.htm**), from 1599. Many "doctors" were very poorly qualified, some having attended a few series of lectures at university, or read a bit about the subject — but even this was not compulsory. Having said that, Scottish education produced many very good doctors, whose work was appreciated around the globe.

An excellent secondary source for doctors, dentists and midwives is P.J. and R.V. Wallis' *Eighteenth Century Medics (Subscriptions, Licenses, Apprenticeships)*, part of the Project for Historical Geography Research Series (1994). Registration of medics started in 1858 with *The Medical Register*, which was then published annually, listing medics, with their address and qualifications (leading you back to the records of the professional bodies). There is also the *Medical Directory for Scotland 1852–60*, which became *The London and Provincial Medical Directory 1861–9*, then *The Medical Directory*.

There are similar annual lists of chemists (from 1869), dentists (1879), midwives (from 1917) and nurses (from 1921) in good libraries. Records of nurses 1885–1930 are in NAS HH2/33–7. If your ancestor was treated in hospital, there might be records of their treatment. These are best sought through **www.scan.org.uk** under the keywords "health" and "health boards."

Freemasons

Freemasonry has dual roots — in groups searching for esoteric knowledge and in lodges of working masons. By the 18th century, it had evolved into a form of Friendly Society whose main roles were social and charitable. Lodges proliferated in Scotland, and membership lists appear in Justice of the Peace records. Some lodge records are in archives and most others are with the lodges, who are now reasonably well disposed towards researchers. But the records will often merely confirm that an ancestor was a freemason and tell you no more, making them rather unrewarding as genealogical sources.

Government officials

An incomplete list of these, with salary and pension details, is in "civil and judicial establishment 1707–1830" (ref. 332) in the NAS Historical Search Room.

Industrial workers

As the 1700s and 1800s progressed, many people were drawn off the land and into the industrial towns, so that by the 1840s, almost a third of Scots no longer worked on the land.

Workers might change industry seasonally, laboring, say, as brickmakers in the summer

Scene in a Scottish hospital in about the 1920s (courtesy of the Crowley Family Collection).

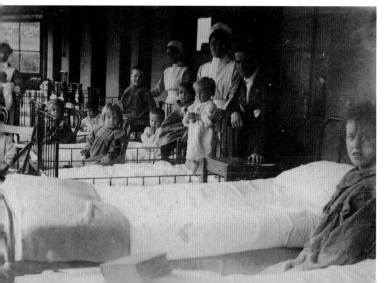

and in the gasworks in the winter. Business records can be sought through **www.scan.org.uk** and through I. MacDougall, *Labour Records in Scotland* (Edinburgh, 1978), which should include Friendly Societies and other organizations aimed at mutual help. Factories treated their employees as day-laborers, so few records were kept; those that exist usually just give names, and perhaps how much was paid. However, if you have time and inclination, they may repay close examination.

Industrial accidents, especially those in the mines, were investigated by sheriff courts and reported in local newspapers. Those many industrial workers who fell on hard times may be chronicled in the records of poor relief (see p. 143).

Innkeepers

From 1756 onwards, anyone selling alcohol had to have a licence from the burgh, if they were in one, or else from the local justice of the peace.

Jacobites

Some lists of rebels who fought on the Stuart side in the 1715 and 1745 rebellions, and in other rebellions such as the Duke of Argyll's in 1685,

are in *Register of the Privy Council of Scotland*, which is printed and indexed from 1545–1691. Names of some 1715 rebels are in the lists made by James Campbell of Stonefield, Sheriff Depute of Argyll, published in N. Maclean-Bristol's *Inhabitants of the Inner Isles, Morvern and Ardnamurchan, 1716* (SRS, 1998). The 1745 rising is better documented. A. Livingstone, C. Aikman and B. Hart (eds.)'s *No Quarter Given — The Muster Roll of Prince Charles Edward Stuart's Army 1745–6* (Aberdeen University Press, 1984) and B. Seton and J. Arnot (eds.)'s *Prisoners of the '45* (SHS, 1928–9) are worth searching. In 2008 the Culloden visitor center **www.nts.org.uk/ Culloden/PPF/Legacy** invited children descended from participants in both sides of that battle to send in their family trees.

Literati

The John Murray Archive **www.nls.uk/jma/ index.html** has over 150,000 items concerning people involved in "literature, science, politics, travel and exploration" between 1768 and 1920.

Lawyers

See p. 99.

LEFT: **Workmen cutting granite in a quarry at Rubislaw, Aberdeen in 1910.**

TOP RIGHT: **The co-operative tailoring factory in Glasgow, crowding the workers in even though it is a co-op.**

BOTTOM RIGHT: **Drawing whisky from its huge casks at the Johnnie Walker Whisky blending plant. However big or small the distillery, most whisky-making tasks have been the same for centuries.**

Shipbuilding

TOP: **An aerial view of Scott's shipbuilding yard, Glasgow.** BOTTOM: **The ship-yards of Dumbarton today, sadly neglected and falling into disrepair.**

Shipwrights at work building the *Queen Elizabeth* at John Brown's Yard, Clydebank. Launched in 1938, she was named after Elizabeth, wife of George VI, and was the largest liner ever built.

The west-coast Scots have always had a close relationship with the sea, right back from the days when their coracles plied the ancient Atlantic seaboard. Merchants created a constant demand for ships for foreign trade, which was met by small shipyards, particularly along the sheltered stretches of the Clyde leading from Dumbarton up into Glasgow. In the 19th century, as iron and steam began to replace wood and sail, Scotland's engineers gained a world-wide reputation for innovative shipbuilding. By 1850, half Britain's iron ships were being built on the Clyde, which, by 1880, was leading the way in steel technology, too. It was not until the 1920s that foreign competition started to dent

Scotland's supremacy — a brief resurgence after the Second World War (when the Clyde benefited from the wartime destruction of the German and Japanese yards) was followed by terminal decline.

Many shipbuilding firms' records are at Glasgow University, but shipyard workers are badly recorded. MacDonald's *Labour Records in Scotland* details some surviving material for shipyard workers and their Friendly Societies, and mentions their unions. Deposited shipping company records, accessible via www.scan.org.uk, may name your ancestors, but are more likely to be useful by giving background information on employers.

Peter Denny (1821–95), from *The Book of Dumbartonshire*. He is shown wearing two foreign decorations, awarded for his services to shipbuilding. His father William built sailing ships in Dumbarton, and Peter and his brothers graduated, with their century, to steam. The Dennys made a fortune for themselves, and helped turn Dumbarton from a tiny burgh into a flourishing industrial town. Many of the ships that connected Britain to her empire were built here, including the *Cutty Sark*, which was finished here in 1869. The key to Denny's success was his fair treatment of his workers, building them a "model" town, Denniestoun, and paying bonuses to anyone, however junior, who came up with innovative ideas. Sadly, shipbuilding has declined, and Dumbarton's glory-days seem to be in the past.

Lunatics

Asylums and madhouses (and their records) generally date from the mid-19th century, with records in the sheriff courts. From 1858, asylums were subject to the General Board of Commissioners in Lunacy, with records in NAS class MC. A "Return of lunatics or idiots at large in the county of Edinburgh" for 1850 is in NAS AD58/114. Also worth searching if you suspect a history of insanity in the family (and, let's face it, who doesn't?) is NAS JC54/13–41, containing reports naming lunatic paupers throughout Scotland. Holders of heritable land who were considered insane had their rights exercised by curators, who were appointed in retours.

Members of Parliament

All known members of the Scottish Parliament to 1707 are in M.D. Young's *The Parliaments of Scotland* (Edinburgh, 1992). From 1707, Scottish MPs at the House of Commons, Westminster, London, are included in *The History of Parliament*, Wedgwood House, 15 Woburn Square, London, WC1H 0NS, 0207 862 8800, www.irinfo.ac.uk/hop/, which currently covers MPs from 1386–1832 and Members of the House of Lords from 1660–1832.

Motorcar owners

Some local archives hold details of early car registration. Dundee Archives's records for Perthshire (1909–11) and Kinross-shire (1904–52) are online at www.fdca.org.uk/registrations.htm. For example:
"527 Mrs. Caroline F. Drummond Forbes, Millearne, Auchterarder, 14 hp Siddeley Side entrance Phaeton body, painted blue with white lines, [weight unladen] 19 cwt, [use] Private, [registered] 17 April 1909, [notes] Trans[ferred]. 23 Feb. 1911 to David Morgan Graham, Pitreuchie, Forfar. (Mar. 5 1912)."

Railwaymen

Scotland's many private 19th-century railway companies' records contain varying degrees of information about their staff (drivers, plate-layers, station masters and so on), though virtually nothing for unskilled employees and

Walter Hooks (1877–1968) with his motor car (courtesy of the MacLeod Family Collection).

the navvies who originally built the lines. NAS BR/RCH(S)/5 will help you guess, by location, which company may have employed your railway ancestors, and company records can then be sought in NAS class BR. For more help see T. Richards' *Was Your Grandfather a Railwayman?* (FFHS, 1989) and the NAS guide on **www.nas.gov.uk/guides/**.

Postmen

Post Office Establishment books date back to 1803 and are in NAS PO1/15–65 up to 1911. The detail staff in main Post Offices including letter carriers, though not sub-postmasters, but many of these were listed in directories.

Schools and Universities

Thanks to the Church of Scotland, all children aged five and upwards received basic education from the 17th century onward, though poor children could seldom afford to remain after eight, unless helped by bursaries.

There were no school holidays, but most children were let off to help their families during harvest time. Besides religious instruction, the schoolmaster (or *dominie*) taught reading and writing, with some Latin for older children, and only in the burghs did arithmetic feature strongly on the curriculum. All this contributed enormously towards forming the "serious-minded" Scottish character that made Lowland Scots natural leaders in the cultural enlightenment of the 1740s and the Industrial Revolution, bringing untold (and often unsung) benefits to Britain as a whole.

The *dominie* was appointed and paid by the kirk sessions or by the burgh. Burgh records contain records of hiring and firing — my probable relative John Paterson was fired from his job as schoolmaster of Selkirk in July 1613, accused by the Minister of being, "*insufficient both for reading, and teaching, and the counsel not liking him, he had been given warning at Candlemas.*" In the countryside, kirk sessions, the records of the heritors and local presbytery

Schoolboys and their *dominie* or master pose for a school photograph in the 1920s (courtesy of the Crowley Family Collection).

that confirmed the *dominie*'s appointment can be equally informative. Schoolmasters often doubled-up as kirk session clerks and later as census enumerators and registrars (for whose conduct see NAS GRO1). From 1847, your schoolmaster ancestor may have belonged to the Educational Institute of Scotland (see NAS GD342), and if he was a schoolmaster in Aberdeenshire, Banffshire and Morayshire from 1832 you can see if they received assistance from the James Dick Bequest Trust, in NAS GD1/4.

Secession churches often had their own schools and schoolmasters, detailed in their own records, and Catholic schools appeared after the 1829 *Catholic Emancipation Act*. In addition to parish schools, you may find "adventure schools," set up by private teachers who "[ad]ventured" their own money in the projects.

Scotland had some orphanages (called hospitals) funded by charitable endowments, particularly George Heriot's School, Edinburgh (NAS, GD421), Dean Orphanage (GD 417), Dr. Guthrie's Schools (GD425) and the Orphan Hospital (GD417). Their records can give names, ages and some information on the children's backgrounds. The *Statistical Accounts* usually refer to schools existing at the time.

State-run mass education was introduced to Scotland in 1872, taking schools away from church control and placing them under new school boards. While in England similar legislation brought education to the masses for the first time, in Scotland, in most cases, 1872 simply saw a small administrative change in an on-going system. The boards' records are divided between local archives and the NAS.

The Society in Scotland for Propagating Christian Knowledge (SSPCK) worked from 1709 to establish church schools to help eradicate "popery and ignorance" in the Highlands and Islands. NAS GD95 records its schoolmasters and school inspections: see also A.S. Cowper (ed), *SSPCK Schoolmasters, 1709-1872* (SRS, 1997).

From 1872 schools kept logbooks, some of which are now kept in local archives, not in the school. At best, though, the logbook will simply be a mere list of names. More interesting are leaving certificates ("highers"), listing each candidate's subjects, grades and marks, in NAS ED36 (arranged by parish), available from 1906 but closed for 75 years. In ED52, for fun, you can see reports on individual schools' meals from 1946.

Fee-paying schools generally keep detailed records of pupils, sometimes including ages and fathers' names. Some of these are published, such as those for Edinburgh Academy, Fettes College and Loretto School, and most also produced rolls of honor commemorating ex-pupils who died in the World Wars.

Scotland's education system produced many potential university students. The oldest universities are St. Andrews (1410), Glasgow (1451), Kings College, Aberdeen (1495), Marischal College, Aberdeen (1593) and Edinburgh (1582). Records of graduates of all but Edinburgh are published; the amount of genealogical information (ages, fathers' names and so on) varies. Many Scots also studied beyond Scotland, at Oxford and Cambridge, but more often in the Protestant universities in northern Europe.

Part of the 1809-13 intake of arts graduates at Marischal College, from J.P. Anderson (ed.), *Fasti Academiae Mariscallanae, Aberdonensis* (New Spalding Club, 1898). The footnotes indicate what some of them did later; in the entries themselves, "f" is for "filius," i.e. "son of."

Alexr. Stirling, f. Jacobi in Tyrie, agricolæ, Abdn.	b, s.
Alexr. Thomson,[11] f. Jacobi, advocati, Abredonen.	b, s, t, m, A.M.
Car. Crombie,[12] f. Alexandri, mercator., Abredon.	b, s, t, m, A.M.
Car. Farquharson, f. Roberti, pastoris de Coldstone, Abdn.	b, s, t, m, A.M.
Car. Ogg,[13] f. Alexandri, fabri ferrar., Abredonen.	b, s.
David Braick, f. Joannis, mercator. in Arbroath, Forfar.	b, s, t, m, A.M.
Geo. [Watson] Black,[14] f. Thomæ, pharmacop., Abredon.	b, s, t.
Geo. Cumine,[15] f. Jacobi dem., in Dysart, Fyfe.	b, s, t, m, A.M.
Gul. Brown,[16] f. Gulielmi, bibliopolae, Abredon.	b, s, t, m, A.M.
Gul. Cadenhead, f. Gulielmi in Hardgate, Abdn.	b, s, t, m, A.M.
Gul. Dawson,[17] f. Joannis in Rathven, Banff.	b, s.

[1] Surg., H.E.I.C.S.   [2] Rector of Woughton, Bucks; D.D., 1845.
[3] Surg., H.E.I.C.S.   [4] See 1792-96; Bishop, Brechin.   [5] Stud. of med.
[6] Sch., Aberd.   [7] Gray math. bursar, 1812; W.S., 1826.
[8] Surg., H.E.I.C.S.   [9] Surg., R.N.   [10] Adv. in Aberd., 1817.
[11] Silver pen, 1810; adv. in Aberd., 1818; Lect. on Scots Law.   [12] Surg. dentist, Aberd
[13] M.A., King's Coll., 1814; sch., Banchory-Ternan; min., Inverallochy.   [14] America.
[15] Adv. in Aberd., 1818.   [16] Distr. of stamps and taxes, Aberd.   [17] Surg., Portsoy.

CHAPTER 11

The burghs

If your ancestors were among the small proportion of Scots who lived in towns or cities, you may well be able to trace them through records that are not available for people living elsewhere. The records make burgh-dwellers rather interesting and desirable ancestors to have.

There were four types of burgh or merchant settlement. The main and most numerous were royal burghs, with charters from the Crown, created from the 12th century onwards. Sometimes, they were created out of nothing, as a means of "civilizing" an area, and in others the status, with its accompanying trade rights, was granted to existing settlements. By 1707, there were 66 of them, ranging from cities to tiny villages. In addition there were burghs of regality, which also had Crown charters; burghs of barony,

which were imitations of royal burghs and had charters granted by the local laird; and, from 1833 onwards, there were police burghs, with police forces and other municipal responsibilities.

17th-century Scotland had no large cities: Edinburgh in the 1650s had a mere 30,000 inhabitants, so crowded into narrow wynds and tenements that it took less than half an hour to walk the city end-to-end. Glasgow, Dundee and Aberdeen had less than 10,000 souls a-piece, and most burghs were vastly smaller. The relative safety and sophistication of burgh life was marred by terrible sanitation, most inhabitants emptying chamber pots from their windows, or using loos that jutted out over the wynds, with terrible consequences for passers by below. In Edinburgh, by 1773, the practice of flinging effluent from windows had been forbidden, but, introducing Dr. Johnson to the city that year, Boswell was still embarrassed at "his being assailed by the evening effluvia" of the city. Not surprisingly, burghs were rife with rats, fleas, lice and diseases such as typhus and summer diarrhoea.

The smallest burghs were little more than hamlets, dominated by the local laird and populated by peasant burghesses, who only practiced crafts once they had attended to their fields and animals. Kilmaurs, Ayrshire, for example, was a burgh of barony, with a charter from the Earl of Glencairn, whose proud burghesses spent their time growing and selling kale.

Edinburgh from the north bridge, 1845, by S.D. Swarbreck.

Johnson and Boswell

Johnson and Boswell.

The curious and engaging friendship between Dr. Samuel Johnson (1709-84) and the Scots lawyer and author James Boswell (1740-95) engendered a desire on the part of the latter to show his country to the former. When Boswell mentioned the plan to Voltaire, "he looked at me, as if I had talked of going to the North Pole," but Johnson was more adventurous, being particularly desirous of seeing the Hebrides, whose ancient beliefs and folklore had been described so admirably in Martin Martin's *A Description of the Western Isles of Scotland*. They made their journey in 1773, traveling in an anti-clockwise circuit encompassing Edinburgh, Aberdeen, Inverness, Loch Ness, Skye, Coll, Oban and Glasgow. Of particular fascination to Johnson (and ourselves) were his encounters with the clan chiefs of the Hebrides.

Both wrote accounts of their journey, Johnson *A Journey to the Western Isles of Scotland* (1775) and Boswell *The Journal of a Tour to the Hebrides* (1786), both as interesting to read now for their historical value as they were at the time for their social comment.

Boswell had blue-blooded Scots ancestry. His great-grandfather, Alexander, Earl of Kincardine, was a prominent Royalist, and about him, Boswell wrote, "*the blood of Bruce flows in my veins. Of such ancestry who would not be proud?*"

The burghs were largely self-governing, with the right to elect baillies (similar to magistrates), run a merchant guild and maybe also craft guilds. Royal burghs could elect MPs and send commissioners to conventions of royal burghs. The greatest privileges of the burgh were trading rights over their hinterlands (or "liberties"), some of which covered entire counties. In addition, until 1672, royal burghs had a virtual monopoly on foreign trade.

Burgesses

Freemen of the burgh, known as burgesses or burgers, were divided into merchants and craftsmen.

Merchants: The members of the burgh's merchant guild dominated the burghs. Merchants spent a lot of time preserving their exclusive rights to foreign trade from the craftsmen below them by keeping control of the

Glasgow's Iron Gate and the old tower of the Tolbooth, about 1845, by S.D. Swarbreck.

The merchants of Edinburgh busy at a horsefair on Bruntsfield Links. Edinburgh Castle can be seen in the background. From a painting by Paul Sandby (1725–1809).

town council. Few merchants specialized in specific commodities — most bought shares in whatever ventures were afoot, usually shares of ships and their cargoes, and then prayed hard that they arrived safely. These shares are recorded in shipping registers, some of which are in NAS class CE and others are in burgh archives.

Trade brought merchants wealth, sometimes equal to that of the highest nobles. As land brought status (and, one should imagine, some fresh air) there were many transitions from merchant to laird, either by purchase of an estate or by marriage to a laird's heiress. Consequently, most burghs were surrounded by a ring of estates owned by merchants.

Most burghs were dominated by small cliques of merchant families. 17th-century Dundee, for example, was dominated by the Goodmans, Haliburtons, Wedderburns and Clayhills.

Craftsmen: ranking below the merchants, they included tailzers (tailors), blacksmiths, skinners, saddlers, cordiners (cordwainers or

shoemakers), weavers, goldsmiths and armormakers. In some burghs, from about 1450 onwards, craftsmen formed craft guilds to prevent competition from non-burgesses tradesmen rather than as any guarantee of quality. Indeed, because they had to produce cheap goods for sale in the countryside, Scottish craftsmen had a reputation abroad for being rather shoddy. Their records may include pension records and payments for funerals.

Craft guilds could be very small — in 1604, Glasgow had a mere 361 guild members, only five in the dyers' guild and only two in the surgeons' guild. The barrier between merchant and craftsman was usually impenetrable and only in 17th-century Glasgow did the rules give craftsmen equal footing with merchants, a measure of egalitarianism that helped the city's great commercial success.

Becoming a burgess: this could be done by patrimony (being the son of a burgess), marriage (marrying the daughter of one), apprenticeship (being apprenticed to a burgess), or redemption (paying for admission). The latter could be an expensive business: in 1600, it cost £67 for a stranger to become a burgess of Edinburgh.

Incomers took several forms, including younger sons of landed families who were not due to inherit land, and also sons of indwellers whose fathers made enough money for them to be apprenticed.

Apprentices (whether sons of outsiders or burgesses) were usually boys aged between 14 and 21, bound to their masters, upon payment of a fee by their families, for five to seven years. Having finished the apprenticeship, one became a journeymen, paid by the day (the word comes from the French for day, *journée*), and might go on to submit an "assay" or "master piece" to become a burgess and (if not a merchant) a master craftsman. Those wishing to join a guild (merchant or craft) had then to trade for four years, two of them unaided by a servant or apprentice or else pay a fine, or, best of all, marry your master's (or another master's) daughter. Those who completed the course were often denoted "B. & G.B.," "Burgess and Guild Brother," and were eligible to stand

for office within the guild, such as that of the deacon.

Using the records

Burgh records usually include their own registers of deeds and sasines (see p. 132), town council minutes and the records of the trade and craft guilds. The records are scattered between NAS (class B), university libraries and burgh archives — look on **www.scan.org.uk**, or ask the relevant burgh archivist. Printed material will be identified in D. and W. Stevenson, *Scottish Texts and Calendars* (SHS, 1987).

Burgh officers in Selkirk prepare for the enduring tradition of the Common Riding, or riding around the boundaries of the burgh's common land. In former times they would go armed, prepared to fight anyone encroaching on the commons.

The prosperous, well-dressed residents of Edinburgh in the late 18th century.

Dumfries High Street in about 1890, its shops and traders were still doing a brisk trade.

Burgess often had voting rights, so will be shown in poll books, which listed voters and said how they voted. Available in local archives, these are useful for indicating when people were alive and for identifying different people of the same surname in the burgh.

Some apprentice indentures are in burgh deeds registers, and others are in NAS RH9/17/274-326. Those on which tax were paid in the period 1710-74 are indexed by the SoG (searchable on **www.britishorigins.net**), and some have been published (such as records of Edinburgh apprentices 1583-1800, published by the SRS). They often give the father's name and trade, and some, such as those of the Incorporation of Gardeners of Glasgow, might cite a "craft genealogy" going back several generations.

The great emphasis on family continuity within burghs makes their records valuable genealogical tools. Records of apprenticeship, or admission as a burgess by patrimony or matrimony, usually provide the father's name, and the latter of course reveals links to the wife's father as well. You can often trace a web of interconnected families through these records. Matrimony was a popular system because, by marrying his daughter to an up-and-coming burgess, the father ensured a comfortable retirement for himself, while the son-in-law gained the experience, social contacts and financial backing of an established family. The result could be seen as a form of matrilineal succession — reminiscent, coincidentally, of ancient Pictish society — whereby you can sometimes trace back several generations most easily through the female line.

Non-burgesses

Indwellers (or "inhabitants") were the "unfree," non-burgess residents of burghs. They paid their taxes but had no say in how the place was run. Most were poor (and were kept so by the

Crail in Co. Fife, now a peaceful seaside town but once a bustling royal burgh whose charter was granted by Robert the Bruce. Its 12th-century harbour was an important port for lobster and herring fishermen, sailing as far as Danzig or Stockholm to sell their catches and load their holds with iron to sell back in Scotland.

system), such as journeymen, servants, carters, night-soil carriers and prostitutes. The well-off, such as nobles and notaries, were often made honorary burgesses.

There were plenty of craftsmen living outside the burghs who had no connection to guilds (though the indentures of the few who were apprenticed may appear in registers of deeds). Some belonged to mutual benefit societies (see MacDougal's *Labour Records in Scotland*), and occasionally they appear in oral history. In 1695, Martin Martin reported a smith in Kilmartin, Skye, who could cure "faintness of the spirits" by laying people on his anvil and then threatening them with his hammer — he was apparently the thirteenth generation of his family of smiths able to exercise this curious power.

Dundee from the Firth of Tay, 1840, emphasizing the royal burgh's reliance on sea trade.

LEFT: **Entrepreneur James Paterson (1830–87).**

RIGHT: **The Tailzers' Guild Minute Book (1820–47) contains admission records of new members, including this entry from April 22, 1820, in which three boys were admitted to the Guild, swearing to uphold its privileges and do all they could to stop its privileges being eroded. The boys were James Evans, eldest son of William Evans, "Taylor, Burgess [of Selkirk] as also Freeman of the said Incorporation [of Tailors];" William Paterson, third son of John Paterson (ditto); and Thomas Hall, son-in-law to John Evans "Taylor in Selkirk Freeman of the said Craft," clearly not a burgess. The page is signed by the three new members and by others including John Paterson and his brother Walter (1790–1876), who was deacon of the Guild. On the next page, William paid "his dues to the Trade and Seat in Church" – a handsome £13 pounds and three shillings! (courtesy of the Scottish Borders Heritage Hub).**

Selkirk is a quiet town in the Borders that became a royal burgh in 1535. It had five guilds: souters (shoemakers), hammermen, weavers, fleshers (butchers) and tailzers (tailors). The craft guild, the Incorporation of Tailzers, was established in 1610 and its records constitute an excellent source for people, like me, who are descended from members.

Local histories are always worth exploring. In Selkirk's case, Craig-Brown's *History of Selkirkshire* (Edinburgh, 1886) commented, somewhat unfairly, that,

"The honest craftsmen knew little and cared less for anything beyond their own ports, liberties and walls ... Cromwell leads his army past their doors, Montrose is defeated before their eyes [at Philliphaugh, a mile away from the town], a dethroned dynasty strikes twice in vain for reparation, but the tailors of Selkirk go on making deacons and admitting apprentices in unbroken enjoyment of the happiness pertaining to people whose annals are dull ..."

On August 10, 1743, my seven x great-grandfather John Paterson, master tailzer of Selkirk, signed the guild's records admitting his son John as a freeman.

This John later served as dean or head of their guild. His own son John was baptized in Selkirk.

The OPR entry for the younger John Paterson in the 18th century reads: *"Novr the 19th 1758 John Patrson [sic] taylor burges in Selkirk and Rebecca Thomson his spouse had a son Baptized named John [born] October the 12 1758, in presence of the Congregation."*

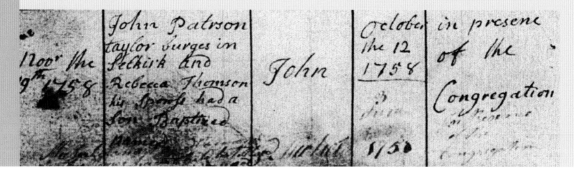

John went on to be a master tailzer and dean of guild too, said by his descendants to have been a good friend of Sir Walter Scott, who was for a time sheriff of Selkirkshire. John married Betty Scott.

"Decr 8 [1786] John Paterson Taylor in Selkirk and Betty Scott both in this parish gave up there Names to be proclaimed in our Church in order to marriage John Curver Tanner in Selkirk Cautioner. They were married Decr 10."

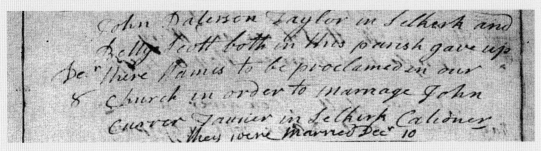

In Selkirk Library are letters by Alexander Johnstone containing reminiscences of John's sons. Of John's son Walter Paterson (1790–1876), he wrote, *"I remember being once in the Old Kirk during the sermon in the Tailors' loft or seat when [Walter] gave a boy such a stroke over the head with his Bible for misbehaviour that it made the whole church ring. This was a common occurrence with him."* Walter's brother William (d. 1798) had apparently walked all the way to London: *"we all liked him, he was so light-hearted and he was singing John O'Badenyon the nicht he left me: he died falling out of a farm cart near Broxburn in Mid-Calder. Their brother was Robert."*

The Patersons were said to have lived in Kirk Wynd in a house that survived until the 1960s. This was confirmed in an early "census," or "Catalogue, Containing the Number of Inhabitants in the Burgh of Selkirk, 16th June 1817" that appeared in *Border Counties' Magazine* and is now online at **www.afhs.ab.ca/data/census/1817/index.html**. John Paterson's house, with seven occupants, is listed six doors away from one Elliott Scott, presumably a relation of his wife's, in "Outer Line, Kirk Wynd."

Robert Paterson (1803–49) became a tailzer like his father, and then an exciseman, stationed at Rochdale, Lancashire, and Whitby, Yorkshire (excisemen were normally posted far from home to lessen the possibility of corruption). He married Elspeth Arnott at Kinnoul, Co. Perth, and had five children. Of these, James Paterson (1830–87) became stationmaster at Alnwick, Northumberland. Goods could easily be transported by railway, yet getting them to and from stations was a logistical nightmare for most people, so James established the firm of Carter-Paterson that specialized in doing just that. The firm was a massive success and soon had branches all over Britain, so James was among the legion of entrepreneurial Scots who made their fortunes in Victorian Britain. He settled in Stoke Newington, London, in a house he named "Melrose," after the abbey that was only a few miles from Selkirk.

The baptism record for Robert Paterson Tailor: *"John Paterson Taylor and Elizabeth Scott his spouse had a Child Baptized upon the 29th May [1803] Named Robert [born] 22 April 1803, In Presence of the Congregation."*

CHAPTER 12

Landholders

Generally, those who held land were better recorded than those who did not, because the acts of buying, inheriting and holding land entailed the creation of records. This makes them useful ancestors to have. Their records can also shed light onto those who occupied their lands.

The upper echelons of the landholding system comprised royalty, and below them were the nobles: dukes, marquises, earls, viscounts and barons. After them came the knights and baronets and then the lairds, whose hereditary titles were tied to the land. All such people usually had coats of arms, and were described as "of" somewhere, such as "James Matheson of Dougaltoun" (those described as "in," i.e. "James Matheson in Dougaltoun," were not land holders). The landowning class included most clan chiefs, some of whom were granted titles.

Original records for tracing landowners are generally quite detailed, though also somewhat redundant as so many of their pedigrees have already been traced and recorded. These are the best places to start looking:

- Margaret Stuart, *Scottish Family History* (1930, repr. GPC 1994).
- Joan P.S. Ferguson (ed.), *Scottish Family Histories* (NLS, 1986), which updates and enlarges on Stuart.
- NLS catalog **www.nls.uk**.
- Catalog of printed works in the SoG **www.sog.org.uk**.
- Catalog of the Royal Historical Society **www.rhs.ac.uk/bibl/bibwel.asp**.

For the peerage, see also:
- James Balfour Paul (ed.), *Scots Peerage* (Edinburgh, 1904-14).

AN ORDINARY OF ARMS

CONTAINED IN THE PUBLIC REGISTER OF ALL ARMS AND BEARINGS IN SCOTLAND; BY

SIR JAMES BALFOUR PAUL

LORD LYON KING OF ARMS

SECOND EDITION

- *Burke's Peerage, Baronetage and Knightage*, published in 107 editions since 1826. The 107th (2003) publication, edited by Charles Mosley, includes the pedigrees of the clan chiefs even if they never received peerages. It is also available online at a subscription website, www.burkes-peerage.net. Burke's also published many editions of the *Landed Gentry of Great Britain and Ireland*, that includes numerous non-titled Scottish families.
- The holdings of the Scottish National Portrait Gallery.
- *The Dictionary of National Biography* and its modern re-write *The Oxford Dictionary of National Biography*.
- P. Bell's *Who Was Who in Edwardian Scotland* (Edinburgh, 1986), which indexes 10 illustrated county biographical dictionaries covering about 2,000 prominent people.
- Lord Lyon's records (see pp. 134-6 and 160).
- Manuscript (i.e. unpublished) sources for landholders include the NAS's collection of genealogies in RH16, the collections of individual family papers in NAS class GD (Gifts and Deposits), and the John McGregor Collection of genealogies and genealogical notes on mainly Highland families, particularly Campbells and MacGregors, in GD50.

Grants of land

The holding, gaining and inheritance of land (or heritable property) generated a great many genealogically useful records. The system was a feudal one, instituted by the Canmore kings, and consequently, its terminology — retours, inquests, clare constat, tailzies, *beneficium inventarii, ultimus haeres* (see pp. 131-2) — is drawn variously from Scots, Latin and Norman French, and can be terrifying for the uninitiated. In most cases, however, the jargon merely describes people inheriting or buying land.

Armstrong. Border Memories, by W. Riddell Carre (1858), 366-369. Chronicles of the Armstrongs, by J. L. Armstrong (New York, 1902).

Arnot of Arnot. Eminent Men of Fife, 14-17. Brief Notices of the Families of Arnot, Reid, etc. (1872).* Burke's Extinct Baronetcies. Complete Baronetage, by G. E. C., ii. 361. The House of Arnot, and some of its Branches, by James Arnot, M.D., Brigade Surgeon-Lieut.-Col. I.M.S., 4to, illust. (Edinburgh, 1918). Notes and Queries, 4th S., v. 92, 135 ; 5th S., i. 144.

of Balcormo. East Neuk of Fife, by W. Wood, 2nd ed., 255-257.

of Fenwick. Paterson's Ayr and Wigton, iii. 247.

of Lochrig. Certificates of Birth and Descent of John Arnot of Lochrig ; Brit. Mus. Eg. Ch., 413, 414. Ayrshire Families, by G. Robertson, i. 13-21. Paterson's History of Ayr, ii. 457-459. Paterson's Ayr and Wigton, iii. 247-248, 599-604.

of Woodmiln and Granton. Cramond, by J. P. Wood, 19.

Arnot-Stewart of Lochridge. Ayrshire Families, i. 20-21.

ARNOT, THE FAMILY OF. The name of Arnot, not a common one in Britain, seems to be most frequent in the counties of Fife and Kinross, in the latter of which it probably had its origin when surnames began to be assumed. Family names were often derived from landed possessions, and the word " Arnaght," from the Gaelic, signifying " high lands," is supposed to have given the family of Arnot their name. The original seat of the Arnots seems to have been the uplands on the southern slope of Bishop Hill, in Kinross-shire, a little east of Lochleven. There the chief of the name had extensive possessions for nearly 700 years ; there still stands, in good preservation, commanding a noble prospect of the loch and the vale of Leven, the stronghold of the family, Arnot Tower ; there are Arnot Hill and Little Arnot ; and in the vicinity there are still many residents of the name of Arnot—branches, no doubt, of the old stock, fondly lingering around the homes of their fathers.

Some chroniclers claim a high antiquity for the family of Arnot, asserting that they obtained their lands on the banks of Lochleven in the time of Kenneth M'Alpin (843–859 A.D.). Of this we shall only remark, that perhaps it might be difficult to *disprove* it. There are traces of the Arnots in charters early in the twelfth century. In the middle of that century, Arnald, son of Malcolm de Arnot, is Abbot of Kelso, and grants lands on Douglas Water " Theobaldo Flammatico," the first notable man of the Douglases (Douglas' Peerage). Arnald was afterwards Bishop of St Andrews, the cathedral of which he is said to have founded—*Legate a latere*—and died in 1163. Sir Michael Arnot, said to have married a sister of the Earl of Fife, was drowned at the seige of Lochleven in 1334. His son was popularly known as "David the Devil," as alleged, from his " untoward looks," but probably also from " untoward deeds "—if traditions still lingering in the vicinity of Arnot Tower can be relied on. David's two grandsons, William and James, were ancestors of two leading branches of the family. William's son, John Arnot of Arnot, who married Marjory Boswell (of

Top: **A section from the bibliography in Maggie Stuart's *Scottish Family History*. This led to finding (LEFT) this fascinating account of the Arnots.**

Some charters survive with their seals intact, such as this one given by Patrick, Earl of Dunbar (1182–1232), to Melrose Abbey regarding a ploughgate (courtesy of the Duke of Buccleuch).

A caibeal (a stone enclosure to house a wealthy family's graves) in the churchyard of Inchnadamph, Assynt. Rather than being purpose-built, this may be part of the original church building, built by Angus MacLeod of Assynt about 1440, on his return from a pilgrimage to Rome. The entrance had been blocked, as the interior, full of the bones of the MacLeod chiefs of Assynt, all jumbled together, was unsafe. Just as well, too, for a permanent and inexplicable drip of water, "MacLeod's Tears," falls from the vault's door. Any descendant of the chiefs on which the drip falls, they say, can expect to die soon after.

Remember that some fairly small farmers and tradesmen held land, and (as is often suggested by their surnames) a huge number of poor families are descended from younger sons of landholders.

Since 1964, unless a will says otherwise, Scottish estates are divided equally among the heirs. Before 1964, unless a will said otherwise, primogeniture, the exclusive succession of the eldest son, applied. Before 1868, wills could not affect the inheritance of land, so the eldest son always inherited. If there were no sons, the daughters inherited equal portions as heirs portioners, and if there were no children, the next eldest brother inherited (if the deceased had older and younger brothers, the younger ones inherited before the elder ones). If no brothers, the sisters became heirs portioners. Once someone has died, the person due to inherit becomes the "apparent heir," until they "complete the title," i.e. complete the process of inheriting the land.

Under the Canmore kings' system the Crown assumed ownership of all of Scotland and became the "superior." By Crown charters, the Crown then *feud* or granted land, either in perpetuity to institutions such as universities or burghs, or to individuals or vassals as heritable property. Recipients of such charters were "subject superiors." They could hold the land themselves or sub-infeudate it, by further charters, to their own vassals or tenants.

Crown charters, granting land to subject superiors, appear in the records of the Great Seal, Privy Seal, and Signatures (drafts commissioning a charter). Abstracts from the *Registers of the Great Seal of Scotland* (RMS or *Registrum Magni Sigilli Regum Scotorum*) have been published

from its start, 1314, up to 1668 (in Latin to 1651). They are indexed for people and places. The abstracts contain much genealogically useful information, and provide reference numbers to the original documents, which are in NAS class C. The period 1668–1919 is covered by typescript indexes to the grantees and lands in the three categories of original records (the Register of the Great Seal, Paper Register and Principality Register). "Signatures" were written in Scots and, although drafts, often give the salient details — names, lands and date. They are in NAS SIG1–2, 1607–1847. For charters granted through the Privy Seal see *ultimus haeres* (page 131).

The "reddendo" section of a charter includes details of the "duty of feu," i.e. what the vassal must pay or do in return for the land. In the Middle Ages land was usually held by *blanche ferme*, in return for occasional payments, or by ward holding, in return for military service. By the late 16th century, most holdings had been converted to *feu ferme*, by which land was held in return for a regular rent of produce or, more commonly, money. Usually, conditions included several sorts of "casualties" or special payments: ward casualties were paid by minors until they reached 21; casualties of marriage were paid until the heir married; casualty of non-entry was paid between the death of the vassal and the entry of his heir to the land, and when he did he paid a casualty of relief.

Charters were also granted by subject superiors to their own vassals. They are usually mentioned in relevant sasines. The records were not registered publicly, so will only be in archives in deposits of family papers. Those in the NAS are, for this reason, indexed in RH6, 1142–1600. Other sources for charters include RH9/15, containing writs of land for Shetland and Orkney, and Miscellaneous Charters and Writs in RH6–8, which must be searched manually. Charters

granted by the Lords of the Isles appear, with annotations, in J. and R.W. Munro's *Acts of the Lords of the Isles* (SHS vol. 22, 1986).

Inheriting land

The inheritance of land by subjects superior was controlled by services of heirs, also called retours, and that of sub-tenants was facilitated by precepts of clare constat (see p. 131). In theory, one could only be given sasine of heritable land once one of these processes had been completed.

Retours or services of heirs: these are records of inheritance of land held by subject superiors,

This postcard of the Clan Menzies shows the clan's tartan together with the arms of the clan's chief. The front of the card has a space for the sender to write a message.

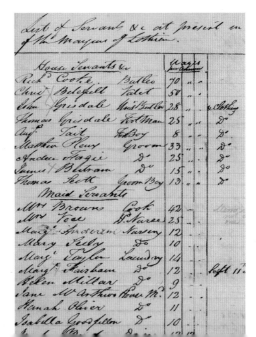

The estate papers of the rich sometimes contain lists of tenants or servants, such as this list of domestic staff employed by John Kerr, the seventh Marquis of Lothian, in 1841.

Technical terms

Heirs of line	those inheriting by normal rules of succession.
Heir of conquest	heir to land that had been purchased.
Heir of destination	heir to lands that had been acquired through a tailzie (see pp. 131-2) or, in exceptional cases, by a will.

i.e. held direct from the Crown. Because they are covered by detailed indexes, it is sometimes possible to trace a line of landowners back using services to heirs alone.

The process started with the heir approaching Chancery. A brieve (or writ) of Chancery would be issued, instructing the sheriff or burgh court to establish, by inquest, who was indeed the true heir. The records (or "repertories") of those courts may contain details of the inquest, including sworn testimony from witnesses (those for Jedburgh sheriff court are published as *Services of Heirs, Roxburghshire 1636-1847* (SRS vol. 69). The verdict, if positive, was then returned or "retoured" to Chancery, who consequently allowed the heir to inherit the land by being given sasine of it. Retours came in several forms, including general retours, whereby the heir was acknowledged generally (by general service), and special retours, whereby someone was acknowledged as the heir to specific pieces of land (special service).

The retours were recorded in Chancery, starting in 1530. They are in Latin (except for the Commonwealth period, 1652-9), up to 1847. Summaries of the retours up to 1700 are published in *Inquisitionum Retornatarum Abbreviatio* (full title *Inquisitionum ad Capellam Regis Retornatarum Abbreviatio*). The period 1544-1699 is also covered by a SGS CD. Both are indexed for people and places. From 1700 to 1859 there are indexes for each 10 years, and from 1860 to the

An unusual source for deaths of the well-to-do are the sadly very rare pre-Reformation books of obituary or "obit. books," recording charitable donors to churches, for whom prayers were said. This entry, from J. Paterson's *The Obit Book of the Church of St John the Baptist, Ayr* (Thomas G. Stevenson, 1848), provides much information on Janet Glover, who died in 1504.

October.

The OBIT of Janet Glover, a provident woman, spouse of the late James Certane, who died in the year of our Lord 1504, on the 3d day of the month of October, who, also, for the good of her soul, has freely given to God and the church of St John the Baptist, and choristers of the same, for obsequies, with *placebo* and *dirige*, and a mass, in chant, in all time coming, six shillings and eightpence of yearly revenue, and for perpetuity, to be annually levied from the above described lands and croft of the said Fergus Kennedy lying at the south end of the same burgh, between the common vennel on the east part, and his lands or croft on the west part, and the common vennel leading from the barn of Thomas Broun, before the parish church of Ayr, on the south part, and the lands of John Dalrumple, now of James Curry, on the north part; which annual revenue, the foresaid Janet acquired from Thomas Reid for a certain sum of money. Present at the premises, John Steill, John Hoge, John Curry, chaplain; Sir Matthew Broun, and Robert Gamyll. Done in presence of Mr Patrick Pethed, notary to each of the premises.

Margaret Michell Schaw, inhabitant.

present there are annual indexes. They are available on SGS CD for the period 1700–1859. The printed and CD versions usually give all salient information about a case, but if you want to explore further you can use the references given in the indexes to order up the original documents in the NAS.

If you don't find what you want, remember some retours between 1303 and 1622 were omitted from the foregoing, but are transcribed in C39/4. Some slightly pre-1700 retours actually appear in the post-1700 records. For 1700–1846 some retours, omitted from the indexes, appear as a supplement to the 1905–6 volume.

Royal burghs and some franchise courts, such as Dunfermline and Dunkeld, issued their own services of heirs. These are not included in the Chancery records, and appear in the records of those burghs and courts instead.

The retour process was also used to appoint guardians for children whose fathers had died. Retours tutory appointed tutors for pupils (boys under 14 and girls under 12) and retours curatory appointed curators for children from those ages up to 21, and also for the mad.

Unfortunately, not all heirs completed the process as soon as their predecessor died. Some waited years or even decades or just occupied the land regardless. In some cases, fathers granted land to their eldest son while they were still living, by deed, to avoid the hassle. But even when a retour is missing, though, there may be a sasine (see p. 132) anyway.

Clare constat: the right of sub-tenants to inherit land was acknowledged by the subject superior by what was called a precept of clare constat. These did not have to be registered, but might be referred to in subsequent sasines, or in family muniments (such as those in NAS class GD, "gifts and deposits"). If found, they

---

Issues of inheritance

A drawback of inheriting land was inheriting associated debts. From 1695, it was possible for an heir, inheriting an estate, to limit his liability to the value of the land and no more. This was done by registering a procedure of *beneficium inventarii*. These are in NAS RD20 for 1689–1850, sadly unindexed.

Ultimus haeres concerns people dying without heirs. The Exchequer (on behalf of the Crown) became the heir, but claims could be made by those with moral rights, such as the widows of intestates, or maternal relatives of intestates who had no traceable paternal cousins. Grants up to 1584 are in the Register of the Privy Seal, and to 1660 in Privy Seal minute books (PS6); there are indexes (in PS3) thereafter and from 1834 records are in E851–70. Petitions are in E303.

---

can be valuable because they tend to recite an heir"s descent from the ancestor to whom the land was granted originally. If the process proved complicated or contentious, a precept of clare constat could be taken to Chancery (the Lord Chancellor"s court) and may appear in the services of heirs.

Tailzies

From 1685, landowners could control what happened to their land by a deed of tailzie (the Scots" equivalent of the English "entail"). These are sometimes referred to in a service of heirs.

Some Fifeshire entries from *Scotland: Owners of Land and Heritages, 1872–3* (HMSO, 1874). Besides giving information on family landholdings, this one-off source can be useful for finding out who owned the land on which many other people's ancestors lived.

Christina	muchty . .	23	100 13	M:
Lyon, Joseph . . .	Woodend, Cowdenbeath, Lochgelly . .	1	25 –	M:
				M:
M‘Ara, Mrs. Eliza . .	Kettle, Ladybank . .	27	95 3	M:
M‘Arthur, Peter . .	Perth	24	40 –	M:
M‘Call, Robert . .	Radernie, St. Andrews .	2	10 18	M:
M‘Cash, Andrew, of Templehall . .	Meadowwells, Ladybank	182	274 6	M:
M‘Cash, James . .	Pitilloch, Falkland .	4	14 10	M:
M‘Callum, Mrs. Christian	Inverkeithing . .	3	19 –	M:
M‘Culloch, Rev. James .	West Kirk Manse, Greenock . .	1	13 –	M:
M‘Culloch, Thomas . .	Cowstrandburn, Dunfermline . .	4	6 –	M:
M‘Dougall, Alexander .	Bogside, Culross . .	5	8 –	M:
M‘Dougall, Alexander S.	St. Andrews . .	5	30 –	M:
M‘Duff, John . . .	Milton, Markinch .	2	14 –	M:
M‘Farlane, Rev. Patrick .	Manse, Pittenweem .	5	60 10	
M‘Farlane, Thomas . .	Carhurly, Crail . .	13	32 –	M:
M‘Gorian, William . .	Dunfermline . .	1	24 18	M:
M‘Gregor, Rev. Alex. .	Manse, Inverkeithing .	16	73 6	
M‘Gregor, John . .	St. Andrews . .	19	1,219 5	M:
M‘Gregor, John, and M‘Intosh, John . .	} St. Andrews . .	2	36 –	
M‘Intosh, Alexander .	Dairsie, Cupar . .	11	102 16	M:
M‘Intosh, Robert . .	Largoward, St. Andrews	3	16 –	
M‘Intosh, Heirs of Mrs.	Rosebank, Markinch .	1	15 –	M:
M‘Intosh, Mrs., wife of Alex. M‘Intosh . .	Dairsie, Cupar . .	2	41 14	M:
M‘Intyre, Allan . .	St. Andrews . .	7	26 15	M:
M‘Kay, William . .	Pilmuir, Largo . .	3	16 12	M:
M‘Kean, William Blair .	Tourville, Inverkeithing .	1	59 –	M:
M‘Knight, Alexander E. .	12 London St., Edinburgh	5	14 –	
M‘Laren, Rev. Alexander	Manse, Kemback . .	12	39 –	M:
M‘Laren, Robert . .	Falkland . . .	3	5 10	M:
M‘Laren, Thomas . .	Hawklymuir, Kirkcaldy .	1	168 7	M:
M‘Lean, Heirs of William	Cowdenbeath, Lochgelly	2	43 10	M:
M‘Leish, James . .	Gartmorn Hill, Alloa .	8	20 –	M:
M‘Leod, Mrs. Agnes, of Burnside . . .	Perth	200	203 –	M:
M‘Nab, Duncan . .	Cupar . . .	3	53 16	M:
M‘Naughton, John . .	Leven . . .	1	57 6	

Sasines usually come in three sections that generally state the same relevant information about the land and people concerned. The term "registers disposition" means that the recipient of a sasine is already in possession of the land concerned. The term "grant ratification" indicates several heirs-in-common acknowledging each other's rights to their shares:

- the introduction sets out who is who and what land is concerned. It names the bailie, who was the legal representative of the grantor, and should not be mistaken for a member of the family.
- the precept reiterates this information. It relates in Latin (except in the burghs) what the bailie would have read aloud in the Scots, Gaelic or English, and ends with a list of witnesses, who often included relatives.
- the confirmation states that sasine had been given and ends with a further list of witnesses.

consent of the superior from whom the land was held.

Sasines and their phraseology seem daunting to the uninitiated: "giving sasine," "instruments of sasine," "taking of instruments," becoming "seised in," "infeft in" or given "sasine of" land all mean basically the same thing. The arcane terminology (rather like that of heraldry) is because, although it is used now of paper records, it arose to describe physical objects and actions. In ancient times, and right into the Middle Ages, ownership of land was signified by being handed a rock or clod of earth from the land concerned. The Scots understood this practice well, for when the ships of the Milesians first approached Ireland at the end of their voyage from Spain,

A tailzie might prevent heirs selling off land, ensure succession by those who would not normally be the legal heirs (such as illegitimate children), or force sons-in-law or maternal grandsons due to inherit family land to adopt the surname of the original owner.

The register of tailzies (NAS RT1) begins in 1688. It is indexed 1688–1833 in the Historical Search Room, and then (in the Legal Search Room) by a manuscript index "Register of Entails" (RT3/1/1–2) that runs from 1688 again right up to 1938. Tailzies could only be broken from 1848 onwards, and these disentails also appear in the registers.

Sasines

Sasine is the Scots word for the act of giving or investing people with entitlement to land, and happened whenever land changed hands. This was often when land was inherited, but vassals of any sort could alienate (sell), wadset (mortgage) or assign (by a marriage contract, for example) their holdings to someone else during their lifetime, provided they had

Sir Henry Raeburn's 1812 portrait of Colonel Alastair MacDonell of Glengarry, a member of one of the great landowning families of Scotland.

their ancestor Heremon, son of Milesius, is said to have severed his own hand and thrown it ashore, so that he could claim possession by having touched it first — an act commemorated to this day by the Red Hand of Ulster.

Less dramatically, sasine came to be given by handing over a symbolic piece of earth, and later by written documentation alone. Up to 1660, sasines were recorded by notaries, though few survive out of the many that must have existed — those surviving for royal burghs are in burgh archives or in the NAS (class B). The NAS holdings for those outside burghs are in NAS class NP. The NAS catalog and D. and W. Stevenson, *Scottish Texts and Calendars* (SHS, 1987) will show you what has been published.

Notaries were not averse to taking bribes to make up sasines that never existed, or lose ones that did. In 1599 the state established the Secretary's Register, which ran until 1609, as a more reliable and secure place for recording sasines. Its records are now incorporated into the two registers that succeeded it, from 1617 — the General and Particular Registers of Sasines. These are all in NAS class RS.

The Particular Register was divided into counties (hence its being "particular"): pages 77-8 of the NAS guide relates particular registers to modern counties and states whether they are indexed up to 1780 (only nine out of 40 are not) and if so for what periods, and whether indexes have been published (24 out of 40 have). Particular Registers that have not been indexed are best searched using the minute books, or, failing these, searching through the register itself.

The General Register should also be searched. It is indexed to 1735. The period 1736-80 can be searched using the minute books, in NAS RH62.

From 1781 onwards, there are printed abridgments of sasines, covering the Particular

A page from the Edinburgh register of sasines.

and General Registers (the latter was abandoned in 1868). These have now been digitized and are fully indexed up to the present, by place (except between 1831-1871) and person. The abridgments usually provide all the information given in the original document, but the originals can be ordered and studied if desired. Some registers of sasines have been microfilmed by the Mormons.

The General and Particular Registers do not include sasine registers in royal burghs until the 20th century. Up till then they are in the burgh registers, with the earliest recorded in Dysart in 1602. The records are generally in Scots. Some are indexed — all this is indicated by the NAS catalog (look up the name of the burgh under class B). Those for Glasgow are at Glasgow City Archives, Aberdeen's pre-1809 are at Aberdeen City Archives and Dundee's pre-1890 are at City of Dundee Archive and Record Centre.

Valuation rolls

Kept from 1643 onwards, these were an aid to taxing people on the land they owned or occupied. They are useful for learning about landowners, whose estate records can then be sought. They sometimes provide direct information on tenants, but generally don't mention sub-tenants.

They are due to be searchable on ScotlandsPeople by 2010. For 1643–1854, they are in exchequer records (NAS E106), arranged by county. L.R. Timperley's *A Directory of Landownership in Scotland c.1770* (SRS, 1976) is based on the 1771 rolls, and is indexed. Various rolls for the 1810s to 1850s are in IRS4 (and identifiable using the NAS catalog). Some turn up in heritors' records too. The records do not cover royal burghs, though for Dunbar, Inverkeithing, Jedburgh, Linlithgow, North Berwick and Peebles before 1855 there are rough equivalents, the cess or stent rolls, in NAS class B.

For 1855–1988 they are more inclusive, omitting only tenants paying less than £4 per year. There are annual valuation rolls covering each county and burgh, detailing each piece of land and buildings, stating who owned and occupied them (naming heads of households). These are divided between NAS class VR and local archives. Some include place name or street indexes, as identified in the catalog, though even with these aids they will be slow to search. They are useful for pinning down when people came and went from homes between the decennial censuses.

Heraldry

The visible symbol of the landed class was heraldry. Heraldry is not confined to the rich — the younger sons of younger sons (etc.) of heraldic lords or clan chiefs were entitled to use arms, but those who were poor simply didn't have the means to display their arms, or perhaps didn't have any great interest in doing so.

Heraldry was introduced to Scotland by the Canmore kings and their Norman followers. It was then a very new idea, for while the concept of painting devices on shields and flags is as old as warfare itself, it was only in the 12th century that the Normans and French started passing the same designs down from father to son. The sons and their descendants later began "differencing" the arms they had inherited by a small mark of cadence or, more commonly in Scotland, by a distinctive bordure placed around the original design.

Besides simply identifying knights on the battlefield, coats of arms became a way of identifying the male lines of families.

Scottish heraldry is regulated, very strictly, by Lord Lyon King of Arms and his heralds, who operate from offices in New Register House. Lyons have been appointed since at least the 14th century, and their office incorporates the much more ancient duties of the Gaelic royal sennachies, who were responsible for reciting the

Arms of the Murrays of Atholl, descended from Freskin from Flanders, who held extensive lands in Moray, from which his grandson Sir William Murray took his name. The double tressure (border) around the shield shows the Murrays' loyalty to the Scottish Crown, whose arms also included a double tressure.
(Painted by Tom Meek and reproduced courtesy of *Family History Monthly*.)

Arms of the Paterson descendants of John Paterson (d. 1679), Bishop of Ross, and his son John Paterson (d. 1708), last Archbishop of Glasgow. The "vulning" (self-wounding) pelicans are emblems of self-sacrificing piety, an example not lived up to by the archbishop who was once described as, "*the most notorious liar of his time, and a vicious, base, loose liver.*" (Painted by Tom Meek and reproduced courtesy of *Family History Monthly*.)

RUTHERFURD, LORD RUTHERFURD

ROBERT, LORD OF RODYR-FORDE, witnessed a charter by David I. to Gervase of Rydel, *circa* 1140.[1]

GREGORY OF RUTHERFURD witnessed two charters of Roger Burnard to the monastery of Melrose of thirteen acres of the lands of Faringdon, in the reign of King William the Lion, and other charters in the reign of King Alexander II.[2]

HUGH OF RODERFORDE witnessed a grant by Philip de Valoniis to Robert de Stutteville of lands of Torpenhow in Northumberland in or before 1215, in which year Philip died.[3]

RICHARD and HUGH RUTHERFURD witnessed a charter of Richard Burnard of Faringdon to the abbey and convent of Melrose in the reign of King Alexander III., 1252.[4]

SIR NICOLAS OF RUTHERFURD witnessed charters by William of Landels and by John of Landels to the church of St. Mary of Melrose, and other charters in the reign of

[1] *Rutherfurds of that Ilk.* [2] *Liber de Melros*, i. 75, 76, 177, 179, 227, 229, 232. [3] Macfarlane, *Original Writs, Adv. Lib.* [4] *Liber de Melros*, i. 299.

genealogies of the kings. Early Lords Lyon were concerned chiefly with ceremonial matters, and also granted and recorded the use of coats of arms, by authority of the king. The first proper record of Scottish heraldry was the armorial compiled by Sir David Lindsay of the Mount in about 1542.

The use of heraldry is controlled by strict rules, but they are easily broken, and by the 17th century the need to regulate the use of arms became pressing. In 1662 an Act of Parliament complained of younger branches of families assuming the arms of their senior cousins without differencing their arms and, "*other mean persones, who can nowayes derive their succession from the families whose names they bear*' assuming those same families*" arms anyway. In 1672, Lord Lyon established a proper "Public Register of all Arms and Bearings in Scotland," which is still maintained today. Details of all arms granted and/or registered to people (and also to

institutions such as burghs, universities and companies) up to 1902 are published in Sir J. Balfour Paul's *An Ordinary of Arms Contained in the Public Register of All Arms and Bearings in Scotland* (William Green and Sons, second ed. 1903), with an additional volume published in 1977 covering up to the 1970s.

Lord Lyon's office is a treasure-house of the genealogies of families entitled to use arms, the best of which have been updated regularly since the

The coat of arms of Rutherford, from J. Balfour-Paul's *Scots Peerage*.

The Lord Lyon, David Sellar, in his tabard (courtesy of the Court of the Lord Lyon).

Arms of the Grahams of Braco, Co. Perth, a scion of the great house of Graham of Montrose.

(Painted by Tom Meek and reproduced courtesy of *Family History Monthly*.)

17th century. The "Public Register of Genealogies" contains two types of record: birthbrieves, which record, where possible, all 16 great-great-grandparents, and linear pedigrees which aim to trace the male line as far back as possible. Early entries tend to be terse (maybe just names and no dates), becoming sometimes over-detailed in the 18th and 19th centuries, including copious notes, for example, of the military achievements, awards and decorations of Napoleonic War officers. The records can be studied at the ScotlandsPeople Centre.

The main rules are simple: don't bear arms undifferenced if you are not the senior representative of the family, and don't bear arms at all if you have not been granted them yourself, or are not descended in the male line from someone who had been. Where heraldry is concerned, male-line descent must be proved with 100 percent, watertight documentary evidence.

In any event, do nothing without having your evidence examined and approved by Lord Lyon. These lions, I am delighted to report, have teeth in the form of extensive powers of criminal jurisdiction — they fine people who misuse heraldry, and seize and destroy artefacts displaying unauthorized arms, sometimes at great cost to their owners.

This is not such an elitist field as you may think. Thomas Innes of Learney calculated in the 1950s that one in every 45 Scots was entitled to bear arms. Lord Lyon does not permit anyone with a "clan" surname to use "clan arms" (which are strictly those of the chief and his proven kin alone), but the clan crest can be used by clansmen and clanswomen who, in Lyon Court's words, *"... are the Chief's relatives, including his own immediate family and even his eldest son, and all members of the extended family called the "Clan", whether bearing the Clan surname or that of one of its septs; that is all those who profess allegiance to that Chief and wish to demonstrate their association with the Clan. It is correct for these people to wear their Chief's Crest encircled with a strap and buckle bearing their Chief's Motto or Slogan. The strap and buckle is the sign of the clansman, and he demonstrates his membership of his Chief's Clan by wearing his Chief's Crest within it."*

Estate papers

Landholders' estate records are important not just for studying landowning families, but also for learning about their tenants or tacksmen and, to a much lesser extent, their tacksmen's sub-tenants. Published estate records (such as many of the Sutherland estate papers that have been published by the SHS) are listed in D. and W. Stevenson, *Scottish Texts and Calendars* (SHS, 1987). Original records are in the NLS, local archives and private hands, and NAS class GD (Gifts and Deposits), with others in RH (especially 9, 11 and 15) and CR (Crown Estate papers for Glenlivet and Fochabers). These can be searched in the NAS catalog under the appropriate reference (GD, etc.) and the relevant family name.

Some are disappointing, but others, such as the 1814 records for Blair Drummond Moss, Kincardine, Perthshire, 1814, name everyone in each family. Another splendidly detailed survey is John Hume's *Survey of Assynt* (see pp. 163–6).

The Forfeited Estate Papers concern estates confiscated from landholders who supported the Stuart risings. They are in NAS E601–63 for 1715, E700–88 for 1745 (look in the NAS catalog under these references and the name of the estate). The estates were administered by factors appointed by the Commissioners of the Annexed Estates and the records can include occupants of the land, rentals, claims and details of how the estates were improved prior to being sold off.

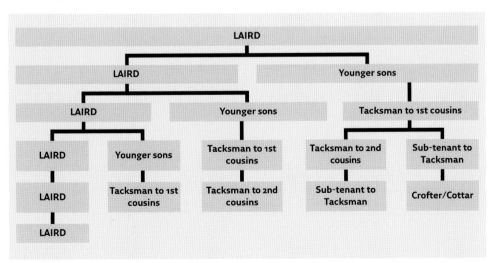

An unusually sympathetic estate factor learns a tacksman's tale of financial woe.

Tacksmen and tenancies

The Scots for "lease" is *tack*, and the larger takers or lessees of land were called tacksmen, sometimes described as occupiers or possessors. Tacksmen form a rural "middle class" between the landowners and their own sub-tenants, the small farmers and cottars.

Many leases were regularly renewed, enabling families of tacksmen to stay put for centuries. Boswell reminds us that, *"the tacksmen or principal tenants, are named by their farms, as Kingsburgh, Corrichatachin; and their wives are called the mistress of Kingsburgh, the mistress of Corrichatachin ..."* The historian John Prebble adds, *"these tacksman took titles from the land they leased, were mac-This of That or The Other, and were as sensitive as sea-anemones on matters that touched their honour."*

Tacks may be found in registers of deeds, and will tell you a little about the tacksman,

Theoretical and truncated chart showing how descendants of the lairds ultimately filled all the available roles in Gaelic society.

what he leased, and how much rent he paid. Some records of them, and the resulting rentals and surveys, survive in the records of the landowner (see under estate papers). Sadly, though, most tacks were never registered — when the tack expired, it was thrown away. Luckily, court records are full of disputes over tacks, especially due to non-payment of rents and consequent evictions.

Dr. Johnson wrote that the tacksman was "commonly a collateral relation of landowner," for landholders generally granted tacks to close relatives, so as to guarantee a good supply of fighting men in times of trouble — the tacksmen were the officers while their sub-tenants were the foot soldiers. After the battle of Culloden, the system began to break down, and Johnson tells us that by 1773, *"the ancient dependent is in danger of giving way to a higher bidder, at the expense of domestick dignity and hereditary power."* But as late as 1785, an English traveler complained, *"the chieftan lets out his land in large lots to inferior branches of his family, all of whom must support the dignity of lairds. The renters let the land out in small parcels from year to year to the lower class of people, and to support their dignity squeeze everything out of them they can possibly get, leaving only a bare subsistence. Until this evil is obviated Scotland can never improve."*

For us, however, the system provides valuable clues for working out likely relationships. While you cannot be dogmatic about what the relationship "would have been," you can be pretty confident, in the absence of any other evidence, that if X MacKie was the tacksman and Y MacKie was the laird, then X and Y were pretty closely connected by blood.

In the same fashion, and for the same reason of breeding up loyal fighting men, tacksmen tended to sublet their land to their own kin, as discussed in the next chapter.

The past comes to life

Working the land, a detail from Hume's *Survey of Assynt*, Map 1 (by kind permission of Lord Strathnaver).

Eadar a' Chalda today.

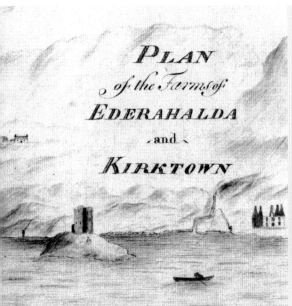

Eadar a' Chalda is shown on the map as a tiny farmhouse up above Ardvreck Castle (by kind permission of Lord Strathnaver).

A sheep watches two men fishing from their boat next to the towering Old Man of Stoer. From Hume's Survey of Assynt, Map 2 (by kind permission of Lord Strathnaver).

Gaelic tradition speaks of seers, such as Kenneth MacKenzie from Uig, Lewis, called Sombre Kenneth of the Prophecies. He could speak with the dead who emerged from the burial mounds at Samhain. Frustratingly, he seems not to have left written records of his conversations and, much as we'd like to ask questions of our deceased ancestors, time always forms a barrier between us and them, and perhaps that's for the best.

But, occasionally, the veil can be pierced, and these are the moments that make genealogy and family history electrifying. While using the maps in Hume's 1774 *Survey of Assynt* to find out more about the MacLeod family, I noticed the title of each map was illustrated. At first, I thought these were quite amusing, but then I noticed, in the background of Map no. 9's drawing of Ardvreck Castle, a tiny farmhouse, with a series of outbuildings, up on the hill. My eyes widened, as once we had walked up that very hill and examined the ruins of those very buildings, silent testimonies of the Clearances: the farm of Eadar a' Chalda!

From Hume's accompanying survey, I learned that Eadar a' Chalda had been home in 1774 to Duncan MacLeod, his wife and two children, and of Alexander

MacKenzie, his wife, four children and three servants. I never dreamed I'd see a drawing from two and a quarter centuries ago, depicting the flourishing settlement just as it was when Duncan and Alexander lived there.

I examined the other maps in more detail, and the more I looked the more wondrous the experience became. I knew the names of the MacLeods and the other inhabitants of Assynt from Hume's 1774 list, and had found out what sort of lives they led. But here in the margins of Hume's maps were pictures of the self-same people, living their lives. I have used some of them, with Lord Strathnaver's kind permission, as illustrations in this book. Perhaps most intriguing of all, the notes accompanying Map 1 includes a description of,
"A Machine call'd a Carscroom being a crooked stick like the Coulter of a plough like the figure here prefix'd and thus pushing before him with both hands and his foot performes the Work like an ebb ploughing; in this severe and tedious manner their tillage is carryed on throughout all the coasting farms ..."

Hume included a sketch of a kilted farmer using his cas-chròm. It was drawn from life: who knows, perhaps it was one of the very MacLeods I was trying to trace.

CHAPTER 13

Farmers and crofters

Most Scottish ancestors were not landholders, so were described as "in," not "of," the place where they lived. Unfortunately, their tenure of land was often informal, providing little security for them and few written records for us. However, even if you cannot trace them back generation by generation, you can still learn a lot about the sort of people they were by studying their social history.

Highland Hospitality by John Frederick Lewis (1805–76).

Farmers

Up to 1700, virtually all (80–90 percent) of Scotland's million or so people lived on the land, evenly scattered between bog and mountain. Roads were virtually non-existent and the meandering tracks linking the settlements were generally impassable save on foot or horseback. The fact that people say carts could travel between Glasgow and Edinburgh in good weather speaks volumes for the situation over the rest of the country.

Arable land was hard to come by, so large villages were rare. Most Scots lived in small hamlets, maybe a dozen or so per parish. Hamlets were called bailies in the Highlands, and farmtouns in the Lowlands (or kirktouns or clachans if they had a church, milltouns if

there was a mill, or cottouns if they supported only cottars).

The tacksmen who leased land generally farmed only part of it themselves and sub-tenanted the rest to small farmers, who did most of the work of actually cultivating the soil and tending the animals. Just as tacksmen were often relatives of their superior, so too might the tacksman's tenants be his own kin. Unfortunately, the difference between knowing this as a general fact and proving it in your particular case may be enormous, the problem being the lack of written records. Sub-tenancies were usually verbal arrangements, and estate papers that list the sub-tenants are very rare.

Cottars and laborers

Below the farmers came the great mass of cottars, also called pendiclers or grassmen. They are sometimes confusingly termed "landless," while in fact, they held land, totally informally, but only a hut with space for a kale-yard or potato patch, and no grazing rights for a cow. Cottars might pay their rent to the tacksman, but were more often under-tenants of the small farmers. In the Highlands, you even find cottars on parts of crofts — not living in a shoe like old Mother Hubbard, but crouched, so-to-speak, in the shoe's toe. They grew what little food their patch would allow, and tried to earn money elsewhere, serving or laboring for those above them, following them into battle when required, and — despite their poverty —

Runrig

Remains of runrig fields below Dun Charlabhaigh on Lewis.

Most hamlets were focused on a farm that might be occupied by a single farmer or husbandman, or were shared between any number of joint tenants as a conjoint tenancy (particularly common in Ross and Cromarty, and the Hebrides). Many joint tenancies operated by runrig: the arable land was divided into strips, and each tenant was allocated a certain number scattered across the whole, to ensure fair distribution of the better and worse land: under periodic runrig, these strips were reallocated regularly by ballot. Rundale was a modification of runrig, whereby larger (but still scattered) blocks of land were allocated between the joint tenants.

as deeply attached to the land as everyone else. Cottars were not always hard-up, for some worked as tradesmen, such as blacksmiths, shoemakers, weavers, carters and potters. In times of poor harvest, they might actually be happier than small farmers, though their conditions never even approached those of their counterparts in the burghs.

Life for 18th-century Ayrshire cottars was immortalized in Burns' *The Cottar's Saturday Night*, in which:

A blackhouse at Arnol, Lewis (LEFT), **preserved in its original state by Historic Scotland. It was called a blackhouse because it had dry stone walls, in contrast to newer buildings such as the cottage below, built with lime mortar and called a whitehouse.**

Sheilings

A group of shielings on the island of Jura.

Many farming and crofting communities had separate areas for summer grazing, with temporary shelters for themselves called sheilings (in Scots) or *airidhean* (in Gaelic, also called *ruigh* in the eastern and central Highlands). Each summer, the community would up-sticks and take their cattle up to the sheilings, to give the grass a chance to grow back around the farms. Writing in 1776, Thomas Pennant describes:

"A bank covered with sheelins, the temporary habitations of some peasants who tend the herds of milch cows. These formed a grotesque group; some were oblong, some conic, and so low that the entrance is forbidden without creeping through the opening, which has no other door than a faggot of birch twigs placed there occasionally; they are constructed of branches of trees covered with sods; the furniture a bed of heath; placed on a bank of sod, two blankets and a rug; some dairy vessels; and above, certain pendent shelves made of basket-work, to hold the cheese, the product of the summer. In one of the little conic huts I spied a little infant asleep."

Pennant missed the point entirely — it was a lovely time of year, when the community mixed together in the warm sun, and many a courtship led to marriage.

"The toil-worn Cotter frae his labor goes,
– This night his weekly moil is at an end,
Collects his spades, his mattocks, and his hoes,
Hoping the morn in ease and rest to spend,
And weary, o'er the moor, his course does
hameward bend."

We learn much about his home, his prayers and his way of life, including what his children are doing:

RIGHT: **A tired cottar carrying his tools home after another long day. This is an 1853 engraving by William Millar of a painting by John Faed.**

"Belyve, the elder bairns come drapping in,
At service out, amang the farmers roun';
Some ca' the pleugh, some herd, some tentie rin
A cannie errand to a neibor town:
Their eldest hope, their Jenny, woman-grown,
In youthfu' bloom-love sparkling in her e'e–
Comes hame, perhaps to shew a braw new gown,
Or deposit her sair-won penny-fee,
To help her parents dear, if they in hardship be."

In the Lowlands, from the 1700s onwards, there was a tendency to consolidate smallholdings into bigger farms. Many families were uprooted, and became hinds (landless laborers), hired at the local feeing fair on six-month or year-long contracts, living with their families in chaumers (lofts over stables), a corner of the farmhouse itself, or in bothies (wooden huts) — the latter being somewhat notorious for the bawdy songs and sexual freedom engendered by their primitive conditions. Some hinds, especially in the Lothians, might be hired on the same farm on a rolling basis all their lives, but the itinerancy of

the less fortunate is often reflected in census returns that show each child in the family being born in a different parish. Hinds often had to supply a female servant or bondager, usually their wife, daughter or sister. Many made the transition to industrial laborers, or fell the short distance down to the bottom of the pile as vagabonds and beggars — often from families that, a couple of generations before, had known their laird as their kinsman.

Besides the OPRs, cottars and hinds may appear in kirk sessions or local court records, and usually the poorer, drunker, randier and more dishonest your ancestors were, the better the chance you'll have of finding them, sometimes with a genealogical detail such as an age or place of birth. Less exciting mentions may include court records of witnesses or General Assembly lists of heads of households, especially those petitioning for the appointment of this minister or that. The kirk sessions may list people in communion rolls; "mortifications" recording bequests of money for charity and the poor people on whom it was spent; laborers hired to mend roads, bridges and church buildings; and the sadly rare "testificates" that recorded where incomers had been born.

The Poor

The term "poor" was reserved for those in need of outside help. The "undeserving poor" comprised vagabonds, drunks and "ne'er-do-wells," whom Knox condemned as "*stubborn and idle beggars who, running from place to place, make a craft of their begging.*" The "deserving poor" were "*the widow and fatherless, the aged, impotent and lamed,*" or simply hard-working families faced with starvation through bad harvests or unemployment. From the 1690s, the deserving poor were the responsibility of the parish, specifically of the kirk sessions and heritors (see below). A caveat in the system was that, to receive relief in the parish, you had to have been born there, or gained right of

A small village school on Easdale Island, Co. Argyll, around the end of the 19th century. Most of the children wear big boots, except for the boy standing on the left who is so poor that he wears little more than sackcloth. It is thought that he belonged to a family of tinkers who lived in the woods (courtesy of Easdale Island Folk Museum).

Heritors

The heritors were the holders of heritable land. On their shoulders, until the system was abolished in 1925, fell the responsibility of paying for the kirk, manse, school and (until 1845) the poor (though they could charge half their expenses to their tenants in a form of local tax). The heritors sat periodically to hear applications for poor relief. Those of their records that survive (in NAS class HR, with some in local archives) can provide a welcome extra layer of detail on the parish and its poorer inhabitants.

Photographed in the late 19th century, this Stornaway woman is laden down with blocks of peat for the fire, but is also busy knitting as she walks. Although many like her would have been very poor, she was probably not so desperate as to warrant help from the parish.

Potato famine

The potato blight that so devastated Ireland in the late 1840s spread to Scotland too. In the Western Highlands, crofters were as dependent on potatoes as their Irish kinsmen. Special Boards were established to help them — records are in the Highland Destitution catalog (NAS class HD, 1847-52) and can include details of wives and children.

settlement by marrying a local man or by having lived there for seven years without causing trouble.

The 1845 Poor Law Act established parochial boards, independent of the church, in each parish (which became, for that purpose, civil parishes). The transition took a few years, so kirk session and heritors' records are still worth searching a few years after 1845. In 1894, responsibility was transferred again, to local councils. The boards' minute books and accounts (which are closed from the 1930s onwards) can provide varying degrees of detail about applicants and what relief they were given, but most useful are their Registers of the Poor. Surviving records are generally held in local archives, and can be sought through **www.scan.org.uk**, and some are in NAS class CO. Registers of the Poor can include name, age, marital status, religion, occupation, name, age and income of spouse, and details of children, siblings and parents. They will say why the application was being made and, crucially, where people were born — particularly useful when seeking famine migrants from Ireland.

Registers of the Poor do not survive for Edinburgh, Dundee City or Aberdeen, but the Glasgow area is superbly well covered,

A restored blackhouse at Colbost Folk Museum, Skye, and the interior of the same building. The blackhouse's design developed from Norse longhouses.

specifically for Glasgow (from 1851), Barony (1861) and Govan (1876), and for other local parishes in Bute, Dunbartonshire, Lanarkshire and Renfrewshire, to 1948. They are at Glasgow's Mitchell Library (North Street, Glasgow, G3 7DN, 0141 287 2999, **www.mitchelllibrary.org**), indexed to 1900. Some other areas' records are online, such as those for Liff and Benvie Parochial Board 1854–65 and Dundee East's poorhouse register (1856–78), at **www.fdca.org.uk**. For more, see K.M. Forbes and H.J. Urquhart's "Records in the National Archives of Scotland relating to Poor Relief, 1845–1930," *Scottish Archives*, 8, 2002, pp. 9–32.

Crofting

Crofting was a type of landholding peculiar to the Highlands and Islands, defined by the 1883–4 Napier Commission as holding land for agriculture or pastoral purposes individually or in common (perhaps by runrig), direct from the

proprietor, at a rent of up to £30 a year. (The same commission defined cottars as occupying homes without agricultural land, worth up to £2.) The system started in the 18th century, when some lairds cut out the tacksmen and started renting land directly to small farmers, allocating each a parcel of the former farm as a croft.

In theory, as long as the rent was paid, the croft passed down from father to son (thus encouraging families to make more effort to look after their land than they had when they knew they might be

A turf-roofed cottage near Stromness in the Orkneys.

Bill Lawson's series of books on the *Crofting History of Lewis* lists the occupants of each croft, township by township within the parishes, compiled from records such as censuses but also, crucially, from living memory. The oral records allowed him to include many Gaelic patronymics (reproduced by kind permission of Bill Lawson).

Tolastadh a' Chaolais 87

Croft No 27

Murdo MacGregor c1770-c1820 [mac Dhonnchaidh]
= (1) Ann MacLeod
1 Donald   1801-   = Catherine MacDonald   Breacleit, Bearnaraigh   >> 27 Tolastadh
2 Norman   1807-93 = Flora MacArthur   8 Tolastadh   >> 12 Tolastadh
= (2) MARY MACDONALD 1773-c1853
3 Alexander   1811-   = Kirsty MacKay   4 Calanais   >> on 29 Tolastadh
4 Malcolm   1811-   = Kirsty MacDonald   Breacleit, Bearnaraigh   >>
5 Mary   1816-77 = Norman MacLeod   Crilals

----------Croft passed to son Donald MacGregor------

DONALD MACGREGOR 1801-   [mac Mhurchaidh Dhonnchaidh] 27 Tolastadh
= Catherine MacDonald 1801- [ni'n Aonghais Thormoid] Breacleit
1 Murdo   1834-
2 John   1837-
3 Ann   1842-
4 Angus   1845-

Donald MacGregor and family emigrated in 1851 to Bruce County, Ontario

----------Croft passed to John MacDonald 8 Old Dun Charlabhaigh------

JOHN MACDONALD 1799-1880 [Ian Dearg mac Iain] 8 Old Dun Charlabhaigh
= Isabella MacLennan 1801-59 [ni'n Alasdair] 18 Tolastadh
1 Marion   1832-60
2 Mary   1835-1910 = John MacIver   59 Breascleit
3 John   1838-   = Kirsty MacDonald   5 Pairc Shiaboist   >> 27 Tolastadh
4 Catherine   1841-dii

----------Croft passed to son John MacDonald------

JOHN MACDONALD 1838-   [mac Iain Dheirg] 27 Tolastadh
= Kirsty MacDonald 1837-1901 [ni'n Iain Dhonnchaidh] 3 Pairc Shiaboist
1 John   1869-   = Rachel MacLennan   16b Tolastadh   >> 27 Tolastadh
2 Angus   1871-   >> Newcastle
3 Annabella   1874-   = Alexander MacLean   55 Breascleit

moved on if the tacksman lost his lease). An exception was the early-19th-century system (called *suidhicheadh*) of allocating crofts for seven years and then rotating the families.

Sometimes, as families grew too big, crofts might be subdivided or parts would be sub-sub-let as homes for cottars (who might often be poor relatives of the crofter, or the previous croft-holder who, for whatever reason, had been unable to keep up the rent).

Kelp

A further motivation for landowners to introduce crofting was the kelp industry. Soda ash (sodium carbonate), made in southern Europe by burning certain plants, especially barilla, was used in many British manufacturing processes, such as glass and soap. The French Revolutionary and Napoleonic Wars (1793–1815) cut Britain off from these supplies, but it was found that the kelp that grew copiously around the Highlands and Islands had similar properties to barilla. As demand soared, so did prices, and lairds encouraged their tenantry to engage in the filthy work of growing, collecting and burning kelp. Some lairds cleared people to live on the coast in crofts deliberately designed to be too small to sustain families through agriculture alone.

On Harris, for example, the relatively fertile west coast is now largely deserted, due to families being cleared away in the 1790s, while the inhospitable, rocky east coast is peppered with crofts built for kelp farmers.

Despite the horrible nature of the work, kelpers flourished, and their tiny crofts became full of relatively healthy, happy children. Then, in 1815, the Napoleonic Wars ended, cheaper Continental minerals flooded back in, the kelp price plummeted and the crofters' incomes evaporated. Worse, they were now stuck on coastal crofts that could not sustain them. As if that wasn't enough, farmers used to collect kelp as fertilizer for their fields, but during the boom they had preferred to burn it for minerals. Consequently, the fields of 1815 were far less fertile than they had been in 1793.

The end of the wars also opened the seas to commercial shipping that offered passage to the colonies. Driven from the land by the collapse of the kelp industry, many people sailed abroad. Those who clung on then had to face the Potato Blight of the 1840s and 1850s, and a further wave of emigration ensued. Many descendants of the crofting families of Harris now live in Cape Breton, Canada.

Gathering kelp along the seashore and burning it for soda ash.

The Clearances

Until a few decades ago, the Highland Clearances were seldom talked about. Descendants of people who had been cleared knew little or nothing of what had happened, and cared less. In 1963, John Prebble's *The Highland Clearances* was published, and awareness of the events of the late 18th and early 19th century came back into sharp focus.

Only a small number of clans took part in the '45, but in the government backlash that followed, all clans lost the right to bear arms, to wear tartans and kilts and for their chiefs to exercise hereditary jurisdiction. The clan system started to crumble.

As government-imposed law and order spread north, the need to sow dragon's teeth (to use your land to raise fighting men) became redundant. Settling in Edinburgh, chiefs quickly forgot their ancient obligations to their kinsmen, and became absentee landowners. Within a generation of the battle of Culloden, few young chiefs spoke Gaelic, many married Lowland wives, and their desire for ready cash soared. Their land was seen simply as a source of revenue, no more. The administrators of the Confiscated Estates of 1745 had shown how lands could be "improved" by abolishing runrig, bringing in Lowland farmers to replace native

The Last of the Clan, by Thomas Faed (1826–1900), showing families forced from their traditional lands, waiting at the quay side for their ship.

Black Highland cows had vanished from the Highlands, but survived in Canada, where they had been taken by several prosperous settlers in the 1770s. During the recent BSE scare, the Canadian government decided to dispose of them, but Canon MacQueen of Barra arranged for some that were not infected to be brought back home. Now they are a familiar sight again in Lewis and Harris.

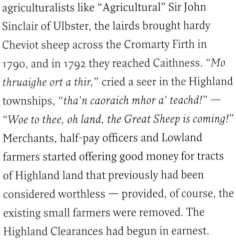

A glimpse of the Highlands as it would have been before the sheep came: black Highland cattle have been reintroduced to areas such as Lochan Lacasdail, Harris, and now graze happily alongside red ones again.

Soldiers from Highland regiments (such as these members of the Highland Light Infantry) were used to enforce the Clearances.

tacksmen, and consolidating land into large farms on which were reared black cattle that could be sold for beef.

Cattle cannot graze everywhere, so for a few decades the pace of change in the Highlands remained only moderate. But it was soon realized that the right sort of sheep could survive practically anywhere. As war with France loomed, the price of meat rose sharply and Highland lairds looked greedily at the profits that could come by replacing their distant kindred with the new, profitable "four-footed clansmen." Encouraged by progressive agriculturalists like "Agricultural" Sir John Sinclair of Ulbster, the lairds brought hardy Cheviot sheep across the Cromarty Firth in 1790, and in 1792 they reached Caithness. "*Mo thruaighe ort a thir,*" cried a seer in the Highland townships, "*tha'n caoraich mhor a' teachd!*" — "*Woe to thee, oh land, the Great Sheep is coming!*" Merchants, half-pay officers and Lowland farmers started offering good money for tracts of Highland land that previously had been considered worthless — provided, of course, the existing small farmers were removed. The Highland Clearances had begun in earnest.

As tacks came up for renewal, they were terminated, and when the tacksman was removed his sub-tenants had no rights at all. Small farmers, crofters and cottars could simply be told to leave their holdings, and go they must. Occasionally, "warning away notices" were issued by the sheriff courts, but usually no paper trail exists. Sometimes people were actively encouraged to emigrate, though usually they were offered alternative holdings on the least desirable land, often by the sea where fishing and (until 1815) kelp farming meant they could still be profitable to the estate.

1792 is remembered as *Blaidhna nan Caorach*, the Year of the Sheep, when tenants in Ross-shire tried driving the sheep back south. They were met by the local yeomanry and three companies of the Black Watch, summoned for fear that the protestors were Jacobites. Thereafter there was little resistance, for everyone knew the Government would support the lairds and their sheep before people.

It's hard to take sides now on the basis of surname or clan loyalty. Within the MacLeod clan, for example, many tacksmen, sub-tenants and cottars named MacLeod were cleared from their ancestral lands, yet MacLeods were among the soldiers who enforced the process. A scion of the Chiefs of Assynt, Donald MacLeod of Geanies (1745–1834), was the sheriff depute of Ross and Cromarty who brought in soldiers in the *Blaidhna nan Caorach* to defeat the tenantry.

The greatest landowner in the northern Highlands, so by default the worst offender in the Clearances, was Elizabeth, Countess of Sutherland (1765–1839), *Ban mhorair Chataibh* or "the great lady of Sutherland," wife of Lord Stafford, who later became Duke of Sutherland. James Loch, her chief commissioner, implemented a ruthless clearance policy with an army of factors and local commissioners. Between 1810–1812, they had cleared most of Assynt, Golspie, Loth, Clyne, Rogart and Dornoch. Prebble wrote that, *"The first white wave of Cheviot sheep broke over the Assynt hills before the people there had time to obey the writs of eviction. To the sound of phrenetic bleating, they pulled down their house timbers and walked with them to the coast where the villages in which they were to live had not been built, the boats from which they were expected to fish had not been launched, the nets unspun."*

Prebble benefited much from the work of Donald MacLeod, a stone mason from Strathnaver, Sutherlandshire, who lived through these dreadful times and later wrote *History of Destitution in Sutherlandshire* (1841) and *Gloomy Memories in the Highlands of Scotland* (1857). *"A large portion of the people of these parishes,"* wrote MacLeod, *"were in the course of two or three years, almost entirely rooted out, and those few who took miserable allotments … and some of their descendants continue to exist on them in great poverty."*

As time passed, clearances became yet crueller. The year 1813 was remembered as *Bliadhna an Losgaidh*, the Year of the Burnings. Until then, people had been allowed to take away their roof timbers, for wood was a scarce commodity in the Highlands. In 1813, fearing the disobedient people might return to rebuild their homes, factors started burning down farms, timbers and all.

In many cases, the year's crops were left to rot in the ground, or to be munched by the incoming sheep. We hear of desperate people creeping back in the winter to scratch for potatoes in the frozen fields, terrified of being caught trespassing. Donald MacLeod wrote that, *"Every imaginable means short of the sword or the musket was put in requisition to drive the natives away, or force them to exchange their farms and comfortable habitations, erected by themselves or their forefathers, for inhospitable rocks on the sea-shore …"*

Nobody knows what numbers were involved. Between 1810–1820, between 5,000 and 15,000 people were evicted in Sutherland alone. Many of those who stayed were given coastal crofts and encouraged to fish, and harvest kelp. Of life on the coast, Prebble tells us that the coastal strips, "were narrow patches on the cliff's edge, or bordered by bog and morass." The arable soil so thin that Donald Macleod wrote, *"In many places the spots the poor people endeavoured to cultivate were so steep that while one was delving, another had to hold up the soil with his hands lest it roll into the sea."*

Seed was blown away, salt and mildew ruined the crops, and cattle trespassed inland,

The Bernera Riot monument on Lewis, erected in 1992 by the islanders to commemorate their ancestors' struggle for rights. The cairn (stone memorial) includes a stone from each croft on Bernera and Tir Mor, and the coping stones at the top are from the crofts of the three men who were tried.

resulting in fines that the crofters could not pay for want of anything to sell. Needless to say, the occasional poaching of a sheep was punishable with transportation.

The Napier Commission

Highland families are a hardy lot. Despite the Clearances, the collapse of the kelp industry and the potato blight, a core population of survivors remained in their ancient lands

The Napier Commission return for crofters in Badnaban, Assynt, Sutherland (NAS AF 50 7/16), filled in by the Sutherland Estate (there were no cottars there). Back in the 1811 census, Badnaban had 10 households (so presumably 10 crofts), six of which were MacLeods. Here, on January 1, 1883, there are nine, of which five were MacLeods — suggesting (superficially, at least) a remarkable degree of continuity throughout a troubled period. Alexander MacLeod (1810–84) is shown here with a two-acre croft, for which he paid £2 rent, making it one of the two largest, though only by a few rods. His souming, the number of animals he was allowed, was four cattle aged a year or more and six sheep. He actually had three cattle aged over a year, one calf and four sheep. His croft supported just one family, his own, comprising six people. These would have been himself and his wife Christina MacLeod and four others, probably including his son and eventual successor Ally Alistair MacLeod (see p. 152).

beyond the mid-19th century. But conditions remained pretty dire, and by the 1870s pressures for social reform were mounting, for by now, rural Scots were not an ignorant peasantry but the products of church schools, very well aware of what was right and wrong, and, more to the point, what was decent. The 1870s and early 1880s saw the outbreaks of civil disobedience such as the Bernera Riot of 1874 on Lewis, and the Battle of the Braes on Skye in 1882, both protests against landlords taking away grazing rights because they wanted the land for game.

The crofters' plight concerned Gladstone's Liberal government. In 1883, he established a royal commission chaired by Lord Napier and usually referred to as the Napier Commission. During 1883, the commissioners traveled through the Highlands and Islands interviewing 775 crofters to discover exactly how they lived and what their grievances were. Transcripts of these interviews are published in the *Report of Her Majesty's Commissioners of Inquiry Into the Condition of the Crofters and Cottars in the Highlands and Islands of Scotland* (1884). A very readable analysis of the findings appears in A.D. Cameron, *Go Listen to the Crofters: the Napier Commission and Crofting a Century Ago* (Acair, 1986, repr. 2005), including a useful list of where and when the hearings were held.

The Napier Commission also sent forms to each estate owner requiring them to fill in details of their crofters and cottars:

- the name of each holder (but not the names of everyone else in the family)
- number of families in each croft
- number of houses on the croft
- total number of people living on the croft
- rent and other dues such as labor that the tenants had to give in return
- area of arable land
- area of pasture

ROYAL COMMISSION HIGHLANDS AND ISLANDS
RETURN respecting CROFTERS and COTTARS on the Estate of *Sutherland* the Property of *The Duke of Sutherland* as at the 1st day of January 188[3]

- souming or summing, which was the number of horses, cows, calves and sheep they were allowed to keep as well as the number they actually had
- the cottars' return asked for names, if their house was on someone else's croft, if they paid rent and if so to whom and what their occupations were.

The forms (save those for the Orkneys and Shetlands, which were lost) are in NAS AF 50 7/1-7/19 (crofters) and 8/1-8/7 (cottars), arranged by county and then alphabetically by estate. They are rather cumbersome to search, but worth the effort.

In the mid-19th century, many crofters clung to the hope that a son enlisting in the 93rd (Sutherland) Highlanders guaranteed that his father's croft would still be there when he returned. John Sutherland of Musie in Rogart, Sutherland, told the Napier Commission, *"as an inducement to my father to enlist in the 93rd Highlanders, my grandfather got a promise of being left undisturbed in his lot during his lifetime, and if his son survived his term of service, he would succeed him. My father joined that regiment and was wounded at New Orleans. On the expiry of his service in the army he returned home and expected to succeed his father as tenant of the whole lot but, to make room for another man who was evicted from a sheep farm, my father was*

summonsed and deprived of the best part of his father's lot."

Alexander MacCaskill, cottar and boatman in Soay said, *"my grandfather went to the army — at least he was forced to go — and his bones are bleaching on a West Indian island and now his grandson (myself) was evicted to a rock or island not fit to be inhabited."*

Nobody liked having to perform labor as part of their rent. John MacCaskill, cottar and shoemaker in Fernilea, Bracadale, Skye, claimed that in spring, summer and harvest he had to labor on the laird's land for up to three days a week at one shilling a day, time he should have spent (at much greater profit) making shoes. Alexander Cameron, cottar in Cuilmore, Skye, said that as part of his rent he had to provide a maid servant for the sheep farm at Drynoch for

Badnaban in the 1970s. Many families were cleared to this coastal settlement in the early 19th century (courtesy of Mrs Nan MacLeod).

Ally Alistair MacLeod, crofter at Badnaban, pictured here on the rocky land from which his family had eked a living for four generations. Some of his ancestors had been cleared from fertile Cnocaneach just prior to 1812 (see p. 35), and were cousins of the Angus and Alexander MacLeod who were cleared thence that year (courtesy of MacLeod Family Collection).

Ally Alistair MacLeod (son of Alexander of 1883) with his wife Mary Ann and their grandson David Service (MacLeod Family Collection).

Barbara Service, daughter of Ally Alistair.

Ally's son Jimmy MacLeod with his sisters Alice and Mary and others, in his fishing boat (MacLeod Family Collection).

Alexander MacLeod was called "Ally Alistair" because Alistair is the Gaelic version of Alexander, Ally is short for it, and he had to be distinguished from his father of the same name. He was born on the family's croft in Badnaban, near Lochinver, on Apri 21,l 1861, and died there on August 13, 1940. His father's father, Angus MacLeod (b. 1756), was in Badnaban by 1811, having been cleared from an unknown location. The family's tradition is that they came from Elphin, about 10 miles (16 km) to the south-west. Angus's wife Margaret was also a MacLeod, whose parents had been cleared to Badnaban from nearby Cnocaneach just prior to 1812.

Asking around in Lochinver, the lady in the post office sent us to see Mrs. Nan MacLeod. Nan had lived in Badnaban for the first 84 years of her life, and married a MacLeod who was not, so far as she knew, related to Ally Alistair. (*"Some people you knew you were related to, and some you weren't."*) She remembered Ally Alistair well. He had three cows, a horse called Lilly, who was used for plowing, and a bull. As a girl, Nan was terrified of the bull, and used to walk a long way around to avoid going near it. Ally Alistair kept sheep on the hills in summer and at the croft in winter, and sold lambs at six shillings apiece at market in August and sheep in October. He took wool all the way to Dingwall, a trip lasting two days, using the money he made there to buy sacks of oatmeal, which were very dear at £3 a sack.

In the Clearances, inland farmers who were moved to tiny coastal patches like Badnaban were told to supplement their living by fishing, and it was fishing that took Ally Alistair all the way round to Lossiemouth on the east coast, where he met and married Mary Ann

White on September 11, 1891, bringing her back, no doubt, in the boat with him. When the First World War came, he served in the Navy, surviving to come back home to his wife and bairns. Nan remembers him in the 1930s with a boat called *The Nain*, selling his fish at the Haddiebank down the coast near Inverkirkaig.

The Badnaban men would fish in all weathers. If a storm caught them, they might have to put in further down the coast, in which case a child would be sent running down to see if they were safe. In the winter, they caught "lovely big lobsters," that were packed in straw and sent to Billingsgate on Mondays, the money coming back on Thursdays. At Christmas the Billingsgate fishmongers sent them colanders as presents.

Ally Alistair's eldest son Jimmy took over the croft after the Second World War and farmed and fished there all his life. It was sold out of the family after he died. The house is now the beautifully renovated home of a local bank employee, while some of its outbuildings stand decaying.

Ally Alistair's last surviving daughter, Mrs. Barbara Service, "Old Babs," left Badnaban with her sister Alexandrina (known as Alice) in the 1930s. They arrived in Glasgow by train and found jobs as domestic servants. Looking back in 2006, a year before she passed away, she said that earning, "ten bob [shillings] a week working in a warm, dry house" in the suburbs of Glasgow, with the prospect of becoming a silver service servant, was vastly preferable to life back home. Besides, they could send money back to supplement their parents' small income. And she had no dewy-eyed sentiment about crofting life, either: *"Cows all over the place knocking down the fences, and mud everywhere,"* she commented. *"It was a dump!"*

50 days a year. His sister had filled this role, but then she married and, having nobody else to do the job, he was first threatened with eviction and then his rent was raised. Charles Cameron, crofter in Acharacle, Ardnamurchan, Argyll, said his rents were so high that his daughter working in England had to send money back: "What she is able to give me helps to pay my rent and to support me."

The people's demands were reasonable. They had all heard about the "Three Fs" that underpinned Gladstone's 1881 Irish Land Act — fair rents, fixity of tenure and free sale (freedom to sell their holdings, or otherwise be compensated for improvements they had made, if they gave their holdings up). They were aggrieved that the best land was devoted to sheep and deer, while they had to make do with the worst.

Gladstone could do nothing about the latter — to this very day crofts remain on poor land, while the rich shoot deer on the most fertile stretches. But he gave them rights, under the Crofters Act of 25 June 1886, allowing crofter and cottar alike the "Three Fs," so that holdings could be passed down in the family, with a Crofters' Commission

to adjudicate on fair rents. Some court cases brought by crofters from 1886 onwards, and by small farming tenants from 1912, can be found in the Scottish Land Court (NAS class LC), which is arranged by county, and indexed (the records are closed for 75 years).

Cutting peat, for use on the fire.

Sometimes sheep were not sheared, but wool was instead "rooed" or plucked by hand, as shown in this picture from Shetland, about 1910.

CHAPTER 14

Clans and tartans

Many Scottish families belong to clans, and many more believe they are associated with one on the basis of a family surname. With the new surge in interest in family history, clans have been reinvented as societies with a strong emphasis on genealogy.

The *Clach MhicLeoid*, the "MacLeod Stone" at Aird Nisabost, Harris. This Neolithic monolith stands boldly on its headland, easily visible from the seaways all around. It became the rallying place of the MacLeods when summoned to arms by the fiery cross.

The clan system

Rather like black holes that can bend space, the clan system had an oddly warping effect on Scottish genealogy and continues to exert a force on Scottish family history that is absent from the genealogies of most other European countries. The main advantage it gives us is that, before the mid-18th century, surnames can usually be localized to very specific areas and connected back to specific traditions and founders. The main disadvantages are that the system encouraged people to adopt surnames that were not theirs, and that once a surname is associated with a clan, many people believe that all bearers of the surname must, ergo, be members of that clan.

The earliest references to clans come from the 1100s (the earliest, apparently, is to the Clanna Morgan of Buchan), though that

probably tells us more about the lack of earlier records than what was actually going on. The term simply means "children" or "family," and the idea derived from the ancient tribal system of the Picts, broken down and modified by the Dalriadan and Viking invasions.

By the time it emerges into recorded history, "the clan" denoted a family, or mixture of local families who, regardless of their actual ancestry, professed a common descent from the clan's founder. They owed allegiance to a chief who was the living representative of the founder, whom they regarded as their senior kinsman. Clans often had several prominent branches, whose kinship was assumed, though could seldom be proved.

During what Dr. Johnson called, "the ages of tumult and rapine," violence underpinned the clan system. The economy, such as it was, was based on farming black cattle, and raiding those of neighbouring clans. Raids led to blood feuds and vendettas, with blackmail and demands for "protection money" thrown in. The famous Glencoe massacre of 1692, when the MacDonalds of Glencoe were massacred by Campbell soldiers to whom they were giving hospitality, was merely one in a web of inter-clan conflicts (the MacDonalds had once killed 100 Campbells by barricading them into a barn near Oban and setting it ablaze). To call his clansmen to arms, the chief would send runners through the region, bearing a blazing or fire-blackened cross. The men would gather and march to war. Actual violence was perhaps less prevalent than posturing, and we know that even blood feuds could be terminated by simple satisfaction of honor — compensation might be paid and signed guarantees would put an end to the vendetta.

Chiefs and clansmen

Chiefs were chosen by their close male-line relationship to previous chiefs. Under the ancient

A romantic view of clansmen and women is shown in this poster for an 1895 drama, *Bonnie Scotland*.

Gaelic system, the new chief could be a son or male-line grandson or great-grandson (or great-great, the limit varied) of any previous chief, chosen on the basis of his ability to lead the clan in battle (under "tanistry," the chief could nominate his successor). By the 1500s, though, most clans had adopted primogeniture, whereby the eldest son succeeded his father. Great chiefs often had lesser ones to serve them: the Clan Rankin's chiefs were pipers to the MacLeans of Col, and the MacCrimmons served the MacLeods of Skye in the same way, with a piping school at Borreraig near Dunvegan. Johnson described the chief as, "*the father of the clan, and his tenants commonly bore his name.*" His power was absolute: "*He told them to whom they should be friends or enemies, what King they should obey, and what religion they should profess.*"

Membership of the clan involved an obligation to fight and a consequent access to land. Genealogy was key to clansmen's belief in their membership of the clan, through which they derived their obligations and privileges.

Dunvegan Castle, Skye, stronghold of the MacLeod chiefs of Skye for nearly 800 years.

compared to MacLeod of Dunvegan who, in 1739, actually sold some of his people as indentured servants in the Carolinas, America).

As the tribal system became incorporated into the feudal system, many clan chiefs, those "rugged proprietors of the rocks," as Dr. Johnson called them, received Crown charters, or charters from their feudal superiors, for their lands. As Prebble puts it, *"The land was his [the chief's], its ownership long since settled by the swing of a broadsword, and although most chiefs had realized that paper now carried more weight in law than steel, their tribal or feudal levies still protected their title deeds."* Some chiefs missed out, though, and found their land being granted to others. By 1590, several clans, such as the Camerons, Macnabs and Macgregors were landless, tenants of other feudal lords, many of whom were chiefs of other clans. Loyalty, however, remained with the chief, not the landlord. Smout quotes the example of the Earl of Huntly calling his tenants to arms in 1562. Among them were many MacIntoshes, but as Huntly's quarrel was not a MacIntosh one, the MacIntosh chief ordered his clansmen to return home — and home they went.

Their precise genealogical connection to the chief determined their hierarchy and precedence, and decided how land was allocated and indeed how they sub-allocated their holdings to their own minor kin. As W.H. Skene wrote in 1891, *"In such a state of society the pedigree occupied the same position as the title deed in the feudal system, and the sennachies were as much the custodians of the rights of families as the mere panegyrists of the clan."*

Clan lands

The clan's link to land was tremendously important, but was never set in stone. The idea that clansmen had inalienable rights to their ancient lands is nonsense. Clan chiefs themselves had no compunction about moving clansmen about. In 1599, when Macdonald of Islay ordered his people to leave Kintyre, they went meekly (his actions pale into insignificance

Highland dancers at the Highland Games, clad proudly in their clan tartan.

Highland and Lowland

The clan system refers primarily to the Highlands, but not exclusively so. Border clans are first mentioned in 1587, but had existed throughout the Lowlands in all but name for much longer. As the Crown weakened from the late 1200s onwards, Highland practices started spreading into Lowland dynasties, whose Norman or French nobles began to behave increasingly like their Gaelic neighbors. Even Robert II's son Alexander Stewart, Earl of Buchan (d. 1394 or 1406) called out his feudal host as if it was a clan, and led fearsome raids on his neighbours, earning himself the nickname, "the Wolf of Badenoch." One means of consolidating local power was by bonds of manrent, of which about 800 survive, mainly for the 16th century, whereby men bound themselves to their feudal superior in the reasonable expectation that they would be granted land as a result. The main tools, however, were tacks or leases granted by Lowland lords, like the Grants and Frasers, to "gentlemen" of the lord's name. These created networks of patronage so akin to the clan system that this is what, effectively, they became. Smout writes that,

"economically, such 'gentlemen' might be little more than peasants, but if they were the kin of the lord they had a family right to protection. When a great family rose to power, his surname rose with him: the rise of the Earls of Huntly in the north-east was accompanied by the rise of all the cadet branches of the family and by the proliferation of small tenants named Gordon throughout the counties of Aberdeen and Banff; when the cathedral of Dunblane fell into the hands of successive bishops surnamed Chisholm, its main offices were also held for generations by clerics surnamed Chisholm. The kinsman," he continues, *"gave earls and barons of his kin all the deep respect due by a son to a father, though he never treated them with the abject deference due from a mere commoner to a remote and mighty lord. The whole atmosphere of kinship was a complex one, compounded both of*

egalitarian and of patriarchal features, full of respect for birth while being free from humility. It appeared uncouth beyond Scotland mainly because it was a legacy of Celtic [i.e. Gaelic] influence unfamiliar to the outside world."

Smout summarized the situation by saying that the difference between Highlands and Lowlands was mainly one of emphasis — Highland clans were based on kinship modified by feudalism and Lowland families were feudal, tempered by kinship. "Both systems were aristocratic, unconscious of class, designed for war."

This fine young man, photographed about 1910–20, only needs a bonnet to complete his Highland dress.

The end of the clan system

The clan system started to unravel in the early 18th century due to forfeiture of land after the 1715 rebellion. Yet it still functioned until the '45, when clan loyalties were a major factor determining the choosing of sides.

Dr. Johnson writes of the situation before Culloden: the clansmen were, *"perhaps not unhappy ... a muddy mixture of pride and ignorance, an indifference for pleasures which they did not know, a blind veneration for their chiefs and a strong conviction of their own importance,"* while the chiefs themselves *"walked out attended by ten or twelve followers, with their arms rattling."* In *The Sea Kingdoms*, Alastair Moffat repeats a story told to him in Skye that, *"appears in no written version"* of the battle of Culloden. As they stood in the sleeting rain, waiting for battle, some of Charlie's men sang the twentieth Psalm, but others recited their genealogy so that, *"while the government soldiers were shouting abuse and challenges ... the clansmen were remembering why they had come to fight. For their families, for their history and the land from which neither was divisible."* In the next few hours, many of them were laid low by Redcoat grapeshot.

Seeing how easily Bonnie Prince Charlie had been able to call out the clans, the state took vigorous steps to wipe them away, ending the chiefs' powers and banning the wearing of tartan.

The clan chiefs played a large part in dismantling the system themselves when they began to look for ways to make the land yield greater profit. When they stopped seeing their clansmen as beloved kinsmen the stage was set for the Highland Clearances. *"The estate perhaps is improved,"* said Johnson, *"but the clan is broken."*

Tartan

Tartan could easily have become a curiosity consigned to museums and history books. Instead, it has been reinvented as a symbol of the Scottish nation, whether Highland or Lowland.

Tartans started off as patterns common to particular Highland districts or settlements. As these areas also happened to have dominant ruling clans, the district's distinctive tartan became associated with these too, becoming specifically clan tartan. The patterns have evolved considerably since then, so some now may bear little resemblance to those used in the past.

Tartan was not found outside the Highlands until the Act of Union in 1707 that formally united Scotland with England, when, according to Sir Walter Scott, Lowlanders started wearing it in protest against the English, paving the way for it to become a symbol of Scottish identity. Calling the clansmen to arms in 1745, Prince Charlie draped himself in Royal Stewart tartan, creating a direct link between tartan and Jacobitism. Consequently, tartan was banned in the aftermath of the '45, and the law was not repealed until 1782. When tartans reappeared, they may or may not have been the same as those worn before 1745. The first published source for tartan is the *Vestiarium Scoticum*, first produced in the early 1800s by the Allen brothers, who claimed to be grandsons of Bonnie Prince Charlie (they weren't; see p. 81). Their book purported to contain descriptions of the distinctive tartans of the clans of 16th-century Scotland, and, forgery or not, it cemented tartans into the heart of Scottish national consciousness. After this came a rash of publications listing district, family, clan, clergy, Highland, Lowland and general tartans, up to 600 in all.

More tartans

- Scottish Tartans Authority
  Fraser House
  25 Commissioner Street
  Crieff, Perthshire
  PH7 3AY
  (0)1764 655444
  www.tartansauthority.com
- Sir Thomas Innes of Learney's *Tartans of the Clans and Families of Scotland* (Edinburgh, 1938; eighth ed., Johnston & Bacon, 1971)

Tartans are recorded at Lord Lyon's Office. While anyone can sell any type of tartan, registered or made up, it is a criminal offence to sell a registered tartan labelled as something it is not, or which represents a registered one inaccurately. As new ones are discovered or invented and accepted, the number registered increases. As Charles MacKinnon of Dunakin put it,

"tartans and Highland dress are today regarded as the emblems not of the Highlands alone but of all Scotland. When we find Smith tartan being advertised, as we do now, it is clear that the great band of Scottish Smiths have joined the ranks of those who claim to be 'entitled' to a tartan of their own. Why not? They were never a clan, but if Kidds and Coburgs can have their tartans, why not Smiths?"

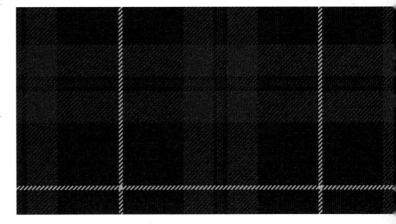

The tartan of the Macleods of Assynt.

Badge "LAUREL". Slogan.— "CREAG AN TUIRC" (The Boar's Rock) Arms.

THE CLAN TARTAN

AB ORIGINE FIDUS

COPYRIGHT W&A.K.JOHNSTON LTD EDIN.

CLAN MACLAREN

The tartan, the arms, and the plant badge, laurel, of Clan MacLaren. The clan's slogan is *Creag an Tuirc* ("The Boar's Rock").

Clan badges

It seems likely that, before the 18th century, plant badges, not tartans, were the main means of telling clansmen apart. Each clan had one: heather for the MacDonalds, fir for Grant and holly for MacIntosh. A list of badges is in F. Adams' *The Clans, Septs and Regiments of the Scottish Highlands* (National Library of Canada, 1965). Each has a story attached to it. The Morrions, for example, use pieces of driftwood. They were hereditary brieves (judges) under the Lordship of the Isles, but fell into relative obscurity after the 17th century. Their Gaelic name is Mhic Gille Mhoire, "sons of the servants of St. Mary," but their traditional descent is from Mores the son of Kennanus, an illegitimate son of the King of Norway who, with his wife and child, was cast ashore on Lewis clutching a piece of driftwood.

The genealogical implications of the clan system

Modern guides to Scots families, such as *Collins' Guide to Scots Kith and Kin* (1953), list many septs or divisions under Clan names. These septs were created for several different reasons. For example, the Clan Chattan's Smiths are descendants of Henry Gow, a Perth smith who once stood in for a missing member of Clan Chattan in a fight against the Clan Kay in 1396. The Beatons, one of 18 surnames listed under MacLeod of Harris (and Skye), were probably originally Bethunes from Flanders, established in Angus by the 12th century and then at Balfour, Fife. A Beaton of Balfour became a physician and settled in Skye, passing his skills on to his descendants there, and as physicians to the MacLeods, they became regarded as a sept of the MacLeods. On the

Sources for clans

The pedigrees of many clan chiefs who received baronetcies or noble titles are in old editions of *Burke's Peerage*. The final printed version of *Burke's Peerage* (2003) for the first time included the pedigrees of all the clan chiefs recognized by Lord Lyon.

- **www.scottishamericansociety.org/id23.html**
  A handy list of the origins of Scottish clans.
- **www.ancestralscotland.com/visit/
  itineraries/Clan_Douglas**
  Includes itineraries for a number of clan tours.
- **www.gsi.org.uk**
  The Gaelic Society of Inverness journals contain some new research on clan origins.

- **www.celts.org/clans**
  Mainly Irish, but includes some Scottish clans, i.e. MacLeod.
- **www.clanchattan.org.uk**
  A gateway to Clan Chattan's many constituent clans and septs and their societies.
- **www.electricscotland.com/webclans/clanmenu.htm**
  A list of clans recognized by Lord Lyon, providing brief histories and links to websites. Electric Scotland's home, the Odom Library, Moultrie, GA, USA, houses the archives of 135 clan societies.
- **www.clan-maccallum-
  malcolm.3acres.org/ScotClanFamily.html**
  A non-comprehensive list of clan societies.

other hand, the Griers are a sept of the MacGregors because of direct descent from a son of the eleventh MacGregor laird.

Clearly, of the world's millions of Smiths, only the descendants of Henry Gow are part of Clan Chattan. The only Beatons who belong to the Clan MacLeod are the descendants of the physician. Only the Griers who are descended from the eleventh MacGregor laird are part of Clan MacGregor. So, if you're a Smith, a Beaton or a Grier, it's not your surname alone but this plus your family tree that will show whether you are part of one of the Clans Chattan, MacLeod or MacGregor. In the absence of a proven pedigree, the best you can do is see where your direct line lived as far back as you can trace them — if this was in the area occupied by these septs, then you may indeed be a member.

Far more worrying for we genealogists is the statement, found in many books on clans, that people who wanted clan protection simply adopted the surname of the local clan and, by inference, ditched their original surname. This would imply that farmer Black one day saw laird, MacDonald, riding over the hill, and declared, "I'm a MacDonald, of proud MacDonald blood, and you're my distant kinsman!" But that is nonsense, of course — in a culture underpinned by genealogical knowledge, no such imposture would ever be believed and the local sennachie would have had Black for breakfast.

People may well have adopted clan surnames that were not originally their own, but where oral history survives, so too will the knowledge that there was not a blood link. In my own experience of oral village history, people often know which people of their surname aren't related. In his *Harris in History and Legend* (Birlin, 2002, 2006), a modern sennachie, Bill Lawson, cites an example from Harris where a change was remembered. At the end of the 18th century, a young boy called MacDonald on the estate of Captain MacLeod was such a good poacher that, when the captain was unable to find deer to hunt, the boy still led him to a herd. The captain rewarded the boy with land to build a house, and bade him call himself MacLeod, which he and his descendants continue to do — but still knowing their original identity.

It's only once such oral knowledge has gone that mistaken beliefs about kinship based on surnames arise.

Bill Lawson's wife Chris told me of a grey area — where oral knowledge was fading, but not gone completely. She has three lines of ancestors now surnamed MacLeod, but who, in their own oral tradition, were called Bànaich ("the fair people"), Glasaich ("the grey people") and Clann 'ic Leòid. The latter definitely considered themselves to be true MacLeods, though without any supporting genealogical evidence. The Glasaich and Bànaich, she thinks, may have been given the surname MacLeod by the minister or estate clerk, simply because they had no proper surname, but lived

The Highland Games in Glengarry, Canada, shows how enduring is the idea of the clan and its associated images of tartan, pipe and band.

in a predominantly MacLeod area. However, nobody can know for sure that they didn't have an earlier tradition of MacLeod ancestry.

Sometimes, lines of clansmen can be traced back to clan chiefs. Bill Lawson told me a story from Tarbert, Harris, of Norman MacLeod of Tarbert (c.1756–1846), whose son Alexander settled in the Philippines and wrote a letter to his aunt Mary MacLeod in Cape Breton, on June 14, 1895. He signed himself,

"Alasdair mac Thormoid mhic Neill mhic Thormoid mhic Thormoid mhic Iain mhic Neill. Am bheil an t-sloinntireachd? (is that pedigree correct?)"

Another descendant of the same family, now in Skye, recited the same pedigree and told Bill that the earliest Neil was "Niall a chaidh a'chrochadh ann a Lit" — Neil who was hanged at Leith. Bill thinks it likely that this was Neill MacLeod, who was hanged there in 1613 (the number of generations works).

This Neil embodied the most characteristic qualities of his clan. His indictment reads, *"from your very youth you being trained up in all manner of barbarous cruelty and wickedness, and following the pernicious example of your godless parents, kinsfolk and country people, having committed innumerable oppressions, heirschipes and violent deeds ... ye accompanied Norman McClaud, your brother, with two hundred barbarous, bloody, and wicked Hielandmen ... in warlike array, with bows, darlochs, two-handed swords, hag-butts, pistols and other weapons ... sentenced to be hanged at the Market Cross in Edinburgh, his head planted on a stake and his lands forfeited."*

Neil, says the indictment, was one of the illegitimate sons of Roderick, last chief of the MacLeods of Lewis. Thus, the MacLeods,

A farmhouse at Cnocaneach, Assynt: originally a MacLeod family farm, then ruined in the Clearances, rebuilt for a shepherd in 1870 and now fallen into ruin again.

descendants of Norman of Tarbet, can be traced back to the MacLeod chiefs of Lewis.

Sadly, many families just cannot make firm links like this. Between your earliest known ancestor and the chiefs of their name there may simply be untold generations who were not recorded, and you cannot know if the male line had always had the surname, or had adopted it. DNA offers hope for many, because genetic tests are proving that many people with clan surnames share the same Y-chromosome DNA, proving a male-line connection with each other.

The MacLeods in Badnaban furnish an example of how a tentative link might be found using some oral history and surviving population lists.

MacLeods in Badnaban

Before the Assynt OPRs start in 1798, few families can be traced back with certainty, but

Malcolm Bangor-Jones's *Population Lists of Assynt 1638–1811* (Assynt Press, 1997) brings together six lists of names: the 1811 census (now held by the Highland Council), compiled by the schoolmaster and (breaking the rules) giving householder's names; a 1774 population list from John Hume's *Survey of Assynt* (NLS Dep. 313/1697 (Sutherland Papers); a 1746 list of heritors and parishioners who did not join the Jacobites in 1745, compiled by the minister (NLS, Saltoun Papers); the 1691 Hearth Tax (NAS E69/23/1), and two lists generated from the legal wranglings of the MacLeods chiefs of Assynt and the MacKenzies, who wanted to seize their land in return for unpaid debts; a 1667 list of tenants and proprietors derived from a Horning (NAS GD305/1/155/71); and a 1638 list of tenants and occupiers, from a Discreet of Removing in the Court of Session (NAS CS7/505 ff.63v-65v). Some of these include patronymics, such as

MacLeod of Badnaban

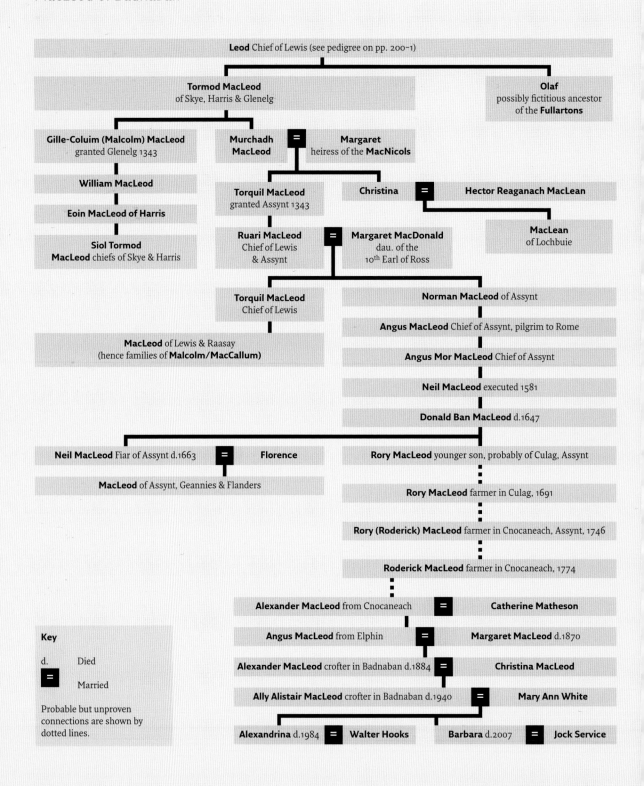

Leod Chief of Lewis (see pedigree on pp. 200–1)

Tormod MacLeod of Skye, Harris & Glenelg

Olaf possibly fictitious ancestor of the **Fullartons**

Gille-Coluim (Malcolm) MacLeod granted Glenelg 1343

Murchadh MacLeod = **Margaret** heiress of the **MacNicols**

William MacLeod

Torquil MacLeod granted Assynt 1343

Christina = **Hector Reaganach MacLean**

Eoin MacLeod of Harris

Ruari MacLeod Chief of Lewis & Assynt = **Margaret MacDonald** dau. of the 10th Earl of Ross

MacLean of Lochbuie

Siol Tormod MacLeod chiefs of Skye & Harris

Torquil MacLeod Chief of Lewis

Norman MacLeod of Assynt

Angus MacLeod Chief of Assynt, pilgrim to Rome

MacLeod of Lewis & Raasay (hence families of **Malcolm/MacCallum**)

Angus Mor MacLeod Chief of Assynt

Neil MacLeod executed 1581

Donald Ban MacLeod d.1647

Neil MacLeod Fiar of Assynt d.1663 = **Florence**

Rory MacLeod younger son, probably of Culag, Assynt

MacLeod of Assynt, Geannies & Flanders

Rory MacLeod farmer in Culag, 1691

Rory (Roderick) MacLeod farmer in Cnocaneach, Assynt, 1746

Roderick MacLeod farmer in Cnocaneach, 1774

Alexander MacLeod from Cnocaneach = **Catherine Matheson**

Angus MacLeod from Elphin = **Margaret MacLeod** d.1870

Alexander MacLeod crofter in Badnaban d.1884 = **Christina MacLeod**

Ally Alistair MacLeod crofter in Badnaban d.1940 = **Mary Ann White**

Alexandrina d.1984 = **Walter Hooks**

Barbara d.2007 = **Jock Service**

Key

d.   Died

=   Married

Probable but unproven connections are shown by dotted lines.

"John MacLeod alias macNeil," John MacLeod son of Neil MacLeod, but in most cases the only genealogical clues are where people lived.

Assynt was inherited by the MacLeods of Lewis in the 14th century and was ruled from the early 15th century by a line of chiefs descended from Norman, second son of Roderick, sixth MacLeod chief of Lewis. In June 1672, the MacKenzies obtained, "letters of fire and sword," and besieged their castle of Ardvreck, and forced them to surrender.

The later lists show many more MacLeods than the earlier ones, with a particular jump between 1691 and 1746 — evidence of people simply taking the MacLeod name, perhaps? Besides natural increase in population, though, the later lists seem to become more inclusive. That of 1746, for example, names all non-Jacobite men able to bear arms, so is far more complete than the 1691 hearth tax, which only names householders who were not exempt from paying due to poverty. Some MacLeods may have

Calder House, by Loch Assynt, an imposing mansion built by the MacKenzies to celebrate their triumph over the MacLeods. Now a ruined symbol of their pyrrhic victory.

Hume's 1774 map showing Cnocaneach and its nearby sheilings: the valley (top right) with wooded sides is the one that the Ordnance Survey maps identify as Bad na h'Achlais (courtesy of Lord Strathnaver).

come in from elsewhere, but there is no recorded reason for immigration, and if anything you'd think MacLeods in this period would want to leave. As the MacLeod surname existed here earlier, there's no sensible reason for looking outside Assynt for the origins of its later inhabitants. Finally, as the MacLeods had lost their power to the MacKenzies, it seems pretty unlikely that anyone would adopt the surname for any expectation of gain. It seems likely, therefore, that the MacLeods in 19th-century Assynt were of the blood of the original chiefs.

My particular interest was in the family of Ally Alistair MacLeod, crofter in Badnaban, Assynt (see p. 152). His grandfather Angus MacLeod married Margaret MacLeod in Assynt on November 14, 1807. Margaret died at Badnaban on February 14, 1870, aged 88, so was born about 1780, when her parents were named as Alexander MacLeod and Catherine Matheson. Having placed a short account of Ally Alistair's life on my website, I was contacted by Roddy MacLeod, who is descended from Margaret's brother Roderick. He told me that, in the 1960s, Kenneth MacLeod, MBE, of nearby Inverkirkaig had recorded some oral tradition, that this same

Alexander was born at Bad na h'Achlais. Hume's *Survey of Assynt* shows that Bad na h'Achlais was a sheiling (a summer encampment where the people went to graze their cattle) on the farm of Cnocaneach. Cnocaneach was $1\frac{1}{2}$ miles (2.4 km) east of Badnaban, and I already knew that families had been cleared from thence to Badnaban.

This placed Ally Alistair's ancestors back in Cnocaneach in the late 18th century. The next challenge was to find a plausible route back through the various population lists, one that did not involve ludicrous jumps, or far-fetched assumptions, to the clan chiefs.

The 1774 list includes an Alexander MacLeod, possibly our man, as a tenant farmer on a conjoint tack at Dubh Chlais, a mile north-east of Cnocaneach. Cnocaneach itself was occupied by four families, of whom three were MacLeods and presumably his relations: Roderick MacLeod, his son Roderick MacLeod, and Roderick MacLeod MacAngus (i.e. Roderick MacLeod, son of Angus MacLeod). We know Alexander was born on the farm of Cnocaneach— since his daughter Margaret was born in 1780, he was probably born about

Cnocaneach (and, behind it, the peaks of Canisp, left, and Suilven, right), seen from Loch Drumswordlin.

the 1750s or early 1760s. The 1746 list combined Cnocaneach and neighbouring Drumswordlin, and shows eight MacLeods, of whom one was probably his father.

- Rorie MacLeod
- Murdo MacLeod souldier
- Alexander MacLeod souldier
- John MacLeod alias MacOnil souldier
- John MacLeod alias macNeil souldier
- Angus MacLeod souldier
- Alexander MacLeod alias Maclein
- Angus MacLeod alias MacAnnish

Rorie is the Gaelic equivalent of the Norman name Roderick. Alexander named his eldest son Roderick, so this was probably his father's name, and here we have a Rorie in 1746 (though all the foregoing were probably very close relatives).

The 1691 hearth tax does not list any MacLeods at Cnocaneach, Drumswordlin, or Dubh Chlais. As people moved about as leases were granted and expired, it makes sense to see where Rorie et al's forbears may have been. The MacLeods in Assynt were:

- Culag: Rorie McLeoid 1
- Leadbeg: Alexander McLeoid 2
- Knockan (not the same as Cnocaneach): John McLeoid 1.

This can't possibly be a comprehensive list of MacLeod householders in Assynt at the time. All the same, Rorie MacLeod of Culag, an old farm barely a mile north-west of Cnocaneach, is at least a plausible ancestor for the MacLeods at Cnocaneach, where the name Rorie/Roderick remained in use for the next century.

The 1667 list, compiled before the MacLeods' fall from power, shows the following of their name in Assynt.

- Elfin: John McCleud brother of the Laird of Assint

- Culag: Rorie McCleud
- Achmelvish: Alexander McCleod
- Claichtoill: Neill Mccleod
- Stoir: Angus McCleod bailzie of Assynt
- Oldini: John and Neill McCleods
- Ardivar: Johne mccleod

Culag was somewhat removed from the conflict at Ardvreck and the presence of an earlier Rorie there suggests a degree of continuity. In 1638, we have:

- Donald mccleod alias neilsone of assint
- Fingoll [Florence] mcleod relict of umqll Neil mccleod alias neilsone of assint
- Neil mccleod her sone and appeirand air
- Alexander Mccleod in Torbreck
- Florence Mccleod in In[v]erchirkak
- Hew mccleod in loch beanache

As with the 1667 list, we have several people identified as members of the chief's family. The others were presumably his kinsmen, holding their tacks in return for military service. Rorie and Culag are not mentioned, but the pedigree of the chiefs themselves does include a Rory, a younger brother of Neil (1592–1633), whose widow Florence and son Neil *do* appear in the 1638 list, as does their father Donald Ban, Chief of Assynt. Nothing is known of this Rory, so he could have been identical with the Rorie who was in Culag by 1667, or else (say) his father or grandfather.

This is a tenuous connection, of course — the aim was never to produce a proven pedigree, as it was clear from the start that this would never be possible. But rather than giving up, this exercise provides a plausible route back through the few records that are available, and shows how one part of Assynt's later population could well have been, as they no doubt believed themselves to be, descendants of the MacLeod chiefs of Assynt.

PART 4

Comings and goings

Scots have been emigrating abroad since ancient times, but there was a mass exodus in the late 18th and early 19th centuries due to the Highland Clearances. Many Americans, Canadians, Australians, New Zealanders and other people from England to South Africa have migrant ancestors who were farmers, cleared off their land by the great estate-owners to make way for more profitable sheep. This section suggests ways of tracing migrant ancestors' places of origin in Scotland, and shows how surnames and DNA can link people today with the ancient peoples who founded Scotland far back in history.

The Thistle, a cutter yacht designed by G.L. Watson and built by D.W. Henderson & Co at Glasgow. From early days Scottish people have set sail across the seas to destinations both near and far.

CHAPTER 15

Emigration

The beginning of the journey at Abercairney station, near Perth, in 1910. The station master is on the left, and in the middle is Andrew Comrie, about to emigrate to Prince Edward Island, Canada. On the right is Andrew's brother John, who saw Andrew aboard his ship in Glasgow.

Scots have been emigrating since ancient times, but a combination of poverty and ill-treatment at home, combined with desire to take up the opportunities offered by the new colonies abroad, caused a mass exodus in the 18th and 19th centuries. While Scotland's population now is just over 5 million, it has been estimated that some 30 million families worldwide are of male-line Scots descent — just under half a percent of the world's population. And that's to say nothing of all the non-Scots families who, like mine, have a Scottish ancestor somewhere in their family tree.

During the Highland Clearances, a surgeon, Robert Knox penned the sarcastic lines, *"the dreamy Celt exclaims at the parting moment from the horrid land of his birth 'We'll maybe return to Lochaber no more.' And why should you return, miserable and wretched man, to the dark and filthy hovel you never sought to purify?"* In a different age, when John Macleod Tutterow of North Carolina was interviewed in James

The popularity of some pastimes is a strong hint that there is a migrant community. Here New Yorkers are playing the Scottish game of curling on a frozen pond.

Hunter's *Scottish Exodus* (Mainstream Publishing, 2005), he provided the clearest reason possible: *"We have been in America for two or three hundred years at best, and oftentimes much less. That's why so many of us are looking to connect with whatever our folks came from. In Skye, I have deeper roots than it's possible for me to have in North Carolina."*

General sources and techniques for emigration

You very much want your migrant ancestors to have been followers of emigration trends, rather than mavericks, as it makes their origins much less difficult to trace. The hardest to track back are young bachelors who struck out on their own, or anyone wishing to evade debts or the law.

When James Loch, Lord Sutherland's senior estate commissioner, was justifying the Clearances, he claimed that, *"in a few years, the character of this population will be completely changed ... the children of those who are removed from the hills will lose all recollection of the habits and customs of their fathers."* Luckily, tradition was more persistent than he thought. The MacDonalds of Bruce County, Ontario, for example, were so numerous that they used by-names, many of which, such as Kelper ("kelp farmer") harked back to life in their native Hebrides.

Top tips for finding the origins of migrant Scots

If you do not know where your Scottish ancestor came from, then start with these techniques that can help you find out.

- Oral history within your family, or gained by contacting distant cousins via sites such as **www.genesreunited.com**.
- Names given to houses and farms may be those of the place of origin in Scotland.
- Record sources in the country of settlement that might shed light on family origins include death certificates of migrants that, in

some states and provinces, provide parents' names. A migrant's will may refer to relatives living back home, or to siblings who had also migrated, but whose origins may be easier to trace than his own.

- DNA matches with people who already know their Scots origins.
- Trace back to your migrant ancestor's first place of settlement in the new country. Find out from local museums and local histories if settlement there was by certain groups at specific times, and if it is known in general where migrants originated. Bear in mind that people often migrated in groups and look at sources (such as censuses) to find out who your migrant ancestors' original neighbors were, and find out if their origins are known.
- Localize the surname in Scotland, using surname dictionaries and clan or surname societies. Look at where the surname occurs most commonly using the regular search facilities on ScotlandsPeople, and telephone directories in libraries or online. Several websites offer access to telephone directories, including **www.192.com**.
- Don't be too quick to assume that the ancestor's point of embarkation, if you find it out, was necessarily near their place of origin. Many Highlanders traveled to Glasgow or even Liverpool before setting sail.

Having said that, the point of embarkation is still a partial clue if no others exist.

- For the better-off, Scottish testaments and services of heirs refer to many relatives who have migrated. Services of heirs contain many references to Scots living outside Scotland, providing links from places of settlement to places of origin, such as David Alexander of Petersburgh, Virginia, who was served heir to his brother James Alexander, wright at Lebanon, Cupar, 1818.
- If your male ancestor married after his arrival abroad, consider whether his wife's family may have traveled out with his own, in which case her origins may be a clue to his. Equally, if the couple arrived already married, you can start by seeking their wedding back in Scotland.

Two pitfalls to avoid:

1 The way surnames were spelled is often a red herring. This was determined by clerks, not the people themselves, so don't fall for the old trick of "Mc" surnames being Scottish and "Mac" Irish; no such distinction ever existed.

2 Ages can be suspect too, especially when emigration societies set restrictions on the ages of people they would help. Not surprisingly, people who fell outside the required range bracket simply lied about their ages.

Online sources

www.abdn.ac.uk/emigration
Aberdeen University's Scottish Emigration Database of over 21,000 passengers who embarked at Glasgow and Greenock for non-European ports between January 1 and April 30, 1923, and other Scottish ports 1890-1960.
www.immigrantships.net/
The Immigrant Ships Transcribers' Guild website.

www.chebucto.ns.ca/Heritage/FSCNS/Scots_NS/Come_Away_In.html
Scots in Nova Scotia.
www.nls.uk/catalogues/online/scotsabroad/index.html
The NLS's page of links to its holdings concerning Scots migration abroad.
www.genealogymagazine.com/scots.html
A reliable essay on Scots migration to the Americas.

To England

While the surname Scott in Scotland can denote the presence of recent Irish settlers, when it occurs in medieval England it often indicates Scots incomers. Its popularity in 13th-century Cumberland, Westmoreland and Northumberland suggests Scottish settlement there, while its presence in eastern England in the 12th century may stem from servants of David I of Scotland, who was also Earl of Huntingdon.

Until James VI became King of England in 1603, Scots were classed as foreign aliens. Migration was not extensive and examples of Scottish families in England, where Scotland was sometimes referred to as "North Britain" or just "N.B.," are exceptions. Some well-to-do migrants applied for English citizenship so as to bequeath property there, and these appear in *Letters of Denization and Acts of Naturalization for Aliens in England, 1509–1603*, edited by W. Page (Huguenot Society of London; vol. 8, London, 1893).

The Napiers of Dorset and Somerset descend from John Napier or Napper, thought to have been a 16th-century Scots immigrant. The surname Galbriath appears in Sussex, mangled by local pronunciation as "Coldbreath." Early 17th-century Chancery records reveal the Scottish birth (though sadly not the exact place of birth) of William Mercer, progenitor of the Mercers of Uxbridge, Middlesex. James VI and I brought many Scots to London with him in the 17th century, and thereafter migration down the road to London, *"the noblest prospect which a Scotsman ever sees,"* as Dr. Johnson described it in 1763, happened in increasing numbers. In the 18th century Scotland's education system was vastly superior to England's, so that century saw a veritable flood of Scots professionals into England as doctors, engineers, administrators and gardeners.

Their numbers included William Paterson (1658–1719), from Tinwald, Dumfriesshire, who founded the Bank of England; James Watt (1736–1819), from Greenock, the pioneer of steam engines, who settled in Staffordshire; Thomas Telford (1757–1834), from Westerkirk, Dumfriesshire, the engineering architect of the Menai Suspension Bridge, Whitstable Harbour, and many other works; John Loudon Macadam (1756–1836), from Ayr, who invented "tarmac;" on a less exalted level, my ancestor James Paterson from Selkirk (see pp. 208–9), founder of the road haulage company Carter-Paterson; and John Forsyth (born in Old Meldrum in 1742), a florist who settled near Hull, whose maternal grandson was the landscape gardener Joseph Forsyth Johnson (1840–1906), whose own great-grandson is the popular entertainer performing under the stage name of Bruce Forsyth.

To Ireland

The early Gaelic Scots were from Ireland, but there was always a backwash of migrants from Scotland across the North Channel, so narrow that the Antrim coast is visible, on a clear day, from the Mull of Kintyre. These included medieval gallóglachs or "foreign warriors," mercenaries from the Hebrides and western Scotland with surnames including MacAllister, MacDonald, MacSweeny, MacSheehy, MacLeod

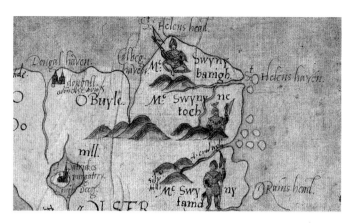

Scottish gallóglachs making their presence felt in Ulster. From John Goghe's "Hibernia," 1567.

rulers of Ulster fleeing abroad to escape charges of treason. James granted their lands to Protestant Undertakers, men who undertook to "plant" the country with Protestant settlers who would "civilize" the wild Catholics by their presence and example. Aside from troublesome septs of Border clans, such as Grahams and Armstrongs, James favored good, hard-working Lowland Presbyterians such as the Montgomerys, Hamiltons, Frazers, Morrisons, Kerrs and Pattersons.

and McCabe, who wielded their two-handed swords for the Irish chiefs against the Normans and were granted lands in payment. The great influx of Scots into Northern Ireland came in the 17th century, once James VI and I had been handed the poisoned chalice of Ireland along with his softer English inheritance. In 1607, the Flight of the Earls saw the principle native

While the Scots migration to England was random, the Scots plantations in Ireland were generally by groups from the Scottish estates of the Undertakers. The identities of the planters themselves were seldom recorded at the time, and church registers in Ulster (and back in their place of origin) are unlikely to have survived. The Undertakers, however, were generally

Clan Campbell

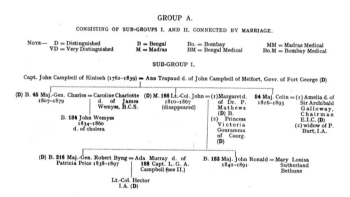

Major Sir Duncan Campbell's *Records of Clan Campbell in the Military Service of the Honourable East India Company 1600-1858* (Longmans, Green & Co., 1925) includes pedigrees of Campbell officers in India, emphasizing how occupations ran in families. The book includes the strange tale of Lieutenant Colonel John Campbell of Kinloch. The ex-Rajah of Coorg, India, had a daughter, Princess Gouramma, whom he persuaded Queen Victoria to adopt. The child ended up being looked after by Lady Login. Queen Victoria wanted the princess to marry Dhuleep Singh, but he

had other ideas, and suggested a union between Gouramma and Lady Login's brother Lt. Col. Campbell. Princess Gouramma died of consumption aged only 23 in 1864, leaving a daughter, later rumored to have been secretly murdered, but who actually grew up normally and married Capt. H.G. Yardley. It was Lt. Col. Campbell himself who vanished. He was last seen leaving, *"his lodging in Jermyn Street one day, carrying a small hand-bag, and from that day to this no trace of him was said to have been found."*

prosperous merchants, army officers or titled nobles, whose Scottish estates can often be traced. With luck, the same surnames will be found there as in the place of plantation, enabling a tentative link to be made back to Scottish soil. In the rare cases where detailed estate papers survive, so much the better.

To Continental Europe

The 16th and 17th centuries saw small but significant emigration from Scotland to Continental Europe, as younger sons of landed and merchant families explored opportunities that existed in foreign armies and ports. In particular, many apprenticed craftsmen and merchants settled in Russia (where an estimated 250,000 people may now have Scots roots), Scandinavia and all round the European coast.

To India

From 1660 to 1947, many British (and thus Scottish) families spent time in India, usually as soldiers but also as administrators, doctors and engineers. Few families stayed there for good, but plenty of Scottish family histories have an Indian component.

The Honourable East India Company (HEICS) controlled parts of India from the 17th century until after the Indian Mutiny of 1857, when it was replaced by the government-run India Office until independence in 1947.

The original records of the HEICS and India Office, including chaplains' returns of baptisms, marriages and burials (there was no General Registration), together with Indian directories and *India Army Lists*, are all accessible at the India Office Library, now part of the British Library. Useful too is the Percy Smith India Index at the Society of Genealogists. The India Office records in fact cover British activities as

The Clayhills

My first encounter with a Scots family who settled in northern Europe was with the Kleighels family of Helsinki. They are descended from Johann Clayhills, a burger and councillor of Tallin, Estonia, in the 18th century, several of whose sons became officers in the Russian Tsars' armies. One of their grandsons, Nicolai Kleighels, became governor general of Warsaw and general adjutant to Tsar Nicholas II in 1910. Johann's father Thomas had settled in Riga, Latvia, and his origins would have been hard to trace had he not taken with him a beautifully illuminated patent, still in the family's hands, issued by the burgh of Dundee on March 31, 1660, "*to protect him against all evil intrigues*" and declaring Thomas to be, "*born in March 1626 ... son of William Clayhills and his wife Margatha Clark*," and stating, "*his grandfather is Thomas Clayhills, from a noble family of Baldovy.*"

The Clayhills family had acquired their estate of Baldovy through money made as merchant burghesses in Dundee. Though well recorded in the senior male line, the junior branch that led to Thomas needed to be traced from scratch, through Dundee's burgh records. Margatha Clark's husband William, "son of Thomas Clayhills, merchant," was admitted a burgess in 1631. Thomas was admitted a burgess in 1582 by right of his deceased father William (Thomas registered his father's testament a few months later). This William Clayhills was admitted as a merchant burgess in 1560, and can be traced back to the earlier Clayhills of the 16th century (see my article "Clayhills Genealogy," *Family History*, 19 no. 157, NS. 132, July 1998. pp. 140-51).

far as Aden, Gulf, Burma, Afghanistan, China, Malaysia and St. Helena. See M. Moir's *A General Guide to the India Office Library* (British Library, 1988) for more detail.

To the Americas and New Scotland

The 17th century saw the opening up of the snowy wastes of Canada by the French in Quebec and the British in Newfoundland, Nova Scotia and Prince Edward Island.

Nova Scotia (New Scotland) was the inspiration

Scottish soldiers in the Napoleonic Wars. Some soldiers who served abroad settled down and stayed there, thus contributing to the Scottish diaspora.

founded in London in 1670, was trading along the shores of Hudson's Bay in north Canada. Many of its employees were Orcadians, already used to the hardships of cold and darkness, and since the company encouraged seasonal work, young men from the Orkneys and Hebrides might sail to Canada each year, then return home with their wages. Being used to speaking both Gaelic (or Norn) and English, islanders proved adept at picking up the language of the Native Canadian Cree People, and some brought Cree wives back with them. Several Hebridean families still have particularly dark complexions as a result, and use the family nickname "Indian."

Hudson's Bay Company records are in the Provincial Archives of Manitoba, Winnipeg (**www.gov.mb.ca/chc/archives/hbca/**), with microfilm copies at TNA, London, but not, strangely, NAS (they have a little material, in RH4/47, for example). Records can be ordered via interlibrary loan. Wills of employees date from 1717 and ships' logs from 1751, but few personnel records exist before 1770. Thereafter they can be extremely useful in establishing places of origin.

Scottish numbers in Nova Scotia were swelled in the mid-18th century by the Ulster Scots, Presbyterians from Ulster who had settled first in New England and who came north at the invitation of Governor Lawrence to take the place of expelled French Canadians.

Especially after the Union of 1707 lifted various restrictions to their movement in the new colonies, Scots settled all over the Americas, but particularly favouring New Jersey, New York, Georgia, South Carolina and Jamaica.

Sons of wealthy Scottish families went as enterprising merchants and pioneers, and poorer Scots went as indentured servants, their passage paid in return for laboring for their

of Sir William Alexander, first Earl of Stirling (c.1570–1640), who found an enthusiastic patron in James VI and I. The colony's royal charter was granted in 1621, and in 1624/5 an order of baronets was created to promote colonization. Wealthy men, such as landholders and merchants, were "invited" to maintain soldiers there and buy land, for which they were given a new hereditary baronetcy of Nova Scotia.

After conflict with the French, permanent colonization did not take off in Nova Scotia until 1713.

Meanwhile, the Hudson's Bay Company,

patron at the other end. Some went because they found themselves on the wrong side of religious or political issues, such as Covenanters after 1690, and Jacobites after 1715 and 1745-6, some of whom were volunteer migrants, others transported prisoners. Some migrants were tacksmen and their tenants, forced to leave by rising rents at home, their leaders fantasizing about establishing their own clans in the Americas.

John Macdonald of Glenalladale (of the MacDonalds of Clanranald), called Mac Iain Oig ("son of young John"), felt an obligation to save his relatives and friends from ever-increasing rents in Scotland. So he bought land on the island of St. John in the Gulf of St. Lawrence in 1772 and took tacksmen and sub-tenants from South Uist, Moidart and Arisaig to settle it. Few such plans came to fruition, however, for once across the Atlantic the tenants realized there was land for all, and no need to oblige themselves to new lords.

A considerable number of Scots took the British side in the American War of Independence. Some British regiments, such as the 82nd and 84th that were raised in America came to Windsor, Nova Scotia, to train and were later disbanded there, the soldiers being given land grants in Hampshire, Halifax, Cumberland and Pictou Counties. Many families who supported the British left America after the war was lost in 1784, and went to Canada. Numbering some 70,000, and known as United Empire Loyalists, they made claims (now at the National Archives of Canada's audit office) for loss of land. The United Empire Loyalists Association of Canada (50 Baldwin St., Suite 202, Toronto, Ontario, Canada, M5T 1L4, 416 591 1783, **www.uelac.org**) offers the best resources to start research.

The Highland Clearances caused a major wave of migration, particularly to Prince Edward Island, the Red River Valley and Nova Scotia (of which Cape Breton is the most easterly extremity). Settlers in Prince Edward Island,

Glengarry, Scotland, a beautiful wild scene, but whose solitude was purchased through the high price of the Clearances.

Duncan S. McIntosh winning a steer-roping contest at Regina, Saskatchewan, Canada, in 1896. He was the manager of a ranch named Glengarry; many Canadian place names reflect migrants' homes in Scotland.

Ontario, included migrants from South Uist and the mainland from the 1780s, and later (1840s) from Skye. A group from Pabaigh, off Harris, were cleared in 1846, having been accused of being illegal whisky distillers (they were, but the real reason for the Clearance was that the land was wanted for sheep). Finding the best land already taken, they settled in the highlands of Loch Lomond, Ontario.

Dr. Johnson wrote in 1773 that when, *"whole neighbourhoods formed parties for removals ... departure from their native country is no longer exile. He that goes thus accompanied, carries with him all that makes life pleasant. He sits down in a better climate, surrounded by his kindred and his friends."* Group migrations are helpful for genealogists because, if the origins of the group are known, then the likely origins of any family within them can be ascertained. Of course, families did not always stay in the first place of settlement. Settlers in (for example) Quebec,

finding the soil very poor, tended to spread out, south into the United States or west into the prairies of Manitoba and the North West Territories (Scots are often credited with having led the colonization of western Canada).

Group migrations from Gaelic-speaking areas ensured the survival of Gaelic in Canada. The 1891 Canadian census revealed some 3,500 Gaelic speakers living near Montreal — where Gaelic survived so too did patronymics, some recording Scottish-born ancestors whose memory has been effaced, by the Clearances, from Scotland altogether.

A notable promoter of early 19th-century migration was Douglas, Earl of Selkirk, who was one of the few landowners genuinely sympathetic to the plight caused by the Clearances. He acquired grants of land in the Red River Valley, settling it with Clearance migrants from Mull, Lewis, Argyll and Sutherland, especially MacLeans, MacGillvrays, MacEacherns and

Livingstones. On the Clearance of Strath Kildonan in 1813, Prebble writes,

"they were offered meagre lots of land on the cliffs at Helmsdale, the choice of becoming herring-fishers or leaving the country altogether. Ninety-six young men and women proudly chose exile – Gunns, Macbeths, Mathesons, Sutherlands and Bannermans from townships between Garlag and Borrobol. In early June they sailed from Stromness where they boarded the emigrant ship, Prince of Wales. Two months later they disembarked at Fort Churchill on Hudson Bay ... They endured a Canadian winter for which even the Highland snows had not prepared them, and they wrote bitterly to their parents advising the old people to give up all thought of a second emigration ..."

But further clearances in 1815 left others no choice but to join them, notably a party led by James Sutherland from Ceann-na-Coille in Helmsdale, who established a new Kildonan there.

Glengarry in Ontario is named after Glengarry in Invernessshire, from which the MacDonnells were cleared. Each farm in new Glengarry was named after the farmers' original homes in old Glengarry, and customs persisted — when war broke out between Canada and the United States in 1812, the fiery cross was sent round the glen, and the clansmen formed a new militia regiment that won laurels in the successful campaign that ensued. The 1852 census of Glengarry (reprinted in F. Adam, see p. 106) shows no less than 3,228 MacDonnells or MacDonalds there, with much smaller numbers of Macmillans (545), MacDougalls (541) and others.

Other causes of migration included the collapse of the kelp industry in the Highlands after the end of the Napoleonic Wars (1815) and the Potato Famine from the 1840s onwards — between 1846-61, probably about 60,000

A useful source for family history researchers are lists like this one of commissioned officers in the Hudson's Bay Company, Canada, from 1872–1881. It includes: James A. Grahame, Chief Commissioner, 1; Charles G. Brydges, Land Commisioner, 3; George, S. McTavish, Inspecting Chief Factor, 4; William Charles, Inspecting Chief Factor, 5; Colin Rankin, Chief Factor, 10; Peter W. Bell, Chief Factor, 11; James S. Coulston, Chief Factor, 12; Richard Hardisty, Chief Commissioner, 13; Archibald McDonald, Chief Factor, 14; Charles Stuart, Factor, 32; Horace Belanger, Factor, 33; John McIntyre, Factor, 34; Roderick Ross, Factor, 35; Robert Williams, Factor, 36; Ewen McDonald, Factor, 37; etc. The number of Scottish names is striking.

Highlanders emigrated due to this, notably from the areas of Glenelg, Knoydart and Morven and the isles of Tiree and Coll. Such migrations are seldom well-documented, but this is not true of the Crofters and Cottars Colonization Board that, in the late 1880s, ran a program to aid migration to Canada, especially Manitoba, and whose records are in the NAS (AF51).

Between four and five million modern Canadians are from Scottish families, almost a sixth of the total population, but rising to almost seven-eighths of the population of Nova Scotia. Notable Scots Canadians include

Canada's first Liberal prime minister, Alexander Mackenzie (1873–8), and the wartime prime minister, William L. Mackenzie King (1935–48).

In the United States some five million Americans consider their families to be of Scots origin, and more than four million others are of Scots-Irish origin — a fraction of the U.S.'s vast population, but many, many more will have some Scottish ancestry. Famous Americans of Scottish ancestry include the industrialist Andrew Carnegie (1835–1919), from Dunfermline; writer Washington Irving (1783–1859), author of *Rip Van Winkle;* and President Woodrow Wilson (1856–1924), whose grandfather was a Scots Presbyterian minister. Less known are the Scottish origins of President George Washington, whose male-line ancestors (who acquired the manor of Washington, Co. Durham) descended from Gospatrick, Earl of Northumberland, a great-grandson of Malcolm II, King of Scots (d. 1034). See the pedigree on pp. 196–7 showing clan origins.

A page from Bill Lawsons' *Register of Emigrants from the Western Isles of Scotland 1750–1900*, volume 1, "The Isle of Harris" (Bill Lawson Publications, 1992). Reproduced by kind permission of Bill Lawson.

```
CAPE BRETON                                                          -21-

Roderick MacKillop                                                  HE 59
    = Ann Shaw
    1 Donald    1801-     (see HE 54)       3 John    1807-   (see HE 58)
    2 Catherine           = Angus Morrison

Roderick MacKillop emigrated from Obbe in the 1840s and settled at St. Ann's, Victoria County.
    ------------------------------

MACKINNON
Alexander MacKinnon 1802-      from Pabbay                          HE 60
    = Mary Morrison 1801-
    1 Donald     1834-     = Lexy MacLeod      4 John      1843-   = Sarah MacLeod
    2 Catherine  1836-     = David Gwynne      5 Roderick  1846-   = Alexina MacLeod
    3 Donald     1841-                         6 Mary      1850

Alexander MacKinnon emigrated from Pabbay in the 1840s and settled at Cape North, Victoria County. His son
Donald settled at Ingonish.
    ------------------------------
```

Whisky

The smoky interior of an illict whisky distillery, reconstructed at the Colbost Folk Museum, Skye.

Back in 1695, Martin Martin wrote from the Hebrides that, besides common *usquebaugh* (whisky), there was also thrice and four-time distilled whisky, the latter *usquebauch-baul*, "*which at first taste affects all members of the body; two spoonfuls of this last liquor is sufficient dose; and if any man exceed this, it would presently stop his breath, and endanger his life.*"

Anyone wondering why whisky was so popular in Scotland has only to go for a walk on a brisk winter's day in flurrying snow or driving rain, and imagine spending the whole time from dawn to dusk bent double, scratching potatoes from the freezing earth, only to return, sodden and aching, to a low, dark hut and a meagre dinner. Small wonder people longed for a wee dram, and that so much was distilled illicitly in sma' [small] stills and sold illicitly in shebeens. Shame on the miserable government that sought to tax it in the first place, when people drank in the main to stave off misery.

We hear a lot about whisky through the efforts of excise officers to catch illegal distillers, shebeen-keepers and larger fry and bring them to book at the Justice of the Peace courts. In the 19th century, sheriff court records include the granting of licences to innkeepers, but many of these used illegal means to obtain stock. Rosemary Bigwood quotes the story of Alexander Lambie, changekeeper (innkeeper) of Inverary, who was caught with five gallons (19 litres) of British spirits for which he had no permit. "*His wife, Florence McKay, denied obstructing the officer when he attempted to gauge the cask but did admit obstructing him when he tried to remove it!*"

When seeking excuses for the Clearances, landlords often cited illegal whisky-distilling. The Countess of Sutherland complained in 1813 of Clan Gunn, "*who live by distilling whisky and are unwilling to quit that occupation for a life of industry of a different sort.*" Converting barley into whisky, however, was a sure way of making some money for people who had little else to sell for cash, and in many poor areas it was an important part of the rural economy.

Scots' migration to the Americas was not just restricted to the north. Robert Harper, originally from Caithness, settled at Rio Gallegos, Patagonia, where he was known as "Robbie the Sheep Shearer."

North American sources

Migrant communities could harbor vicious feuds. This 1844 cartoon, "Jamie and the Bishop" shows Scottish-born journalist James Gordon Bennett railing against the Catholic bishop of New York, John Hughes. Another Scotsman is offering Jamie support — once he's finished scratching his back against a lamppost — while an Irishman with a gin bottle and a club is offering to defend the bishop.

A. Baxter's *In Search of your Canadian Roots: Tracing Your Family Tree in Canada* (Genealogical Publishing Co., 1999)

is a fine guide to tracing back to migrant roots. Particularly useful are petitions and grants for land in the Canadian national and provincial archives, as described by Baxter. Those for Quebec and Ontario date from the 17th and 18th centuries respectively. B.D. Merriman, *Genealogy in Ontario, Searching the Records* (Ontario Genealogy Society, 3rd ed. 1996) is very useful for Scottish settlement there. See also D. Dobson's *Directory of Scottish Settlers in North America, 1625–1825* (GPC, 7 vols, 1984–1993) and D. Whyte's, *A Dictionary of Scottish Emigrants to Canada Before Confederation* (Ontario Genealogical Society, vols 1–4, 1986–2005).

For the United States, see D. Whyte, *A Dictionary of Scottish Emigrants in the USA* (Genealogical Publishing Co., 2005). A good tip for Scots who fought in the US army in the First World War (1917–18) is to look at their draft registration cards, which include date and place of birth and the birthplace of the father (searchable at **www.ancestry.com**).

Pembina Post, a Hudson's Bay Company trading outpost in Manitoba, 1860. Many Scots men and Canadians of Scottish descent worked here.

To the Antipodes

The explorer Captain James Cook gave Scottish names to several Pacific island groups he discovered in the 1770s, such as New Caledonia ("New Scotland") and the "New Hebrides," now Vanuatu.

Cook's main discovery, of course, was Australia. The American War of Independence discouraged Scottish migration across the Atlantic, and turned the bows of transportation ships south toward New South Wales. The first migrants were mainly criminals sentenced to transportation, from the First Fleet (1787) onward. Cases were heard in the High Court of Justiciary, where precognitions (cataloged in the NAS online catalog) contain most salient details. Registers of prisoners in NAS HH21 can also be helpful. Transportation itself was organized in London, recorded in TNA convict transport registers 1787–1870, copies of which are on microfilm in NAS RH4/160. Lists are chronological by the ship's departure, and Scottish prisoners are usually near the end of the list for each ship.

Only about three percent of transportees to Australia were Scots, but the first six governors of New South Wales were Scottish, setting a pattern for heavy Scots influence in Australia's development. Before long, New South Wales and Van Dieman's Land (Tasmania) were starting to attract better-off voluntary Scottish settlers, such as doctors, engineers and brewers. In 1827, Peter Cunningham wrote *Two Years in New South Wales*, encouraging many to go, and advertisements in the *Edinburgh Courant* spoke of, "*the climate of Italy, the mountain scenery of Wales and the fertility of England.*" From the 1830s, poorer migrants started coming too, attracted perhaps by the promise of a better climate than Canada, and by free passages, especially those offered to skilled farm laborers and unmarried girls from 1832.

Several of these young women preparing for a ceremony at the Chinese temple in Sydney, Australia, in the 1940s were Chinese–Scottish–Australians, with a grandmother from Aberdeen.

Darien scheme

Colonization was not always successful. In 1693, William Paterson (founder of the Bank of England) established the Company of Scotland Trading to Africa and the Indies, aiming to colonize Darien (the Isthmus of Panama) as a world-wide trading center. Many Scots with money to invest in shares contributed to its half-a-million-pound capital, and 1,200 souls volunteered to migrate there on five ships, setting sail from Leith in 1698. The land was impossible to cultivate — nobody had bothered testing the scheme in advance — and within seven months 400 of the colonists were dead. Fever and famine followed, but 11 more ships had already set out, arriving to find the surviving colonists in complete despair. Only one ship came back safely; the scheme was abandoned and the Company bankrupted. Indeed, the entire Scottish economy was so badly damaged that some argue it triggered the dissolution of the Scottish Parliament and led to the 1707 Act of Union with England. A list of those who died in Panama is in NAS, GD45, and some papers have been published by the SHS and Bannatyne Club.

The schemes succeeded — by 1839, Melbourne was described as a "Scottish settlement."

Scottish settlement of neighboring New Zealand kicked off in 1806 with one George Bruce, who jumped ship there, having been flogged a week earlier. By the 1850s a quarter of New Zealand's immigrant population spoke with Scottish accents; half of Otago, on South Island, was Scottish by 1871.

The Highlands and Islands Emigration Society helped some 5,000 people, especially those affected by the Potato Famine in western Scotland, settle in Australia in the period 1852–57. Its records are in NAS HD4/5 (see **www.scan.org.uk/researchrtools/ emigration.htm** (note the extra "r" between "research" and "tools"). The Society forced people to repay the cost of passage on arrival, but often found them very badly-paid jobs — immigrants tended to escape as soon as they could, and this led to groups breaking up. Unlike Canada, groups of migrants tended not to colonize specific areas, so Scottish regional identities were not preserved in the same way.

Migration was not always completed in one journey. The Scots of Waipu, New Zealand, sailed there in 1851 under their charismatic leader Rev. Norman MacLeod. They came from St. Anne's, Cape Breton, Nova Scotia, where they had settled after being cleared from Sutherland in 1817. The website of the Waipu House of Memories **www.waipumuseum.com** tells the extraordinary story of their travels over half the globe.

Today, about one and a half million Australians, seven percent of the total population, are of direct Scots descent. About one million New Zealanders, just under a quarter of the population, are from Scottish families, this overlying a core immigrant population that may have been as much as 30 percent Scottish. Several of New Zealand's prime ministers have been Scots, including Shetland-born Sir Robert Stout (1884–1930).

The Bicentenial (1988) Scotland Australia Cairn or *Carn na h-Alba is Astrailia* in Rawson Park, Mosman, Sydney, made of stones sent by the ministers of each Scottish parish and four Scottish cathedrals. The final stone came from Ulva, birthplace of Lachlan MacQuarie, fifth governor of New South Wales, who is often described as "the father of Australia" (courtesy of Jeremy Palmer, www.anzestry.com).

A Norwegian–Scots Australian

The Australian descendants of Roy Hovelroud knew they had Scottish heritage, but were unsure quite how — especially as their surname was Norwegian. Roy's 1906 Queensland birth certificate reveals the answer: his father, John Williamson Hovelroud (pictured here, with his wife Helen), was born at Blairgowrie, Perthshire. His age (42 in 1906) places his birth back in about 1863/4. John married in Queensland, too. The Queensland marriage record helpfully provides his age, place of birth (mis-transcribed as "Blan Gowrie") and his parents' names, James Hovelroud and Margaret Hovelroud née Souter. Jeremy Palmer of **www.anzestry.com**, who researched this case, found the family in the 1881 census on ScotlandsPeople. John Hovelsroud seems to have been a bit younger than he claimed, for he was 14 (so born about 1866), but is definitely the right person as his parents were James and Margaret Hovelsroud.

The story has a strange twist: Jeremy discovered that John was born to James and Margaret out of wedlock — James then moved in with Jane Crockett by 1871 and married her in 1873. Jane died in childbirth later that year, leaving James free to revert to his old girlfriend, Margaret, in March 1874. Jeremy later traced back to James's grandfather John, a Norwegian mariner who settled in Scotland in the mid-19th century.

CHILD	
Name	Roy Williamson
Sex	Male
Date of Birth	3 November 1906
Place of Birth	Stoneleigh Street, Albion
FATHER	
Name and surname	John Williamson Hovelroud
Occupation	Wheelwright
Age and birthplace	42 years Blairgowrie, Perthshire, Scotland
MOTHER	
Name and maiden surname	Helen Elizabeth Shaw formerly Lester
Age and birthplace	25 years Carlisle, Cumberland, England
PREVIOUS CHILDREN OF RELATIONSHIP	
Names and ages	Dorothy Margaret May 5 years
Jane Gladys 3 years
Vera Ellen 1 year
INFORMANT	
Name, description or relationship, and residence	H.E. Hovelroud, Mother, Stoneleigh Street, Albion

	Bridegroom	
When and where married	14 September 1900 At The Registry Office, Toowong	
Name and surname	John Williamson Hovelroud	Helen Eli…
Marital status	Divorced	Spinster
Birthplace	Blan Gowrie, Perthshire, Scotland	Carlyle, N…
Occupation	Wheelwright	-
Age	36 Years	21 Years
Usual residential address	Holme Street, Toowong	Holme Str…
Parents		
Father's name and surname	James Hovelroud	Thomas
Mothers name and maiden surname	Margaret Williamson Souter	Mary Mu…
Father's occupation (if recorded)	Contractor	Glazier
Rites used	Civil Law	
Names of witnesses to marriage	J.I. Tricker
Annie Hughes	

CHAPTER 16

The origins of Scotland's people

Scotland's people have diverse and fascinating origins, from the aboriginal Picts, the Britons of Strathclyde and the Gododdin, to the waves of invaders — Dalriadic Scots, Angles, Vikings, Normans and French. All went into the great mixing pot that created the modern Scots. The early dynastic pedigrees referred to in this chapter are the very earliest Scottish connections to which even the proudest families, or keenest genealogists, can aspire.

A terrifying vision of Pictish warriors, painted by Peter Jackson (1922–2003). The real ones were certainly fierce enough to halt the Romans in their tracks.

The Picts

The term *Picti,* or "painted people," was first coined by the Romans in 297 CE, for the unconquered inhabitants of Caledonia, "the wooded land" north of the Firth of Forth. The nickname arose due to the native Britons' custom of painting themselves with blue woad prior to battle (hence the related name, *Pretani,* for the ancient British people as a whole). To this day, Scotland's ancient people are referred to as "the mysterious Picts."

The idea of fierce Celts peopling Britain has long been discredited. Equally, assertions in the old chronicles that the Picts were from Thrace, Greece, are wrong — these arose when a classical reference to the *picti,* or "painted," Agathyrsi of Thrace was mistranslated as "Pictish Agathyrsi." We know now that the Picts were simply the indigenous inhabitants of Scotland. They weren't mysterious, either. Their ancestors were the Cro-Magnon hunter-gathering cave-dwellers of the Ice Age, who had followed the reindeer north from southern Europe when the ice melted, 10,000 years ago. Cut off by the rising sea, our ancestors became, unwittingly, British. By 9,000 years ago, they had reached Rum in the Outer Hebrides where, at Kinloch, the remains of a settlement of wood

The Burghead Bull from Morayshire is one of some 30 bulls found carved at the seventh-century CE fort there. They were set in the walls of the fort and would have been brightly painted, perhaps for ritualistic purposes, or as the emblem of the ruling family.

and skin huts, stone hearths and barbed stone arrowheads bear evidence to their presence.

About 6,000 years ago, their numbers were supplemented by incomers from Portugal and north-west Spain. Distantly descended from Middle Eastern farmers, they brought with them grain, plows, pottery, sheep, goats and cows, all transported up the Atlantic seaboard in stick-and-hide coracles. These incomers erected standing-stones and even stone houses, like those at Skara Brae, Orkney, inhabited about 3100–2600 BCE, and complete with under-floor drains. Nearby at Maes Howe you can see one of their great chambered tombs, aligned to the winter solstice.

The Romans recorded the names of Scotland's tribes — obvious precursors to the later clans — including the Cataibh or, "people of the wild cat" in Sutherland; the Votadini in the eastern Lowlands; the Verturiones north of the Forth; and the Caledonii from the Tay up to the Great Glen, whose capital may have been Dunkeld (Co. Perth), the, "fort of the

Caledonians." Tacitus provides a vivid picture of the chariot-driving, strong limbed, red-headed Picts who faced the invading Romans at Mons Graupius (somewhere between Perth and Inverness) in 84 CE. The leader of their hastily-assembled confederation was Calgacus, to whom Tacitus imputes the first recorded Scottish speech:

"we, the most distant dwellers upon earth, the last of the free, have been shielded till today by our very remoteness and by the obscurity in which it has shrouded our name. Now, the farthest bounds of Britain lie open to our enemies... our wives and sisters, even if they are not raped by enemy soldiers, are seduced by men who are supposed to be our friends and guests..."

Calgacus was defeated, but the Romans never subdued the Picts, withdrawing to the Antonine Wall, between the Forth and the Clyde, and then falling back in 180 CE to Hadrian's Wall. Most of north and east Scotland beyond the Forth coalesced into a realm that the Romans called Pictavia (Alba). It seems to have

The author investigating the great stone circle at Calanais, Lewis. In 1684, John Morisone wrote of a local tradition that, *"these were a sort of men converted into stone by an enchanter..."* Calanais was started around 3,000 BCE and completed a few hundred years later.

had two parts, one centred on Inverness and the other, the "Metae," probably based at Forteviot near Perth. There, its rulers, holding the nominal High-Kingship, inaugurated at the nearby hill of Scone.

The High Kings' names, preserved in the *Pictish King List*, start with the semi-mythical Cruithne, son of Cinge, "father of the Picts," in about 1000 BCE. The earliest names are in fact eponyms, names taken from places — "Cruithne" was from the Irish for "Britain." But after them come what are probably the real names of kings, presumably those of the Verturiones tribe, followed by genuine High Kings from Roman times onward. Many of the kings used the throne-name Bruide, in honor of the goddess Bride, whom they presumably worshipped. Succession was matrilinear, with kings being chosen from the sons of daughters of previous kings. These princesses are not named in the King List so we cannot draw a family tree, but we know that the later kings, including Kenneth MacAlpin (d. 858), were

somehow descended from the earlier ones, and ultimately from the semi-legendary Cruithne.

St. Columba is alleged to have converted King Bruide (son of a Pictish princess and the Welsh king Maelgwn Gwynedd) to Christianity in the 560s, and to have baptized all the Picts by the shores of Loch Ness. In reality, conversion took much longer, and paganism never vanished completely. The goddess Bride, for example, continued to be worshipped under the new name "St. Brigid."

The Picts had an equivocal relationship with the neighboring Dalriadans of modern Argyll. Dynastic alliances between the two produced a confused situation, for male-line Dalriadan princes with royal Pictish mothers were eligible candidates for both thrones. The mixed-blooded Kenneth MacAlpin and his immediate successors united the two realms into the kingdom of Alba. Opinion remains divided whether Kenneth was a Pictish king who overcame the Dalriadans (the modern view) or a Dalriadan king who conquered the Picts (the old view). At any rate, his

In the Iron Age (roughly 600 BCE onwards), homes were often built defensively. Some lived in brochs, while others took to the water, living on crannogs built on artificial islands in the lochs. From these they would sally forth to hunt in the forests and cultivate their fields. This is a reconstruction that you can visit on Loch Tay, Perthshire.

successors abandoned matrilinear succession, and the Picts' language, akin to modern Welsh, gradually gave way to Irish Gaelic. Dalriadic ancestry became so closely identified with power that claims to Pictish ancestry are very rare. The Grahams once claimed descent from Grim, a Pict chief alive in 420 CE. The MacNaughtons' patronymic, "son of Nechtan," harks back to two Pictish kings of that name. One version of the Duffs' and Wemyss's origins traces them to Connall Cerr, son of the Pictish king Eochaid Bruide. But while few families claim Pictish ancestry, DNA studies suggest that the bedrock of Scotland's people remains predominantly Pictish to this day.

The Angles

Angles from Schleswig and southern Denmark were invited to Britain by the Romans as mercenaries to fight the Picts. When the Romans left, they took control of East Anglia and expanded north, led by two dynasties claiming descent from the god Woden, creating

the north-eastern kingdoms of Deira and Bernicia. These were later united as the Kingdom of Northumbria, under Ethelfrith of Bernicia. His son St. Oswald captured Edinburgh from the Picts in 638 and penetrated as far north as the Grampians. The Picts fought back at Dunnichen in 685 and Athelstaneford (East Lothian) in 750, when a great white cross of

The broch of Dun Charlabhaigh, Lewis, possibly the royal seat of the rulers of this part of the Hebrides, is so well preserved that you can still walk up its 2,000 year-old staircase.

clouds appeared in the blue sky, signifying St. Andrew's support for the Pictish king Unuist. The Picts won, and the saltire flag of St. Andrew still flies in Scotland. The Northumbrians eventually lost the Lothians to the Vikings and then to the Scots kings, whose possession of the region was sealed by the Battle of Carham in 1018. The Anglians' English dialect developed into Lowland Scots, the tongue of Burns, while to this day (with slight inaccuracy) the Highlanders call Lowlanders *Sassenachs* — "Saxons."

The Aberlemno Stone depicts the Battle of Dunnichen (Nechtansmere), near Forfar in Angus, at which the Pictish king Bridei mac Bili defeated his cousin Ecgfrith of Northumbria in 685 CE.

The Kings of Dalriada

With its long arm stretched out across the Irish Sea, Argyll (*Earra-Ghàidheal*, the Coastland of the Gaels) had always enjoyed close contact with Ireland. Gaels from Ireland were certainly settling there from the second century CE. The old term for the Irish was "Scots." Niall of the Nine Hostages, King of Ulster, was supposedly the first to call Dalriada *Scotia Minor;* thereafter, the term effectively transferred across from Ireland to what we now call Scotland.

Legend holds that Scottish Dalriada was founded by Fergus Mac Feredach, an Ulster prince descended from Heremon son of Milesius, in the fourth century BCE. However, Fergus and the dynasty he spawned may have been made up to give a veneer of antiquity to the new monarchy created there by Fergus Mor Mac Earca in the Roman period. Legend makes the second Fergus a direct descendant of the first. A more plausible genealogy makes him a son of Muireadach, King of Ailech (Co. Donegal), a grandson of Niall of the Nine Hostages. But this does not preclude the possibility of the second Fergus's mother having been Earca, daughter of an earlier Gaelic ruler of Dalriada.

Gododdin, Strathclyde and Galloway

Dun Altcluith, "the fort of the rock of Clyde," the great basalt Rock of Dumbarton, seat of Ceretic Guletic and his descendants, the ancient British kings of Strathclyde. The kingdom's spiritual center was nearby, where Govan parish church now stands.

The tribe known to the Romans as Votadini, and to themselves as Gododdin, dwelt in the Lothians, based first at Traprian Law, East Lothian, then at Din Eidyn, "the fort of the rock face" — Edinburgh. Their king Mynyddawg Mwynfawr's heroic raid into Yorkshire is the subject of the great poem *Y Gododdin* (at **www. gutenberg.org/etext/9842**). Another Gododdin king, Lot Luwwdoc, "Lot of the Hosts," was allegedly husband of King Arthur's half-sister Anna. An old Welsh pedigree (no. 16 in Harleian Mss 3859) alleges Lot's descent (if "Letan" is indeed Lot) from Caratacus of the Catuvellauni, who led the resistance to the Roman invasion in 43 CE. Whatever the truth behind their kings' ancestry, the brave realm of the Gododdin was overrun, first by the Picts and then, in 638, by the Angles.

To the west of the Gododdin, "Cumberland," the land of the "Cymry" (Britons), stretched from the Forth of Clyde down to the Lake District. When the Romans abandoned Hadrian's Wall in 410 CE, the region became dominated by Ceretic Guletic. His pedigree (no. 5 in Harleian MS 3859)

indicates Romanized British roots, his father Cynloyp (Quintilupus) being grandson of Cluim (Clemens).

Ceretic's son Cinuit divided the realm between his own sons, Dumngual Hen and Tutgual. Dumngual Hen and his descendants ruled Strathclyde, until Owain the Bald was killed at the Battle of Carham in 1018, and the realm was absorbed into Scotland. The surname Wallace, borne by the great hero of Scottish nationalism, Sir William Wallace (1274-1305), is Gaelic for "foreigner" and probably denotes someone of Strathclyde descent. Tutgual, meanwhile, ruled Galloway and the Isle of Man but his successors lost the former and their heiress conveyed the latter by marriage to the royal house of Powys, Wales. Galloway fell to the Angles and Vikings, but re-emerged as an independent state under a ruler of unknown origins, Fergus of Galloway (d. 1161). Through dynastic marriages, his great-great-granddaughter Devorgilla of Galloway became heiress of the Scottish throne, passing it and Galloway to her son King John I Balliol (d. 1268).

Ancient sources

The oldest chronicles of Scottish history, including versions of the *Pictish King List*, are collected in William F. Skene's *Chronicles of the Picts, Chronicles of the Scots and other Early Memorials of Scottish History* (HMSO, 1867), available from **www.kessinger.net** or at **http://books.google.co.uk/**. Later, rather fanciful Scottish histories were spun out of these old chronicles by John of Fordun (d.c. 1384), Walter Bower (d. 1449) and Hector Boece (d. 1536), the first and last being available at **www.archive.org**. Skene's introduction is a lucid account of how and why they did so. Political expedience lay at the root. Ancient British legend tells of brothers Albanus and Brutus, who settled Britain, Albanus being the first colonizer of Scotland. In 1136, however, an English subject, Geoffrey of Monmouth, completed his politically-motivated *History of the Kings of Britain*. He related that Brutus alone colonized Britain and gave Scotland to his youngest son, Albanactus, thus "proving" Scotland was subservient to England. To counter such claims, Fordun and his successors never made up genealogies, but they did manipulate existing ones to try to show ever greater antiquity for the Scottish kingship.

The "second" King Fergus, from the series of portraits of all the kings of Scotland from legendary times to the reign of Charles II, by Jacob Jacobsz de Wet (d. 1697). On display at the Palace of Holyroodhouse, Edinburgh, they form what is, in effect, a visual pedigree, one of the grandest of its kind in the world.

The descent from the second Fergus down to Kenneth MacAlpin, who united Dalriada and Pictland to create Alba, is shown on pages 196-7. Kenneth's own descendants gradually gained control of their neighbors, but lost Cumbria south of Hadrian's Wall to the English in 945. True unification of Scotland's races came later — when William the Lyon (d. 1214) addressed his people, he still did so not as "Scots" but as "his faithful subjects, French, English, Scots, Welsh (i.e. Strathclyde British) and Gallovidian."

Milesian origins

Because the Dalriadan Scots were of Irish origin, so too were their genealogical traditions. Virtually all noble Irish families traced their ancestry back to the legendary sons of Milesius (Mil), a king in northern Spain (descended, in turn, from Noah), and his wife Scota, daughter of an Egyptian pharaoh. Their sons Heber and Heremon, Amergin and Ir, with their uncle Ithe, invaded Ireland, capturing it from the god-like Tuatha de Danann. The latter fled through the ancient burial mounds to the Underworld, re-emerging into modern times as Fairies. For a full discussion of the legend, see my book *Tracing Your Irish Family History*.

In Scottish versions of the legend, Milesius became confused with his ancestor Goidel Glas

The great rock of Dunnad

The great rock of Dunadd (Dunmonaidh), the seat of the ancient Kings of Dalriada, stands out impressively above the Moine Mhor, in Argyll, dominating the sea-loch of Crinan. The signboard says that, *"you may feel this is a remote place, but in the seventh century the fort of Dunadd was the centre of a network of communication. Traders brought rare minerals from the Mediterranean for illuminating manuscripts, dye from the Loire, and tin from Cornwall. This was the royal stronghold where the king could drink imported wine out of delicate glass beakers from the Continent and eat meat flavoured with spices from France."* There are also more remains of weapons here than anywhere else in Britain, for the kings were in contact with Vikings, Northumbrians, Irish and Picts.

Clambering up through the narrow rocky defile that was the fort's great natural defence, you encounter a rock carved with a boar, a line of ogam and a hewn-out footprint. The Kings of Dalriada were inaugurated by placing their foot in this, and thus the hard-won and hard-kept power of the kingship was passed on. Placing your own foot in it (it's actually a rock-cast replica protecting the original, but no matter) you certainly feel very royal, and can stand surveying your lands, cattle, the wide Moss and the glittering sea beyond. As most people of Scots blood are descended, one way or another, from the Dalriadic kings, the feeling of connectedness with the ancient landscape is seldom as absurd as it may appear initially.

— Walter Bower thought Scota's husband was called "Gaythelos," and that one "Mycelius Espayn" came later, but the mistake is obvious and the original Irish tales are much clearer.

Through Fergus Mor Mac Earca, the kings of Scotland and their cousins the Mormaers (Earls) of Moray (the ancestors of MacBeth) claimed descent from Heremon, son of Milesius. Many clan chiefs and mormaers also claimed Milesian descent, mostly from the same Ulster kings as Fergus. There is a simple logic behind the notion of invading warlords bringing their kinsmen with them, and DNA studies have started finding male-line Y-chromosome matches among different Scottish families claiming Milesian descent. For example, many Campbells, whose clan once claimed descent from Dairmuid Ua Duibhna of the Ulster dynasty, have Y-chromosome DNA matching Irish families claiming descent from the Ulster kings.

It is certainly true, however, that some claims to Milesian roots were fabrications encouraged by the Christian monks who recorded them. They even made Cruithne, first king of the Picts, into a great-grandson of

At the inauguration of Alexander III in 1249, the royal sennachie recites the king's descent from Fergus Mor Mac Erca. A detail of an illuminated manuscript (courtesy of the Master and Fellows of Corpus Christi College, Cambridge).

Partholon, a four-times great-grandson of Noah and thus a cousin of Milesius. Dr. Johnson was very cynical about the accuracy of all the old Gaelic pedigrees, writing that, *"the nation was wholly illiterate. Neither bards nor sennachies could write or read; but if they were ignorant, there was no danger of detection; they were believed by those whose vanity they flattered."* Such behavior, when it really occurred, jars with modern genealogical practice, but in the medieval Christian mind everyone had to be descended from Noah somehow. And, in any case, the Church found that asserting different dynasties' kinship through their alleged Milesian roots was as good a way as any to foster a sense of national unity and promote peace.

Pages 196–7 show a pedigree, heavily abridged, of the Milesian Kings of Ulster, and the different branches from which many prominent Scottish families claimed descent. The chart cannot show all such claims made by Scottish families, and nor does it imply that all such claims are accepted by genealogists now. It is instructive, however, for many alliances were forged on the basis of a perceived kinship between clans, based on the Milesian framework. Nor does the pedigree imply that the families themselves stuck to their claims consistently, for many have changed their minds due to better ideas or new scholarship.

Gaelic genealogies can be decidedly slippery. The Campbells once (falsely) claimed descent from King Arthur. Among the clans claiming descent from Kenneth MacAlpin's family are the MacGregors. They said their ancestor, Griogar, was Kenneth's younger son, but this claim is not heard of before 1512, while elsewhere we find them asserting their descent from Pope Gregory the Great. They are probably, actually, descended from the abbots of Glenorchy, the kin of St. Fillan (of the Milesian royal house of Leinster, Ireland). Griogar most likely never existed, but in the 17th century the belief in him was strong enough for various clans claiming descent from him to pledge fellowship based on their perceived blood ties. Later, moves were even made to merge all the "Siol Alpin" into one common clan — a plan that failed when nobody could agree who the chief should be.

The last King of Scots of the male line of Kenneth MacAlpin was Malcolm II (d. 1034). His daughter Bethoc married Crinan, hereditary lay abbot of Dunkeld, and was mother of Duncan I. Such lay abbots, or *co arbs*, belonged to the male-line kindred of their abbey's saintly founders. Because Dunkeld was founded by St.

Columba, it has been inferred, very plausibly, that Crinan was a male-line descendant of St. Columba's kin, closely descended themselves from Niall of the Nine Hostages (the generations between St. Columba and Crinan are not recorded). From Crinan and Bethoc descend the later Scottish kings, while from a younger branch, settled in Northumberland and Durham, come a number of sons who took surnames based on the estates they held. These include the Washingtons of Washington, ancestors of president George Washington (d. 1799). Another son married the heiress of the Nevilles and took their surname. Thus, like President Washington, Richard Neville, Earl of Warwick, the famous "Kingmaker" (d. 1471), seems to have been a male-line descendant of Niall of the Nine Hostages.

Another branch allegedly coming down from the Ulster kings leads to Somerled, lord of Kintyre. His male-line pedigree is stated differently in various sources, and DNA studies suggest that, if he was of royal Ulster descent, it was not through the direct male line. What is certain is that his wife Raghnailt was sister of Godfrey, King of Man and the Isles. In 1156, Somerled asserted his independence, assembling a fleet of 80 ships, defeating Godfrey and making himself ruler of the seas from Man to the Butt of Lewis. Somerled's son Randal, Lord of the Isles, was father of Donald, ancestor of the MacDonald Lords of the Isles. They ruled as vassals first of Norway and then of Scotland, but were in reality independent sovereigns in all but name. They had their own judges and bards, some of whom founded Hebridean septs and clans. The MacDonalds' power was crushed by James IV in 1494, but in the vacuum that followed many other local clan chiefs, such as the MacLeods, became semi-independent despots in their own right.

Scota and Milesius (Gaythelos) sail to Ireland, from a 15th-century manuscript of Walter Bower's *Scotichronicon* (courtesy of the Master and Fellows of Corpus Christi College, Cambridge).

Milesian Roots

Milesius

Heber

Kings of Munster hence **Mormaers of Lennox**, hence **MacFarlanes**

Heremon

Fedhlimidh Rachtmar (29 x great-grandson of Heremon) H.K.I. d. AD 119

Conn of the Hundred Battles H.K.I. d.157

Cormac Ulfhada H.K.I. d.266

Cairbre Lifechar H.K.I. d.284

Fiacha Strabhteine H.K.I. d.322

Alechia dau. of Updaire King of Alba = **Eochaidh Dubhlen**

Colla Uais H.K.I.

Niall of the Nine Hostages H.K.I. d.c.450

Conall Galban

Eoghan King of Ailech d.465

Fergus Cendfota

Muireadach King of Ailech = **Erca** daughter of **Loarn** King of Dalriada

Feidlimid = **Eithne of Dalriada**

Muirceartach Mor Mac Erca H.K.I.

Oengus

St Columba (Colum-Cille) d.597

Fergal H.K.I.

MacInnes

Connor prince of Limavady

Niall Frasach H.K.I.

Pictish princess possibly dau. of K. Constantine of the Picts

Annselan granted Buchanan by Malcom II

Aodh Athlaman King of Ailech d.1033

Buchanan / Munro

Methlan ancestor of **MacMillan**

Constantine I K. of P&D. d.876

dau.

SLOL ALPIN

Lay Abbots of Dunkeld where St Colomba's relics were kept

Malcolm I K. of Alba d.954

= **Run** K. of Strathclyde

Heiress of Lamont = **Aodh Anrathan** Lord of Badenoch

Dubh K. of Alba d.966

Kenneth II K. of Alba d.995

Aodh Alainn

Duff (disputed)

Malcolm II K. of Alba d.1034

Boite

Niall ancestor of **MacNeill** of Barra

Giollachrist

Duinsleibe

Crinian the Thane Lay abbot of Dunkeld d.1034

Lachlan Oge

Ferchar

Suibhne ("Sweeny")

MacLachlan

Malcolm

Sorley

Dugal

Maolmuire

Ladman

MacSorley

Ewen

MacSweeny alias **MacQueen**

Malcolm

Clan Ladman (Lamont)

MacEwen of Otter

Robertson Skene

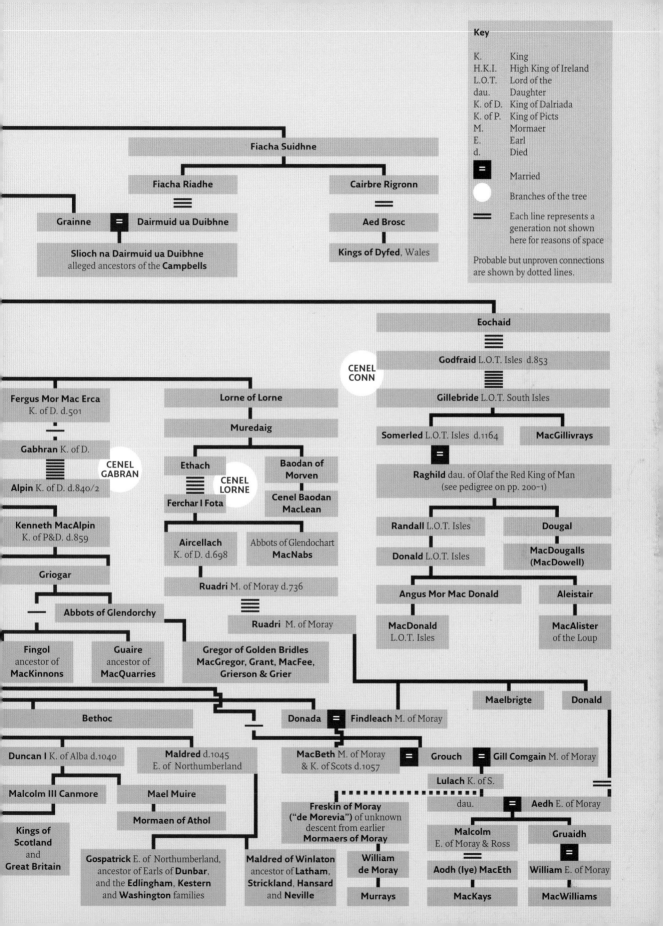

Key

K.	King
H.K.I.	High King of Ireland
L.O.T.	Lord of the
dau.	Daughter
K. of D.	King of Dalriada
K. of P.	King of Picts
M.	Mormaer
E.	Earl
d.	Died
■=	Married
○	Branches of the tree
≡	Each line represents a generation not shown here for reasons of space

Probable but unproven connections are shown by dotted lines.

Fiacha Suidhne

Fiacha Riadhe ≡

Grainne = **Dairmuid ua Duibhne**

Slioch na Dairmuid ua Duibhne alleged ancestors of the **Campbells**

Cairbre Rigronn ≡

Aed Brosc

Kings of Dyfed, Wales

Eochaid ≡

Godfraid L.O.T. Isles d.853 ≡

CENEL CONN

Gillebride L.O.T. South Isles

Lorne of Lorne

Muredaig

Fergus Mor Mac Erca K. of D. d.501

Gabhran K. of D.

CENEL GABRAN

Alpin K. of D. d.840/2

Ethach ≡

CENEL LORNE

Ferchar I Fota

Baodan of Morven

Cenel Baodan MacLean

Somerled L.O.T. Isles d.1164

MacGillivrays

■=

Raghild dau. of Olaf the Red King of Man (see pedigree on pp. 200–1)

Kenneth MacAlpin K. of P&D. d.859

Aircellach K. of D. d.698

Abbots of Glendochart **MacNabs**

Randall L.O.T. Isles

Dougal

Griogar

Ruadri M. of Moray d.736

Donald L.O.T. Isles

MacDougalls (MacDowell)

Abbots of Glendorchy

—

Ruadri M. of Moray ≡

Angus Mor Mac Donald

Aleistair

Fingol ancestor of **MacKinnons**

Guaire ancestor of **MacQuarries**

Gregor of Golden Bridles MacGregor, Grant, MacFee, Grierson & Grier

MacDonald L.O.T. Isles

MacAlister of the Loup

Maelbrigte

Donald

Bethoc

Donada = **Findleach** M. of Moray

Duncan I K. of Alba d.1040

Maldred d.1045 E. of Northumberland

MacBeth M. of Moray & K. of Scots d.1057 = **Grouch** = **Gill Comgain** M. of Moray

Malcolm III Canmore

Mael Muire

Lulach K. of S.

dau. = **Aedh** E. of Moray

Mormaen of Athol

Freskin of Moray ("de Morevia") of unknown descent from earlier **Mormaers of Moray**

Malcolm E. of Moray & Ross

Gruaidh

Kings of Scotland and Great Britain

Gospatrick E. of Northumberland, ancestor of Earls of **Dunbar**, and the **Edlingham, Kestern** and **Washington** families

Maldred of Winlaton ancestor of **Latham, Strickland, Hansard** and **Neville**

William de Moray

Murrays

Aodh (Iye) MacEth

MacKays

■=

William E. of Moray

MacWilliams

The MacDonald, Lord of the Isles, holding court, his clan's heather badge in his helm; by McIan, from J. Logan's *The Clans of the Scottish Highlands* (1845).

Vikings

Vikings from Norway were settling in the Orkneys from at least the 780s, and pillaged St. Columba's island monastery of Iona in 795. They established kingdoms in York, Dublin, Waterford, the Nordreyar (or Northern Isles, including the Orkneys), the Suthreyar (Southern Isles, including the Hebrides), and the Isle of Man, the latter two later being combined into a realm called Innesgall. Like the kings of Norway, these kingdoms' rulers were descended from the Ynglings, who had ruled at Uppsala (in modern Sweden), and claimed descent from the Norse god Frey. The Hebrides remained

Norwegian until Alexander III of Scots won the sea battle of Largs in 1263. The Orkneys, despite having been inherited by the Scottish Sinclair family, remained part of the Kingdom of Norway until a treaty of 1469.

Highland tradition speaks of Gunn, Leod and Leandres as, "three sons of the King of Denmark," a figurative way of saying they were of Viking origin. Leandres was ancestor of Clan Gillanders or Anrias, from whom descend many Rosses, Frasers and Barrons. The Nicholsons and Mathesons are probably of Viking origin. The Morrisons claim descent from a, "son of a King of Norway," but their patronymic, MacGille Mhoire, suggests a Gaelic origin. Paul Balkason, the Norse Sheriff of Skye in the 11th century, is probably the ancestor of the Mac Balks or MacPokes, and of the MacKillops of Bernera, Harris.

The use of ancient genealogies

This chapter has focused on royal and noble genealogies. As we have seen, many Scottish clans and families are actually offshoots of such dynasties. In addition, in a small country like Scotland, where the royal family often intermarried with its nobles, it isn't a great surprise to find royal blood in non-royal families. Mathematically, anyone with Scottish blood is almost certainly descended from the early medieval kings, while any Dark Age king who has any living descendants must (on the basis of statistics) be the ancestor of all Scots alive today.

The royal and noble genealogies are also worth studying because they comprise a form of map of whence and when the people concerned moved, and by inference how the families subject to them would have behaved. For every Norman nobleman coming north to settle newly feudalized lands in the Lowlands, for example, dozens of Norman retainers and servants followed. For each royal family that crossed the seas from Norway or Ulster to the Hebrides or Dalriada, hundreds of ordinary families followed. Each marriage recorded between royal Picts and Scots, Highland chiefs and Norman lords, was mirrored and matched by many others, unrecorded, among their retainers and followers. This tells us a lot about the way the constituent races of Scotland intermingled. These genealogies are therefore the best indicators we have of what many ancient Scottish families would have been like.

The same is true for clan genealogies. People with clan surnames will not waste their time by studying the genealogies of the chiefs of their name. You may not know exactly how you connect to the main stem, but the chief's pedigree again provides a sort of map of the clan's alliances and connections. For example, the early pedigree of the MacLeod chiefs shows intermarriages with families including the

Now a very rare breed, Hebridean sheep are thought to have been brought to the Western Isles by the Vikings, of whose fabled horned helmets they are so curiously reminiscent.

A restored Norse mill at Shawbost by Loch Roinavat, Lewis. We know it is of Norse origin because the grinding wheels were horizontal, not vertical. "*Bost*" is a Norse word for a small farm and is now very common in Hebridean place names. Some 126 Lewis place names have Norse origin, of which 99 are unadulterated Scandinavian.

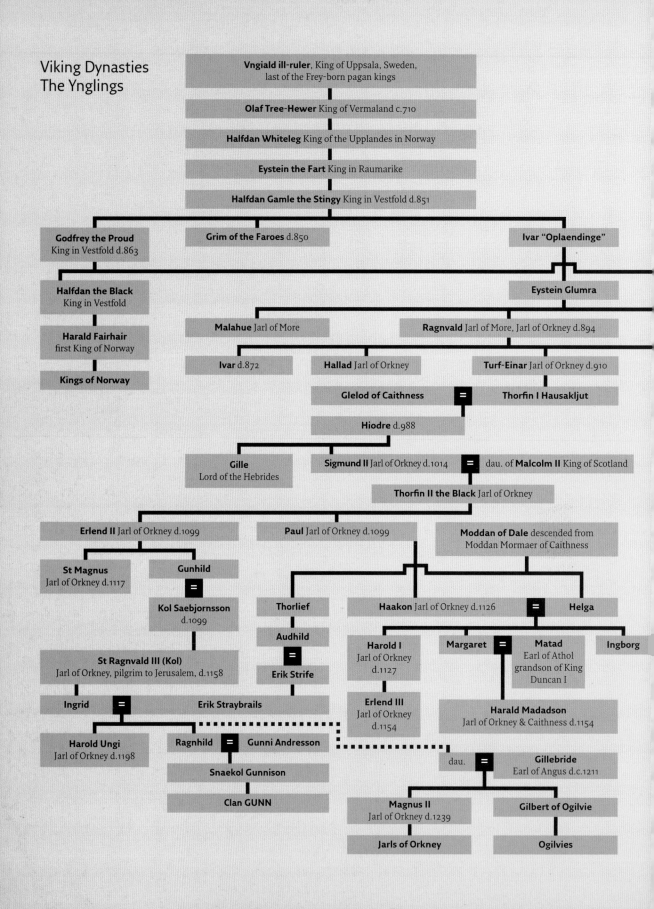

Viking Dynasties
The Ynglings

Vngiald ill-ruler, King of Uppsala, Sweden, last of the Frey-born pagan kings

Olaf Tree-Hewer King of Vermaland c.710

Halfdan Whiteleg King of the Upplandes in Norway

Eystein the Fart King in Raumarike

Halfdan Gamle the Stingy King in Vestfold d.851

Godfrey the Proud King in Vestfold d.863

Grim of the Faroes d.850

Ivar "Oplaendinge"

Halfdan the Black King in Vestfold

Eystein Glumra

Harald Fairhair first King of Norway

Malahue Jarl of More

Ragnvald Jarl of More, Jarl of Orkney d.894

Kings of Norway

Ivar d.872

Hallad Jarl of Orkney

Turf-Einar Jarl of Orkney d.910

Glelod of Caithness = **Thorfin I Hausakljut**

Hiodre d.988

Gille Lord of the Hebrides

Sigmund II Jarl of Orkney d.1014 = dau. of **Malcolm II** King of Scotland

Thorfin II the Black Jarl of Orkney

Erlend II Jarl of Orkney d.1099

Paul Jarl of Orkney d.1099

Moddan of Dale descended from Moddan Mormaer of Caithness

St Magnus Jarl of Orkney d.1117

Gunhild = **Kol Saebjornsson** d.1099

Thorlief

Haakon Jarl of Orkney d.1126 = **Helga**

Ingborg

Audhild = **Erik Strife**

Harold I Jarl of Orkney d.1127

Margaret = **Matad** Earl of Athol grandson of King Duncan I

St Ragnvald III (Kol) Jarl of Orkney, pilgrim to Jerusalem, d.1158

Ingrid = **Erik Straybrails**

Erlend III Jarl of Orkney d.1154

Harald Madadson Jarl of Orkney & Caithness d.1154

Harold Ungi Jarl of Orkney d.1198

Ragnhild = **Gunni Andresson**

dau. = **Gillebride** Earl of Angus d.c.1211

Snaekol Gunnison

Magnus II Jarl of Orkney d.1239

Gilbert of Ogilvie

Clan GUNN

Jarls of Orkney

Ogilvies

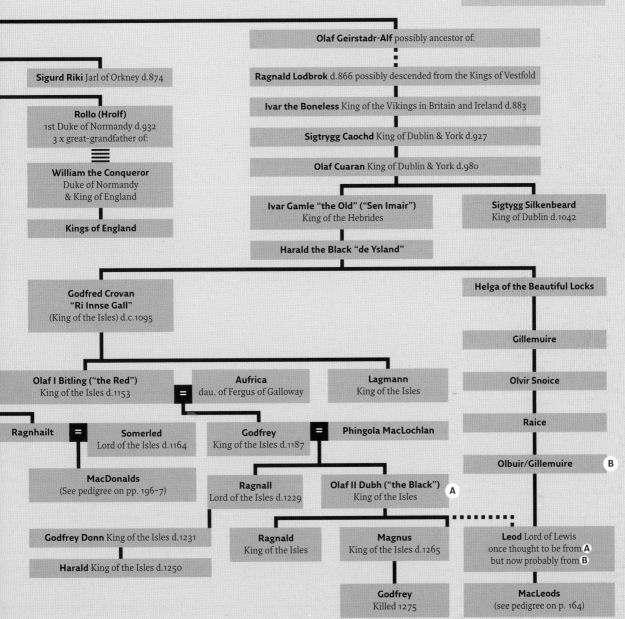

MacDonalds
(See pedigree on pp. 196–7)

MacLeods
(see pedigree on p. 164)

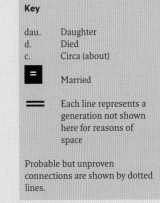

Key

dau.	Daughter
d.	Died
c.	Circa (about)
◼=	Married
==	Each line represents a generation not shown here for reasons of space

Probable but unproven connections are shown by dotted lines.

Olaf Geirstadr-Alf possibly ancestor of:

Sigurd Riki Jarl of Orkney d.874

Ragnald Lodbrok d.866 possibly descended from the Kings of Vestfold

Rollo (Hrolf)
1st Duke of Normandy d.932
3 x great-grandfather of:

Ivar the Boneless King of the Vikings in Britain and Ireland d.883

William the Conqueror
Duke of Normandy
& King of England

Sigtrygg Caochd King of Dublin & York d.927

Olaf Cuaran King of Dublin & York d.980

Kings of England

Ivar Gamle "the Old" ("Sen Imair")
King of the Hebrides

Sigtygg Silkenbeard
King of Dublin d.1042

Harald the Black "de Ysland"

Helga of the Beautiful Locks

Godfred Crovan
"Ri Innse Gall"
(King of the Isles) d.c.1095

Gillemuire

Olaf I Bitling ("the Red")
King of the Isles d.1153

Aufrica
dau. of Fergus of Galloway

Lagmann
King of the Isles

Olvir Snoice

Raice

Ragnhailt

Somerled
Lord of the Isles d.1164

Godfrey
King of the Isles d.1187

Phingola MacLochlan

Olbuir/Gillemuire

Ragnall
Lord of the Isles d.1229

Olaf II Dubh ("the Black")
King of the Isles

Godfrey Donn King of the Isles d.1231

Ragnald
King of the Isles

Magnus
King of the Isles d.1265

Leod Lord of Lewis
once thought to be from
but now probably from

Harald King of the Isles d.1250

Godfrey
Killed 1275

MacLeods

LEFT: **The 16th century tomb of Alistair Crotach MacLeod at Rodel, Harris, includes a vivid depiction of the birlinns in which the MacLeods, the MacDonalds, and the Vikings before them had controlled the Isles.**

OPPOSITE RIGHT: **The tombs of the MacLeods of Lewis are at the Eaglais na h-Aoidhe, built in the sixth century by St. Catan, a follower of St. Columba on the narrow isthmus that juts out east of Stronoway into the Minch. Local people are urgently seeking funds for restoring this extraordinary church(www.eyechurch.org). The surviving grave slabs, now standing against the walls of the ruined kirk, are thought to be those of Roderick VII (d. 1498)** (OPPOSITE LEFT) **and his daughter Margaret MacKinon (d. 1503), who was mother of the last Abbot of Iona. Margaret's brother Torquil was driven from Lewis in 1506 by Lord Huntly, starting the inexorable decline of MacLeod power there.**

The slipperiness of the early clan genealogies is very well illustrated by the Clan MacLeod. Their ancestor Leod was a Viking who held the Hebrides under the Kingdom of the Isles. When Alexander III defeated the Vikings at the Battle of Largs in 1263, Leod's successors retained their lands, but ruled henceforth as Gaelic chiefs, using the Gaelic patronymic MacLeod.

It was widely held that Leod was a younger son of Olaf the Black (d. 1237), Viking King of the Isle of Man. Iain Mor MacLeod of Dunvegan (chief 1626-49) styled himself "John McOlaus," i.e. "[descendant of] Olaf" in 1630 and his son Iain Breac (chief 1664-93) quartered the Manx arms with his own. The theory of Leod being Olaf the Black's son was first stated explicitly by Sir George MacKenzie, first Earl of Cromarty (d. 1714), an astonishingly bad genealogist, and gained widespread acceptance. This theory has since been both challenged and defended, and recently, David Sellar, now Lord Lyon, proposed a new theory in "The Ancestry of the MacLeods Reconsidered," *Transactions of the Gaelic Society of Inverness*, vol. LX, 1997-8.

Sellar showed that Leod is never mentioned in the records of the kings of Man, and his heirs were never considered as heirs to the hotly disputed Manx throne. In contrast, the Gaelic elegies or "praise poems" composed on the deaths of several 17th- and early-18th-century MacLeod chiefs state Leod to have been son of Olbair/Olbuir, the son of Raise/Raoige, son

of Olbair Snaithe/Olbiur. An earlier (and therefore more likely to be accurate) pedigree was recorded in Ireland by MacFirbis, and concerned Christina MacLeod, wife of Hector MacLean and granddaughter of Leod. This gives Leod's father as Gillemuire, son of Raice, son of Olbair, son of Gillemuire. The latter Gillemuire's mother was *"Ealga fholt-alainn ingean Arailt mic Semmair rig Lochlan"* — "Ealga [Helga] of the beautiful locks daughter of Harald son of Semmair, king of Lochlan." Sellar argued that Leod was therefore the son of someone called Olbuir or Gillemuire and grandson of Olvir Snoice. Leod's Manx ancestry came through Olvir Snoice's grandmother Helga of the Beautiful Locks, whom (Sellar showed) was a sister of Godfred Crovan (d.c.1095), King of the Isle of Man, and daughter of Harald the Black of Iceland, son of Ivar the Old (*Semmair* being *Sen Imair* — "Old Ivan"), King of the Hebrides ("*rig Lochlan*"). The pedigree of Viking Dynasties on pp. 200-1 will help you follow this.

Sellar argued that the MacLeods, knowing themselves to be of Manx descent, were confused by the pedigree of the Manx kings that appeared in Camden's *Britannia* (1586), showing Olaf the Black to have been grandson of Olaf the Red. Perhaps the MacLeods thought that these two Olafs, grandfather and grandson, were the same as the two Olbairs in their pedigree. Despite Sellar's work, Leod is still given (at the time of writing) as Olaf the Black's son on the website of the Associated Clan

MacLeod Societies (**www.clanmacleod.org/about-macleods/index.php**) and is enshrined in their published genealogies. The latest edition of *Burke's Peerage* reports the new theory, but erroneously, making Leod the son of Helga by a different Viking, Olvir Rosta. Under the circumstances, a certain amount of confusion is inevitable, and it all goes to show how slippery the clan genealogies can be.

The MacLeods have two main branches, in Skye and Lewis, said (by Sir George MacKenzie) to be descended from Leod's sons Tormod and Torquil respectively. This too appears to be wrong. Leod appears in the *Orkney Saga* as, "Ljotulfr, who was the chief in Lewis" in 1154, but his son Tormod MacLeod was chief only in Skye and Harris, while the MacNicols held sway on Lewis. It was Tormod's younger son Murchadh (as shown in the pedigree on p. 164 of the MacLeods of Badnaban) who married the heiress of the Norse MacNicols, and produced a son and heir, the real Torquil, who inherited Lewis. John Morisone's *Description of Lewis* (c.1688) speaks of, "*Macknaicle whose onlie daughter ....* [MacLeod] *... did violently espouse, and cutt off immediatelie the whole race of Macknaicle and possessed himself of the whole Lews.*" (Morisone says the violent espouser was Torquil, but he seems to have been in error.) Local folklore suggests that the daughter only became an heiress after her wedding. Murchadh is said to have spotted the rest of the Nicholsons sailing off the

Shiant Isles in their galley, rammed it with his own and drowned the lot of them!

By 1343/4, Torquil MacLeod was holding Lewis as a vassal of John MacDonald, Lord of the Isles, who in turn had submitted to David II of Scotland. Through this connection, Torquil received a royal grant of Assynt, and his descendants formed a separate clan, the Siol Torcaill. The heir of the MacLeods of Skye remains at Dunvegan Castle to this day. Harris genealogist Bill Lawson writes that while, "*there are many MacLeod families still on [Lewis] who are aware of their connection with the Chiefs, there are no written proofs of their genealogies. Such proof could only be expected to have been preserved in a land-owning branch of the family, living away from the turmoil of Lewis itself, as in the family of Raasay. The line through Malcolm Garbh of Raasay is now recognized by the Lord Lyon as the senior representative of the MacLeods of Lewis, with Torquil MacLeod of Tasmania as the chief. No doubt this is the closest branch of the MacLeods able to show a detailed pedigree (though there is now some dispute over whether Malcolm of Raasay was indeed a son of Malcolm X), but there must be many more MacLeod families in the islands with a closer tie to the MacLeod chiefs, whose pedigrees are equally genuine, but incapable of proof.*"

The Fullartons are said to be descended from Olaf, a supposed son of Leod, while a family of Malcolm claim descent from the MacLeods of Raasay.

Mathesons and Rosses. 19th- and even 20th-century genealogies of crofting MacLeods from the traditional clan areas show intermarriages to people with exactly the same surnames, suggesting patterns that have been going on in those same families, albeit largely unrecorded, for centuries.

The Norman dynasties

The marriage in 1069 of the Scottish king Malcolm III Canmore to St. Margaret, sister of Edgar the Atheling, started a long trend of English influence north of the border. Edgar had been born in exile in Hungary, and the Leslies and Drummonds both claim descent from Hungarians who came to Scotland with Margaret and Edgar, taking their surnames from the lands they were granted.

Malcolm and Margaret's son David (d. 1153) married Maud, a great-niece of William the Conqueror and daughter of Waltheof, Earl of Huntingdon in England. David inherited Huntingdon and grew up in England; when he became King of Scots, he journeyed north with a band of Norman followers (especially tenants of his great English estates) and made several of them feudal lords in Scotland.

For example, the Comyns settled in Roxburghshire, and became Cummings. A Norman family who settled at Gordon, Berwickshire, became Gordons. Hugh de Moreville (d. 1162), from Morville near Valognes in Normandy, became Constable of Scotland, and through his influence came the Hayes or Haigs, ancestors of Earl Haigh, from La Hague near Morville. Slightly later came the De La Hayes, Earls of Erroll and Kinnoull, originally from La-Haye-Belefond, near St Lô in France. The St. Clairs, from Saint-Clair-sur-Elle near St. Lô, became the Sinclairs, Earls of Roslin, Orkney and Caithness. King David's godson David Olifard spawned the Oliphants of Gask.

The Balliols came from Picardy in France, and produced two kings, John Balliol and his son Edward. John's claim to the throne was through his mother Devorgilla, daughter of Margaret of Galloway, a great-granddaughter of David I. His rivals the Bruces were descended from Robert de

The ruins of Dryburgh Abbey, Roxburghshire, founded in 1150 with the support of the Norman lord Hugh de Moreville, who had become the main landowner in the area. Hugh later joined the abbey as a novice, dying there in 1162. His son, also called Hugh (d. 1173/4), was one of the knights who killed Archbishop Thomas Becket in Canterbury Cathedral in 1179.

Brus (d. 1141) from Brix in Normandy, whose family became lords of Annandale (Dumfries and Galloway), and who gained their own dose of royal blood through the marriage of Robert's grandson to Margaret of Galloway's sister Isobel. The Lindseys and Grahams, who took their surnames from Lindsey and Grantham in Lincolnshire, were also early 12th-century arrivals, presumed to be of Norman origin because of French first names.

A new influx of Franco-Normans came under David's successors Malcolm IV and William the Lyon. These included the families of Barclay, Menzies, Fraser, Montgomery and Colville, names so closely associated with Scotland now that it seems extraordinary to think they were ever from anywhere else.

The Stewart dynasty

Another foreign import of David I's was Walter FitzAlan (d. 1177), Steward of Scotland, whose descendants remained hereditary Stewards and adopted the title as their surname. Walter the High Steward (d. 1327), fifth in descent from Walter FitzAlan, married Marjory, daughter of Robert the Bruce, in 1315, and their son became King Robert II in 1371. The royal Stewart or Stuart line remained on the throne until James VII and II was overthrown in 1688, and the senior line expired in 1807 with the death of his grandson Henry, Cardinal of York, younger brother of "Bonnie Prince Charlie."

A lot of nonsense has been spun about the Stewarts' origins, reinforced in Shakespeare's *Macbeth*, such as the claim that the first Walter's father was Fleance, son of Banquo the Thane, supposedly in turn a male-line descendant of Corc, King of Munster, a descendant of Heber son of Mil. The Stewarts woke up one morning in 1807 to find that the genealogist George Chalmers (1742–1825) had completely disproved this.

The Royal Stewarts gave Scotland many lines of lairds, and several families of dukes, such as the Dukes of Buccleuch, descended from James, Duke of Monmouth (d. 1685), an illegitimate son of Charles II, who live to this day at Bowhill House near Selkirk.

The Palace of Holyroodhouse, Edinburgh, seen from Arthur's Seat, one of the principal homes of the Stewart dynasty.

Bowhill House, residence of the Dukes of Buccleuch.

CHAPTER 17

Genetic evidence

The genetic mapping of Scotland is an infant subject, but so far it has already produced some fascinating results. DNA tests can show how you are connected to Scotland's ancient people, to family groupings such as clans and to other people with Scottish roots the world over.

An idealized image of courtship and love in the Highlands.

An introduction to DNA tests

DNA tests look for mutations that arise when human genetic material changes. There are two sorts of genetic test available: one on what is called "deep ancestry" and the other on genetic markers on the male-line Y chromosome. The first will tell you how you fit into the genetic map of the human race, that is, what is the broad group that your ancestors belonged to, whether Picts, Scots, Vikings and so on. Genetic markers, on the other hand, are more specific in that they identify individual families, such as the Ua Neill and the MacDonalds. Within these unique markers, even more minor mutations have arisen, enabling geneticists to identify different branches of families.

Tests are carried out on the Y chromosome that men inherit from their father, he having inherited it from his father, and so on; also on the mitochondrial DNA (mtDNA) inside the X chromosome that both men and women inherit from their mother's egg, she having inherited it from her mother, and she from her mother in turn. If you imagine your ancestry as a giant fan, then, the two lines you can study are the extreme edges, the male line going up the left side and the female side going up the right.

"Deep ancestry" and how it works

Once genetic mutations have been identified, they are dated by multiplying the number of mutations by an average time over which

mutations are believed to have occurred. The results can be compared for accuracy with other dating techniques, such as carbon dating. Placing the resulting DNA signatures geographically involves seeing where samples are distributed nowadays, and also where most mutations on the original mutations are found. Generally, the more sub-mutations found in one area, the longer it is likely to have been there.

Almost all male-line Y-chromosome DNA in Europe can be broken down, by its unique mutations, into eight groups. Each is descended from a very ancient male-line ancestor, only five of which are found in any quantity in the British Isles. Of these, Haplogroup R1b, called variously "Oisin" or the "Atlantic Modal Haplotype," predominates in Ireland and Scotland, and is also found extensively in Cornwall, the Basque region and (to a lesser extent) the rest of Spain. This strongly suggests that it was indigenous to the original Ice Age settlers of Europe, its distribution up the western seaboard of Europe being reinforced by coastal trade between Ireland and

north-west Spain, which may also have been instrumental in the northward spread of agriculture. The areas of highest concentration also equate to the building of Megalithic and Neolithic monuments, perhaps indicating that the ideas behind them spread within an interrelated population. R1b is lower in the Western Isles of Scotland and in England, probably due to influxes of Vikings, Saxons and later peoples.

The predominance of R1b in Scotland could be due to Scots flooding across the North Channel from Ulster, displacing the Picts almost entirely, or both "races" could simply have had the same genes in the first place. The latter is generally thought far more likely.

The dominant female-line mtDNA signatures found in Scotland so far are coded H, K, X and U, derived from Ice Age hunter-gatherers in Europe. These are from Scotland's original post-Ice Age settlers. Large doses have also been found of J and T. These have been linked plausibly to the spread of the Neolithic Revolution, indicating that farming reached Scotland about 6,000

DNA tests would not tell you directly whether you were related to the pipe-smoking old lady or Willie Dewar, 90 when this photo was taken in 1890. But under the right circumstances a comparative test between you and their living descendants would determine if there was a genealogical relationship (courtesy of Easdale Island Folk Museum).

DYS19 14, DYS385a 11, DYS385b 15, DYS389i
DYS392 14, DYS393 13, DYS426 12, DYS437
DYS441 15, DYS442 17, DYS444 12, DYS445 1
DYS448 19, DYS452 30, DYS454 11, DYS455
DYS460 11, DYS461 12, DYS462 11, DYS463 1
DYS464c 17, DYS464d 18, DYS635 23, YCAIIa

My only recent Scots ancestors come through my mother's great-grandmother Mary Ann Collingwood Paterson, whose grandfather Robert was born in Selkirk in 1830 (see p. 99). The surname Paterson can mean, "devotee of St Patrick," or simply, "son of Patrick" (or Peter). Sometimes the surname is an anglicization of the Clan Pheadirean, a sept of Clan MacAulay; sometimes it isn't. Despite its likely Gaelic origins, the fact that my Patersons were from the eastern Borders, an area invaded by the Angles, made me rather worried that my "Scottish" roots might have been more Angle than Scot.

I wanted to learn about the genetic male-line origins of my Patersons. I am not a male-line Paterson myself — my mother's Paterson ancestry comes through her father's mother's mother, Mary Ann Collingwood Paterson, so I needed to find a fairly remote Paterson cousin who carried the male-line, Y-chromosome "Paterson" DNA. Luckily, I knew one, my 81-year-old cousin, Tinka Paterson, a grandson of Mary Ann's brother. Tinka very kindly agreed to have a DNA test performed by www.familygenetics.co.uk.

A quick swab inside his cheek, and several weeks later, the results were crystal clear: Tinka's Haplogroup was R1b, the Atlantic Modal Haplotype, the predominant genetic signature of the Picts and Scots. It's not exclusive to them, for many R1b signatures are found in England too, where families of ancient British extraction survived the Roman, Anglo-Saxon, Viking and Norman invasions. But I was delighted to find that Tinka's DNA was not distinctively Angle or Viking but instead was strongly suggestive of Gaelic origins.

Going into Tinka's origins in more detail, Family Genetics were able to provide a 37-marker DNA signature for his Y chromosome. Marker DYS19, for example, had a result of 14, while marker DYS385a had a result of 11, and so on. These numbers can be entered into various comparative databases, such as www.ysearch.org, www.ybase.org, www.smgf.org and www.ancestry.co.uk/dna. Annoyingly, the different testing companies don't work to the same standards, requiring some of the markers to be converted, using help given on the sites and from Family Genetics themselves.

On the formidable Ysearch database, many near matches appeared. Some of these are matches to people who, back in the old days, i.e. two or three years ago, had only had 10 or 12 markers tested. These matches are about as useful as saying that if you've a couple of legs and two eyes you must be distantly related to your cat. Interestingly, however, an eight/10 match was found with someone descended from a William Patterson, "born about 1680 in Scotland." The closest match I found, however, was someone who had had a 67-marker test, of which 29 markers could be compared with the ones of Tinka that had been tested. Out of these 29 markers, there was a "genetic distance" of two, which means that two markers differed by one each (their result for DYS 458 was 17, and Tinka's 18, and on DYS 392 the other

DYS389ii 30, DYS391 11,
DYS438 12, DYS439 12,
DYS446 15, DYS447 25,
DYS456 15, DYS458 18,
DYS464a 15, DYS464b 15,
YCAIIb 21, GATAH4 21

person was 13 and Tinka 14). Therefore, their genetic signature, as far as it can be compared, was virtually identical save for a couple of mutations that could have arisen, Family Genetics estimates, in the last 19 generations.

Encouragingly, the almost-matching person was another Paterson, Colin Paterson, whose male-line descendant was a John Paterson, born about 1797 in Carmichael, Lanarkshire, only 32 miles (51 km) from Selkirk! John became Provost of Peebles, and two of his sons migrated to Melbourne in 1854. Nineteen generations at an average of 30 years per generation is 570 years ago, suggesting a connection since 1438 — which is well within the period when hereditary surnames were being used in the Lowlands.

These results don't tell me anything precise in genealogical terms, but they do make sense. I know my Patersons were in Selkirk since at least the 1500s. The surname is supposed to be a Gaelic one, from the west coast. The nearest genetic match to Tinka is from Carmichael — if you draw a line from Selkirk to the west coast, Carmichael is about a third of the way along it. The results suggest, therefore, that my medieval Paterson ancestors may well have migrated east, from the west coast, via the Carmichael area — vague, but considerably better than nothing at all. And they proved a biological connection to a new-found cousin on the other side of the world that could never have been found through written records.

ABOVE LEFT: **The list of Tinka Paterson's 37 genetic markers.**

ABOVE RIGHT: **John Paterson, born in 1797 (courtesy of Colin Paterson).**

years ago, mainly via what seems to have been very busy maritime activity up and down the Atlantic seaboard.

Just as some DNA signatures are distinctively Scottish, others aren't. Bryn Carr of **www.FamilyGenetics.com** tells me of a client who, *"took great pride in being quite stereotypically Scottish. My first conversation with him was an explanation of the price, to convince him that we weren't trying to 'rip him off' — 'I am Scottish, you know, you won't get anything past me!' he said. We*

found after the testing that he in fact belonged to a rare subgroup of Haplogroup J2, a largely Mediterranean group. He was quite surprised at first but once he learned more about the group he was excited about finding this hidden part of his past."

Clan DNA

The DNA signatures referred to here are very general ones, because they are very ancient and carried by many people in Scotland. Much more recent mutations on the Y chromosome can enable geneticists to distinguish different male lineages within these wider groups. When these mutations seem only to have arisen a thousand years or so ago, they start to become linked to surnames and clan names, which also, and very conveniently, tend to follow male lines.

One distinctive mutation within the R1b group is found within significant proportions of MacDonalds (25 percent), MacDougalls (33 percent) and MacAlisters (40 percent). All three clans claim male-line descent from Somerled, Lord of the Isles, so possibly Somerled himself was the originator of this genetic signature. Estimates vary, but over 200,000 men of Scots descent worldwide carry Somerled's genes, including the clan chiefs of those three names.

Many clan chiefs, and the original Scots royal house itself, claimed male-line descent from the O'Neill or Ua Neill kings of Ulster. Studies at Trinity College, Dublin, have identified a strong genetic marker that has been found in many men from Irish families claiming Ua Neill descent, and that same marker has been found in many of the Scots families making the same claim. These claims, then, seem not to have been as far-fetched as some cynical genealogists thought. Ironically, the O'Neill family themselves, descendants of the later Ua Neill kings, don't share the marker: at some point,

The ancestry of Elvis Presley (1935–77) has been traced back to Andrew Presley, who left Aberdeenshire after the 1745 rebellion. This indicates that many Aberdeen Scots should have very similar Y-chromosome profiles to the rockstar.

perhaps, one of their wives became pregnant by someone else, and introduced a different Y-chromosome signature into that line.

The "Somerled" gene does not conform to the Ua Neill norm either, despite the traditional pedigrees that take his male line back to the same Ua Neill roots. This may mean that his pedigree is simply wrong, or that one of Somerled's male-line ancestors had an unfaithful mother. As Somerled is a Viking name, though, and there are a number of somewhat contradictory accounts of his precise lineage, these results may suggest that his male-line ancestry was Viking and his Ua Neill ancestry came originally through his mother or grandmother, the pedigree having been "smoothed out" later to change a female-line connection into a male-line one.

That big groups of families and clans turn out to share the same distinctive male-line Y-chromosome DNA may seem odd, but there is a convincing explanation. In societies dominated by war, the chances of any individual man surviving to adulthood,

marrying a healthy wife, having access to fertile land and producing children who would survive were increased enormously by belonging to a powerful family. When a warlord came to power, he usually did so with the backing of his male-line kindred. He and his kin then gained the pick of the land and the women. Their sons inherited a massive advantage, and their genes could thus flourish. Even if the warlord's men had not slaughtered the other men in the region, the losers had less access to land and food, and thus less chance of bringing up healthy sons to pass on their genes. In addition, they had no means of preventing the winners from raping their wives, thus increasing the winners' gene pool and reducing that of the losers even further. Geneticists are finding increasingly that great swathes of populations all over the world have been affected thus: vast numbers of male lineages must have died out altogether, and what is left is a relatively small number of male-lineages. Most of us are descended, up the male line, from thugs.

Female lineages do not tend to behave the same way. Women are more likely to survive violent take-overs, becoming the mistresses or wives of the victors. While male-line DNA tells the story of conquests, the female lines speak more of continuity, albeit in often horrible circumstances. Your father's father's father's ancestor may well have been a conquering Scot, or Pict, or Viking who traveled a long way to reach Scotland. But along your mother's mother's mother's line you are more likely to be descended from women who had lived in the same area for thousands of years, possibly since the end of the Ice Age.

Viking DNA

Studies of DNA in areas dominated by Vikings have produced interesting results. In the Orkneys and Shetlands, only about 60 percent of men carry the R1b signature (compared to 84 percent in the Pictish heartlands from Fife up to the Moray Firth), while the other 40 percent have signatures (characterized by one expert as "Sigurd" and "Woden") that link them to Viking roots. The female-line results are broadly similar, suggesting that the Vikings brought their own women with them from Scandinavia, rather than raping and enslaving the existing females of the Isles. Hebridean DNA, by contrast, suggests more violent conquest, for 22 percent of men with Viking male-line DNA is matched by only 11 percent of women with Viking female-line DNA. Down in Argyll, the Viking signature becomes very faint — only 7 percent for men and 2 percent for women.

A giant model of one of the Lewis chessmen stands guard over the baggage carrousel at Stornoway Airport, Lewis, a vivid reminder of the Viking presence in Scotland. The original chessmen, carved in walrus tusks by an unknown Norse craftsmen, were found in the sands at Ardroil, Uig, in 1831 by Malcolm MacLeod of Penny Donald, a local Presbyterian farmer. Thinking they were elves, MacLeod sent for a merchant from Stornoway, who gave him a £30 reward. Apparently, the treasure had been hidden a couple of hundred years earlier by the Red Gillie of Ardmore, who had stolen them from a boy whom he had murdered, who had stolen them in turn from a ship anchored in the bay where the sailors had played chess with them. They are now divided between the National Museum of Scotland and the British Museum.

How to have a DNA test

A number of firms have made DNA testing available to all, at a reasonable price. Make sure you have at least 37 markers tested.

Since women do not have Y chromosomes, for a woman to learn about her father's male-line ancestry, she must have her father tested, or else someone who shares his male lineage, such as her brother, brother's son, her father's brother and so on.

To learn about the genetic origins of other lines, you need to be creative. For the male-line origins of your mother's mother, you need to trace and perform a test on your grandmother's brother, or his son, or her father's brother's son and so on.

Such tests are useful if you and someone else with the same surname think you are related, and want to prove it. If your marker signatures match up, then you are related. If they do not match, either your genealogy is wrong or a "non-paternal event," such as an illegitimacy or undisclosed adoption, has taken place. The tests are also useful if you do not know (due, say, to illegitimacy) what your male-line ancestor's surname was. If your Y-chromosome signature

One of the berserker figures from the Lewis chess set. In his battle-frenzy he is chewing his shield and his eyes are popping out. Not the sort of chap you'd want to meet in person, but his genes are likely to have prevailed over many others and are in many of us today.

matches one or more living person, their surname will probably be the same as that of your mystery ancestor. Finally, if you are tracing the origins of a migrant ancestor with a common name, a precise DNA match to people of that surname still living in Scotland is going to give you a massive clue as to where your migrant's original home was.

Useful websites

- **www.FamilyGenetics.co.uk** Manchester-based DNA-testing firm with considerable expertise in Scottish genetics.
- **www.FamilyTreeDNA.com** American-based firm, home to a number of Scottish family and clan projects.
- **www.scottishdna.net/c-dna.html** John A. Hanson's Scottish Clans DNA project, aiming to bring together DNA projects concerning Scottish clans and families.
- **www.scotlandsfamily.com/dna-testing.htm** Dr. James Wilson of Edinburgh University is the discoverer of the Atlantic Modal Haplotype and founder of EthnoAncestry (**www.ethnoancestry.com/ info.htm**). His firm has developed a number of tests

to distinguish Y-chromosome ancestry that is Pictish (two different signatures very common in Pictish areas that are rarely found elsewhere), Viking, Dalriadan (from the O'Neills) or from Somerled himself.

- **www.geocities.com/mcewanjc/** Dr. John McEwan's study of his surname's origins, looking in detail at traditional pedigrees that trace the MacEwans, MacLachlans, Lamonts, MacSorleys and Irish MacSweeneys back to a branch of the O'Neills of Ulster, and then examining genetic evidence to see if these traditions were correct. He is still working on the project, but it looks as if tradition is being exonerated.

Useful addresses

National repositories

Court of the Lord Lyon
New Register House
Edinburgh EH1 3YT
www.lyon-court.com

General Register Office for Scotland (GROS)
New Register House
3 West Register Street
Edinburgh EH1 3YT
0131 3340380
www.gro-scotland.gov.uk

Mitchell Library
North Street
Glasgow G3 7DN
0141 2872999
www.mitchelllibrary.org

National Archives of Scotland (NAS)
H.M. General Register House
2 Princes Street
Edinburgh EH1 3YY
0131 5351314
www.nas.gov.uk

National Library of Scotland (NLS)
George IV Bridge
Edinburgh EH1 1EW
0131 6233700
www.nls.uk

National Library of Scotland Map Library
Causewayside Building
Salisbury Place
Edinburgh EH9 1SL
0131 6233700
www.nls.uk/maps

National Register of Archives of Scotland
Housed at NAS (above)
www.nas.gov.uk/nras/

ScotlandsPeople Centre
New Register House
3 West Register Street
Edinburgh EH1 3YT
www.ScotlandsPeoplehub.gov.uk/

Scottish Life Archive
National Museum of Scotland
Chambers Street
Edinburgh EH1 1JF
0131 2474076
www.nms.ac.uk

Sheriff Clerk's Office
Commissary Section
Sheriff Court House
27 Chambers Street
Edinburgh EH1 1LB
0131 2252525

The National Archives [of Great Britain] (TNA)
Ruskin Avenue
Kew
Richmond
Surrey TW9 4DU
020 88763555
www.nationalarchives.gov.uk

Regional repositories

Aberdeen City Archives
(includes Kinross)
Dunbar Street
Aberdeen AB24 3UJ
01224 481775
www.aberdeenshire.gov.uk

Angus Archives
Hunter Library
Restenneth Priory
By Forfar DD8 2SZ
01307 468644
www.angus.gov.uk/history/archives

Argyll and Bute Archives
Kilmory
Manse Brae
Lochgilphead
Argyll PA31 8RT
01546 604774
www.argyll-bute.gov.uk

Argyll and Bute Library
Library Headquarters
Highland Avenue
Sandbank
Dunoon PA23 8PB
01369 703214
www.argyll-bute.gov.uk

Ayrshire Archives Centre
Craigie Estate
Ayr KA8 0SS
01292 287584
www.ayrshirearchives.org.uk

Clackmannanshire Archives
26-28 Drysdale Street
Alloa FK10 1JL
01259 722262

Clydesdale District Libraries
(includes Lanark)
Lindsay Institute
Hope Street
Lanark ML11 7NH
01555 661331
www.southlanarkshire.gov.uk

Dornoch Digital Archive
Dornoch Library
Carnegie Buildings
High Street
Dornoch
Sutherland IV25 3SH
0186 2811079
www.highland.gov.uk

Dumfries and Galloway Archives
(includes Kirkcudbright and Wigtown)
Archive Centre
33 Burns Street
Dumfries DG1 2PS
01387 269254
www.dumgal.gov.uk/
dumgal/Services. aspx?id=40

Dumfries and Galloway Health Board Archives
Easterbrook Hall
Crichton Royal Hospital
Dumfries DG1 4TG
01387 244228

Dundee City Archives
21 City Square
Dundee DD1 3BY
01382 434494
www.dundeecity.gov.uk/
archive

East Dunbartonshire Council Information and Archives
William Patrick Library
2-4 West High Street
Kirkintilloch G66 1AD
0141 7768090
www.eastdunbarton.gov.uk

East Lothian Council Local History Centre
Haddington Library
Newton Port
Haddington EH41 3HA
01620 823307
www.eastlothian.gov.uk

Edinburgh City Archives
Department of Corporate Services
City of Edinburgh Council
City Chambers
High Street
Edinburgh EH1 1YJ
0131 5294616
www.edinburgh.gov.uk

Falkirk Council Archives
History Research Centre
Callendar House
Callendar Park
Falkirk FK1 1YR
01324 503778
www.falkirk.gov.uk

Fife Council Archive Centre
Carleton House
The Haig Business Park
Balgonie Road
Markinch KY7 6AQ
01592 583352
www.fife.gov.uk

Glasgow Archives
(Includes Dunbarton and Renfrew)
Glasgow City Archives and District Libraries
Mitchell Library
North Street
Glasgow G3 7DN
0141 2272405
www.mitchelllibrary.org

Highland Council Archives
Inverness Library
Farraline Park
Inverness IV1 1NH
01463 220330
www.highland.gov.uk

Moray Local Heritage Services
East End School
Institution Road
Elgin IV30 1RP
01343 569011
www.moray.gov.uk/
localheritage

New College Library
Mound Place
Edinburgh EH1 2LX
0131 6508957
www.lib.ed.ac.uk/sites/
newcoll.shtml

North Highland Archive
Wick Library
Sinclair Terrace
Wick
Caithness KW1 5AB
01955 606432
www.highland.gov.uk

Orkney Library and Archive
44 Junction Road
Kirkwall
Orkney KW15 1AG
01856 873166
www.orkneylibrary.org.uk/
html/contact.htm

Perth and Kinross Council Archive
A. K. Bell Library
York Place
Perth PH2 SEP
01738 477012
www.pkc.gov.uk/archives

Scottish Borders Heritage Hub
(Includes Berwick, Peebles, Roxburgh, Selkirk and some for Midlothian)
Kirkstile
Hawick TD9 0AE
01450 360 699
www.scotborders.gov.uk/
council/specialinterest/
heartofhawick

Shetland Islands Shetland Museum and Archives
Hay's Dock
Lerwick
Shetland ZE1 0WP
01595 695057
www.shetlandmuseum
andarchives.org.uk

Stirling Council Archive Service
5 Borrowmeadow Road
Springkerse Industrial Estate
Stirling FK7 7UW
01786 450745
www.stirling.gov.uk/index/
access-info/archives.htm

Thurso Library
Davidson's Lane
Thurso KW14 7AF
01847 893237
www.highland.gov.uk

West Lothian Council Archives and Records Management Centre
9 Dunlop Square
Deans Industrial Estate
Livingston EH54 8SB
01506 773770
www.westlothian.gov.uk/
tourism/1488/archives/

Organizations

Burns National Heritage Park
Murdoch's Lone
Alloway
Ayrshire KA7 4PQ
01292 443700
www.burnsheritagepark.com

Co Leis Thu?
Seallam! Visitor Centre
An Taobh Tuath (Northton)
Isle of Harris HS3 3JA
01859 520258
www.seallam.com

Guild of One Name Studies (GOONS)
Box G
14 Charterhouse Buildings
Goswell Road
London EC1M 7BA
0800 0112182
www.one-name.org

Hudson's Bay Company Archives
Provincial Archives of Manitoba
130-200 Vaughan Street
Winnipeg, MB
CANADA R3C 1T5
204 9454949
www.gov.mb.ca/chc/archives
/hbca/

Jewish Genealogical Society of Great Britain
33 Seymour Place
London W1H 5AU
020 77244232
www.jgsgb.org.uk

Ordnance Survey Library
Room C454
Ordnance Survey
Romsey Road
Southampton SO16 4GU
0845 6050505
www.ordnancesurvey.co.uk

Royal College of Physicians of Edinburgh
9 Queen Street
Edinburgh EH2 1JQ
www.rcpe.ac.uk

Royal College of Physicians and Surgeons of Glasgow
234-242 St Vincent Street
Glasgow G2 5RJ
0141 2273234
www.rcpsglasg.ac.uk/
archives.htm

Royal College of Surgeons of Edinburgh
Nicolson Street
Edinburgh EH8 9DW
www.rcsed.ac.uk

Royal Marines Museum
Eastney Barracks
Southsea PO4 9PX
0239 2819385
www.royalmarinesmuseum.
co.uk

Scottish Catholic Archives
Columba House
16 Drummond Place
Edinburgh EH3 6PL
0131 556 3661
www.catholic-heritage.net

Scottish Jewish Archives Centre
Garnethill Synagogue
129 Hill Street
Glasgow G3 6UB
0141 3324911
www.sjac.org.uk

Society of Genealogists (SoG)
14 Charterhouse Buildings
Goswell Road
London EC1M 7BA
020 72518799
www.sog.org.uk

The History of Parliament
Wedgwood House
15 Woburn Square
London WC1H 0NS
0207 8628800
www.ihrinfo.ac.uk/hop/

Armed services records (for last 80 years)

Army Records Centre
Ministry of Defence
Historical Disclosure
Mail Point 400
Kentigern House
65 Brown Street
Glasgow G2 8EX
0141 2243030

Royal Air Force Personnel and Training Command
Branch PG 5a(2) (for officers) and
P Man 2b(1) (for non-officers)
RAF Innsworth
Gloucestershire GL3 1EZ

Royal Marines Historical Records and Medals
HRORM
Room 038
Centurion Building
Grange Road
Gosport
Hampshire PO13 9XA
023 92702126
www.royal-navy.mod.uk/
server/show/nav.4330

Royal Naval Personnel Records Office
Ministry of Defence
CS(RM)2
Navy Search
Bourne Avenue
Hayes
Middlesex UB3 1RF
020 85733831

Index

Acknowledgments

My copious thanks go to Denise Bates and Louise Stanley at Collins for commissioning this book, Helena Nicholls and Charlotte Allen at Collins for their care of it, and my agent Anna Power for her unfailing support. Nicola Chalton and Pascal Thivillon of Basement Press have edited the manuscript beautifully, and Meredith MacArdle has done a fine job sourcing some of the illustrations. Much rich material in this book has come from the Crowleys and their relations, especially Scott Crowley, Moira Crowley, Valerie Weeks, Kay Cullen, Barbara Davis, Karen Crowley and Alistra Chalmers. David Sellar, Lord Lyon King of Arms, kindly pointed me in the right direction concerning the origins of the MacLeods. I would also like to thank Siân Ahlås; Malcolm Bangor-Jones; Rosemary Bigwood; Helen Borthwick (GROS); Bryn Carr; Jim Ebling; Margaret Farr; Richard Gollin; Kenny Graham; Brian Lambie; Bill and Chris Lawson; Nan MacLeod; Roddy MacLeod; Andrew Martin of the NLS; Jeremy Palmer; Jenny Parkerson (NLS); Colin Paterson; Tinka Paterson; Rosemary Phillip; Suzanne Rigg; Alan Robson of Clan Gunn; Lord Strathnaver, DL, Master of Sutherland; Sigurd Towrie; Alexes Weaver; Dee Williams (GROS); and the volunteers of the Historic Assynt Trust.

Picture credits